D1067436

A Biographical Dictionary
of the British Colonial Governor

Volume 1: Africa

A Biographical Dictionary

of the British

Colonial Governor

Volume 1: Africa

ANTHONY H. M. KIRK-GREENE

Senior Research Fellow in African Studies
St Antony's College, Oxford

HOOVER INSTITUTION PRESS
Stanford University, Stanford, California

This edition first published in 1980 by
THE HARVESTER PRESS LIMITED
Publishers: John Spiers and Margaret A. Boden
16 Ship Street, Brighton, Sussex

British Library Cataloguing in Publication Data

Kirk-Greene, Anthony Hamilton Millard
   A biographical dictionary of the British colonial
   governor.
   Vol. 1: Africa
   1. Governors – Great Britain – Colonies – Biography
   I. Title
   325'.3'0922   JV1009

   ISBN 0-85527-383-6

Hoover Press Bibliographical Series 61

Printed in the United States of America by
Vail-Ballou Press, Inc., Binghamton, N.Y.
All rights reserved
International Standard Book Number: 0-8179-2611-9
Library of Congress Catalog Card Number: 80-81949

For

B. E. S.- S. and G. W. B., who, as Governors,
    first directed me to write on Africa;

J. S. C. and M. J. H., who, as mentors,
    first taught me to write on Africa;

J. J. T. and D. M. W., who, as editors,
    first encouraged me to write on Africa;

P. D. and L. H. G., who, as colleagues,
    first guided me to write on African proconsuls.

Contents

FOREWORD

Even in the heyday of empire the men who built, ruled and developed the colonies were seldom written about. A few Governors wrote their memoirs and a few others had biographies written about them. But most of the men who administered Britain's colonies had to be content with short sketches in the annual *Colonial Office List* or occasionally an entry in the *Dictionary of National Biography*. Anthony H. M. Kirk-Greene's present study therefore breaks new ground and should be greatly welcomed by scholars, students and librarians. While David Henige's *Colonial Governors from the Fifteenth Century to the Present* . . . (University of Wisconsin Press, 1970) is precisely what its sub-title suggests, a useful but plain list, Anthony Kirk-Greene provides full biographical notes. Previously, to obtain additional data, a student had to go far afield. Information in the *Colonial Office List* is often incomplete. The detail found in obituaries, published reminiscences, and similar material is often scattered and hard to find. This new dictionary provides information on a variety of matters, including the Governors' education, their geographical origins, their career patterns, and so forth. It is the first of its kind for any colonial power, and will further enhance the reputation that the author has already gained for himself as one of the foremost experts on the British Colonial Service in Africa.

British Governors were a diverse lot. They differed widely in their career structure, their political views, their personal idiosyncrasies. But between them, they also had a great deal in common. They helped to determine the shape of British colonialism in Africa; wittingly or unwittingly, they contributed to the foundations of post-colonial Africa. These men were part of Africa's history; they were state builders of Africa, and they not only administered the colonies, they laid down the infrastructures of ports, railways, roads, they developed schools and hospitals systems and helped to bring Africa into the modern world and the money economy. Men of two continents, they are inextricably involved in the history of their mother countries and of the colonies they governed. This study should prove to be invaluable as a work of reference for libraries. It should likewise be of great use to students of the British empire and of African history, and to all scholars interested in the study of administration and elite sociology.

Peter Duignan
Africana Curator,
Hoover Institution,
Stanford, California

Glossary

b.	— born
Bt.	— Baronet
ch.	— children
CB	— Companion of the Most Honourable Order of the Bath
CBE	— Commander of the Most Excellent Order of the British Empire
CIE	— Companion of the Most Eminent Order of the Indian Empire
CMG	— Companion of the Most Distinguished Order of St Michael and St George
CVO	— Commander of the Royal Victorian Order
d.	— daughter; died
d/o	— daughter of
DBE	— Dame Commander of the Most Excellent Order of the British Empire
DC	— District Commissioner
DD	— Doctor of Divinity
DO	— District Officer
D.Phil.	— Doctor of Philosophy
DSO	— Distinguished Service Order
DNB	— *Dictionary of National Biography*
FFPS	— Fellow of the Faculty of Physicians and Surgeons
FRCS	— Fellow of the Royal College of Surgeons
FRGS	— Fellow of the Royal Geographical Society
FRS	— Fellow of the Royal Society
GCMG	— Knight Grand Cross of the Most Distinguished Order of St Michael and St George
GCSI	Grand Knight Commander of the Star of India
GCVO	— Knight Grand Cross of the Royal Victorian Order
GBE	— Knight Grand Cross of the Most Excellent Order of the British Empire
h/m	— headmaster/mistress
Hon.	— the Honourable
ISO	— Imperial Service Order

JP	—	Justice of the Peace
KC	—	King's Counsel
KCB	—	Knight Commander of the Most Honourable Order of the Bath
KCMG	—	Knight Commander of the Most Distinguished Order of St Michael and St George
KCSI	—	Knight Commander of the Most Exalted Order of the Star of India
KCVO	—	Knight Commander of the Royal Victorian Order
KBE	—	Knight Commander of the Most Excellent Order of the British Empire
KG	—	Knight of the Garter
Kt; Knt	—	Knight Bachelor
KT	—	Knight of the Most Ancient and Most Noble Order of the Thistle
Litt.D.	—	Doctor of Letters
LL.D.	—	Doctor of Laws
m.	—	married
MBE	—	Member of the Most Excellent Order of the British Empire
MC	—	Military Cross
MD	—	Doctor of Medicine
MP	—	Member of Parliament
MVO	—	Member of the Royal Victorian Order
OAG	—	Officer Administering the Government
OBE	—	Officer of the Most Excellent Order of the British Empire
obit.	—	obituary appearing in *The Times* (London)
OCRP	—	Oxford Colonial Records Project (papers)
OCRP/t	—	Oxford Colonial Records Project (tape recording)
PC	—	Provincial Commissioner; Privy Counsellor
QC	—	Queen's Counsel
RUC	—	Royal Ulster Constabulary
s.	—	son
s/o	—	son of
VC	—	Victoria Cross
w/o	—	wife/widow of
y	—	younger

INTRODUCTION

1 *The rationale and the sources*

The need for this book both derives from and has contributed towards a parallel project, the research undertaken in connection with my extended essay 'Governorship and Governors: the British Colonial Experience' for the concurrent composite volume *The African Proconsul* edited by L. H. Gann and Peter Duignan (Free Press, 1978). Embarking on the basic research for that project in 1975/6, it at once became apparent that, in the absence of any single work of inclusive reference, the collection of comparative biographical data on the British Colonial Governors in Africa was indispensable to the construction of some form of collective profile on which to base interpretations of the data. Such a perception of an essential tool was heightened by working on two complementary papers on the British Colonial Governor in Africa; while the value of its format was confirmed by the needs generated from contemporaneous work on a socio-career profile of the Governors-General of Canada.[1]

The preliminary career data thus assembled and marshalled in 1975/6, relating to some fifty gubernatorial careers in Africa between 1900 and 1960, have now been extended to cover the biodata of the 200 or so holders of the post of Governor or its Colonial Service equivalent in the British African territories between c. 1875, the eve of Partition, to 1968, the date when the last of Britain's tropical dependencies in Africa became independent.[2] What we now have is a primary biographical source-book for the study of the British Colonial Governor in Africa. If Africa accounted for less than a third of the colonial governorships at the height of Britain's empire, in size, prestige and volume the continent was second to none in its Colonial Service recruitment and rewards. Among the other colonies, only Ceylon and Palestine up to the late 1940s, Malaya up to the mid-1950s, Jamaica and Trinidad up to the mid-1960s, and Hong Kong and the Bahamas to the present day, could compare with Nigeria, Kenya, the Gold Coast and, from 1920, Tanganyika as the plums of the Service. As Robert Heussler observed in his seminal study of Oxford's pre-eminence in recruitment for the Colonial Service, its African character was so pronounced that 'the name "colonial service" normally suggests administration in tropical Africa more than in any other part of the world'.[3] In terms of Colonial Office responsibility and Colonial Service presence, it was Africa that reflected the lion's share.

At a time when more and more interest is being taken in the transfer of power and the legacy of the colonial period, today in the *dramatis personae* as well as an earlier and exclusive concern with institutions, and at a time when acceptance of the argument is gaining ground that in order fully to understand the imperial experience one needs to know who the imperialists were by way of provenance and how their careers were fashioned in the field, there would seem to be a justifiable need for a work of reference on Africa's supreme proconsular cadre. Such is the rationale of this first biographical dictionary of the British Colonial Governor in Africa, and for its successor volume on Britain's governors in the rest of the colonial empire.

But if this is the first work of this nature (there is no reference to anything like it in such standard works of reference as R. B. Slocum's *Biographical Dictionaries: an International Bibliography* (1967, Supplement 1972) or the Gale Research Company's *Master Index of Biographical Dictionaries* (1975–6), with its 725,000 entries, or in the survey of collective biography discussed by Lawrence Stone in his landmark analysis of prosopography,[4] it is by no means the first biographical work to include the British Colonial Governor. Three sources stand forth as the *sine qua non* of any research connected with biography of Britain's proconsuls. These are the *Colonial Office Lists*; *Who's Who* and its companion decennial *Who Was Who*; and the *Dictionary of National Biography*. In addition, there is one comprehensive listing of over ten thousand names, David P. Henige's *Colonial Governors from the Fifteenth Century to the Present* (1970), together with illuminative tables in half a dozen further important sources relating to the British Colonial Governor.[5] All these sources have

4

furnished relevant and corroborative data for this volume. Each of them demands a word of explanatory comment, and if on occasion the writer has detected errors in one, omissions in another or contradictions between the rest, this in no way dissuades him from paying tribute to their exceptional value or deludes him into believing that the present work can lay claim to total infallibility. The author will welcome notice of omissions, corrections and additions.

The *Colonial Office List* was published annually, except for the war years 1941–5 and for 1947, from 1862 to 1966. Between 1926 and 1940 it was issued as the *Dominions Office and Colonial Office List*, companion volume to *The India Office and the Burma Office List* (1937), itself the successor to *The India Office List* (1886). The *Colonial Office List* for 1952 was issued in paperback only. Individual maps started appearing in these *Lists* in 1875 and continued as a feature until 1940. For economy reasons, they were omitted when publication was resumed in 1946, but in 1948 they were presented as a special *Supplement*.[6] In the post-colonial period, two related listings have also appeared in restricted form. In 1967 the Commonwealth Office published *H.M.O.C.S: Records of Service of Senior Staff*; this did not appear again.[7] Since then, Governors of the reducing number of dependent territories have from time to time been provided with a simple roll-call of names, drawn up for official reference purposes only, entitled *List of Senior British Expatriate Officers serving in Dependent Territories*.[8]

After 1966 some of the information has continued in the *Diplomatic Service List* (1966), which replaced *The Foreign Office List* (1823), and in the varyingly named *Commonwealth Relations Office List* (1951), *Commonwealth Relations Office Year Book* (1966), *Commonwealth Office Year Book* (1967), and *Yearbook of the Commonwealth* (1969).[9]

The Colonial Office List could not, by virtue of the sheer size of the Colonial Service, be a complete listing of all persons currently in that Service: in the period following World War II these rose from 11,000 to 18,000 serving officials.[10] Inclusion in the 'Record of Services' section was therefore restricted, especially after 1946, to officers with a minimum of ten years' service. Sometimes an officer's name was removed on retirement, sometimes it was retained after retirement if he had achieved a knighthood, sometimes it persisted until his death. Unexpectedly, and disturbingly, not every Governor has featured adequately in the *Colonial Office List*: for instance, basic information on neither Sir Samuel Rowe nor Herbert Ussher, V. S. Gouldsbury nor Sir William Griffith, all holding governorships on the West Coast between 1867 and 1888, has been located, and information on the staff of the three High Commission Territories of Basutoland, Bechuanaland and Swaziland was not generally included after their transfer to the Dominions Office in 1925, until the Territories were retransferred to the Colonial Office in 1961. Nonetheless, the *Colonial Office Lists* constitute an essential work of first reference, and by and large do not disappoint in their reputation as 'the Red Bible of the Colonial Service'.[11]

Nearly every Colonial Governor attains an entry in *Who's Who* (inexplicably, Sir Gilbert Carter is one who did not), the classic biographical dictionary of Great Britain's and, in later years, the world's elite. Published annually from 1849, it has since 1897 been most valuably supplemented for the researcher by the periodically issued *Who Was Who*. What this latter biographical tool does is to repeat the biographee's last entry from *Who's Who* and then add the date of his death. The first three of these volumes covered the periods 1897–1915, 1916–28, and 1929–40. Thereafter they have appeared decennially. Since the last *Who Was Who* volume goes only as far as 1970, it has been necessary to consult every *Who's Who* since 1971 to bring this present list up to date (1979).

While virtually all Colonial Governors feature in one of these two key works of reference, the same cannot be said of the *Dictionary of National Biography*. Here only *la crème de la crème* earn inclusion. Out of the two hundred or so careers in this volume, spanning a near-century of Colonial Governance in Africa, less than fifteen per cent appear in the *DNB*. Having said this, three qualifications are necessary. First, the bulk of the *DNB* entries (29,120 of them, to be precise) appear in the original twenty-two volumes of the *DNB*. These take the story only up to 1900, a year so early in Colonial Service history — barley the age of consent in the history of African governorships outside the ancient West African Settlements of The Gambia, Sierra Leone and the Gold Coast, and not much more than the year of the birth of territories like Nigeria, Kenya, Uganda, Nyasaland—that only a handful of African Governors could have qualified. In the event, Sir Gerald Portal alone did. Where the British Colonial Governors in Africa have gained admission, they are to be found in one of the seven *Supplements*. These cover, in the first, the omissions up to 1900, and thereafter every ten years, according to the year of death, spread over Supplements II (1901–10) through VII (1951–60). Secondly, certain Colonial Governors included in the *DNB* are excluded here because they did not hold an African governorship: eg in successive pages of Supplement VII one finds Grigg, Grimble and Gurney, only one of whom can earn a place in this volume. Finally, the *DNB* too operates on a decennial basis—in arrears. Since several distinguished Colonial Governors died in the 1960s and the last volume of the *DNB* does not go beyond 1960 (published in 1971), we may anticipate further biographical essays of this classic genre when the 1961–1970 volume appears in a few years' time. Meanwhile, the hiatus is partially filled by a novel device of *The Times*. This has recently published two volumes, together containing some 2,500 obituaries reprinted from its own pages, of world figures who died between 1961 and 1975.[12] While Colonial Governors do not come off too well in the face of such stiff competition, nine of their number are featured in the first volume.

So much for the basic sources for biodata on British Colonial Governors.[13] To establish a list of who was Governor of which territory from when to when (see Appendix), five kinds of authorities are available. Most—but, inexplicably, not all—editions of the *Colonial Office List* carry a list of names of the Governors of each territory from the founding of the colony or protectorate. Some of these go back to the seventeenth century, eg Bermuda (1612), Barbados (1625), Jamaica (1660), Bahamas (1673). A comparable but infinitely more laborious source is the annual *Statesman's Year Book*, which first appeared in 1863. Thirdly, there is the admirable compilation by David Henige, *Colonial Governors from the Fifteenth Century to the Present: a Comprehensive List* (1970). Any mistakes Henige contains are easily rectified by cross-checking so that, provided the researcher will treat this source with circumspection as well as with the respect it deserves, its many advantages comfortably outweigh such occasional shortcomings as incorrect (Weinholt Hodson, Tunstal Chaplin), incomplete (D. P. Chaplin, H. R. Brooke-Popham) or inaccurate (see below, pp. 8–9) presentation of names and dates. Inevitably in an American work, and in marked contrast to the latterday editions of the *Colonial Office List*, it includes the first and family names of every one of its 11,000 Governors: as Henige acidly but accurately observes, 'The lists of Governors of British colonies in the annual *Colonial Office Lists* are unduly simplistic in many cases, unnecessarily complex in others, often distorted, and admittedly incomplete'.[14] Fourthly, there are the various official Colony Handbooks, for example, the pre-war *Handbook of Sierra Leone* (1925) and *The Gold Coast Handbook* (1937) or the post-war *Nigeria Handbook* (1953) and *Handbook of Tanganyika* (1958). Published by individual governments, they contain, almost *de rigueur*, a list of all the previous Governors of the territory (the pre-war Uganda and Nyasaland volumes are virtually unique in omitting this information). Finally, there are the standard histories of the territory or the region, most of which include an appendix giving the names of the successive Governors: eg Lady Southorn's *The Gambia* (1952), Kenneth Ingham's *The Making of Modern Uganda* (1958), Michael Crowder's *The Story of Nigeria* (1962), Sir Alan Burns' *History of the British West Indies* (1954), E. A. Walker's *A History of South Africa* (1957).[15]

In cases of contradiction in the data derived from an amalgam of these sources, it has been necessary first to establish what the error is; secondly, why it occurs; and thirdly, to which source to accord priority, in the absence of personal knowledge or enquiry. A common discrepancy between Henige and the *Colonial Office Lists* relates to the actual years of a governorship held: for instance, Stanley's term of office in Southern Rhodesia, Stack's in the Sudan, and Nathan's in the Gold Coast, or his confusion over the attribution of the titles of High Commissioner and Governor in both Northern and Southern Nigeria between 1900 and 1914. The reason for such disagreement is frequently to be found in the distinction between the date of appointment to a governorship and the date of assumption of office. While this is often a matter of several weeks, during which time the senior official of the colony acts under the title of 'Officer Administering the Government' (OAG) just as he does when His Excellency is out of the country on leave or attending a constitutional conference, it can on occasion be a longer period. For example, Burns was never Governor of Nigeria, as given in Henige's list: he simply acted during the absence of the substantive governor's leave. Nor was Crawford ever Governor of Kenya, as Henige has it. Again, in the case of Shuckburgh to Nigeria and Bourdillon to the Sudan, the appointment was announced but was then superseded by other reasons of state, so that technically it never became anything more substantial than 'Governor designate. Because of this kind of easy confusion among differing authorities, the date adhered to in this book is, insofar as the available information allows, that preferred by the Colonial Office itself, namely the year in which a Governor actually assumed office. This is not only in keeping with official practice for dating the salary and pension implications of promotion to a governorship but also allows inclusion here of an entry showing an acting governorship during an interregnum, often an important moment in the grooming of a potential governor (see below).

In cases of discrepancy over other career postings and promotions prior to the attainment of a governorship, precedence has been given to the date shown in the *Colonial Office Lists* over that included in *Who's Who*. The reason for this apparent partisanship is important. An entry for *Who's Who* is drafted by the biographee himself. Human memory is fallible —unlike the Colonial Office records on an officer's personal file—so that 'Provincial Commissioner 1936' may, in fact, refer to a temporary promotion not gazetted until 1937. Just now and again, too, one comes across in *Who's Who* claims to having been 'Colonial Secretary 1903–07' or 'District Commissioner 1923', or even 'Governor and Commander-in-Chief of Uganda, 1910–11': cross reference to the *Colonial Office List* at once makes it clear that these were at the most acting appointments, not held in substantive rank for maybe a further two to six months. Such a nicety may seem too jejune for mention in the lordlier context of *Who's Who*, but for the Colonial Office scribes it was a proper matter, if not of life and death at least of bread and butter. Nor, by the way, is *Who Was Who* or the *Dictionary of National Biography* above simple errors: in the latter H. H. Johnston's death is given as 31 August instead of 31 July, while in the former Twining's date of death appears as 21 June instead of 21 July and Sir Bryan Sharwood Smith's name appears spelled incorrectly.

These, then, are the sources on which scholars interested in Colonial Service history have during the past decade or so drawn to provide some valuable interpretative analysis of the origins of the British Colonial Governor. For the limited numbers of the nineteenth century, John W. Cell in his *British Colonial Administration in the Mid-Nineteenth Century: the policy-making process* (1970) has extended the analysis of provenance undertaken by Henry L. Hall in his *The Colonial Office* (1937). For the period at the turn of the century, R. V. Kubicek has interesting comments on gubernatorial appointments in his *The Administration of Imperialism: Joseph Chamberlain at the Colonial Office* (1969). A pioneer review of the origins of the Colonial Governor from 1919 to 1939 was undertaken by Kenneth Robinson—albeit in but a few pages of text—in his *The Dilemmas of Trusteeship* (1965). This has been twice extended, first by J. M. Lee, who, in his *Colonial Development and Good Government* (1967), took the data up to 1960, and now by the present writer in his comparative table isolating sixteen selected social, educational and career indices for eighteen of the leading British Colonial Governors in Africa between Sir Harry Johnston's appointment in 1891 and Sir Walter Coutts' retirement in 1963.[16] By far the most explicit and impressive analysis of gubernatorial origins is that by Ian F. Nicolson and Colin A. Hughes in their paper 'A Provenance of Proconsuls' (*Journal of Imperial and Commonwealth History*, October 1975, 77–106) covering a cohort of 214 Colonial Governors throughout the British Empire, from the Caribbean to the Pacific and from the Mediterranean to the Antarctic, between 1900 and 1960. Today, with this *Biographical Dictionary of the British Colonial Governor*, detailed analysis of many other aspects of their Service career as well as further forms of collective biography and composite profile of the Colonial Governor will be possible without the need for elaborate extra research. Although these data have not been computerized, the variables do lend themselves to straightforward coding and computer-based statistical formulation and interpretation.

2 *The text*

This Dictionary comprises nearly 200 biographical entries of the Governors of Britain's African territories, from the eve of the Scramble to the morning after the transfer of power. These territories totalled twenty, variously styled Colony (eg Gold Coast, Kenya), Protectorate (eg Nyasaland, Somaliland); Colony and Protectorate (eg Nigeria, Sierra Leone, Kenya); Self-governing Crown Colony (Southern Rhodesia); Mandated or Trust Territory (Tanganyika); High Commission Territory (Basutoland, Bechuanaland, Swaziland); and Condominium (Anglo-Egyptian Sudan). Geographically, these were distributed as:

West Africa:	The Gambia, Sierra Leone, Gold Coast, Nigeria;
East Africa:	Uganda, Kenya, Tanganyika, Zanzibar, Somaliland, The Sudan;
Central Africa:	Northern Rhodesia, Nyasaland, Southern Rhodesia;
Southern Africa:	Bechuanaland, Basutoland, Swaziland;
South Africa:	Cape Colony, Natal, Orange River, Transvaal.

This list corresponds with the official listing of 'Governorships Open to Members of the Colonial Service',[17] supplemented by six additional posts. Two of these, the Sudan and Southern Rhodesia, did not come under the aegis of the Colonial Office. Finally, the four colonies in South Africa did not survive the 1910 Union. The three High Commission Territories, too, were in a somewhat special category. However, the Governors of all twenty African territories are included here, not only for completeness but also because at one time or another in every one of them save the Transvaal a Colonial Service Governor, past or future, was to hold office. Furthermore, in most cases he had also served as an administrator in a 'straight' Colonial Office territory.

One further point needs to be made about the nomenclature of the Sudan administration. Exceptionally (Indian governorships offer a certain parallel) the officer in charge of a Province in the Sudan was styled a Governor, so that at any one time the Sudan could point to between six and nine Governors, all responsible to a Governor-General. For the purpose of this Dictionary, only the Governor-General (ie the official recognized as the Sovereign's representative in the territory, as with a Colonial Governor) has been included, and not the holders of subordinate office whose responsibility and title in the Colonial Office territories approximated to that of Provincial Commissioner or Resident. If Richard Hill's otherwise admirable *A Biographical Dictionary of the Anglo-Egyptian Sudan* (1951) at first sight seems slightly disappointing in its handling of the Sudan's Governors-General, it must be attributed to the longevity of the country's proconsuls: seven out of the nine Governors-General appointed since 1899 were still alive fifty years later and so were disqualified from inclusion.

The period covered in this Biographical Dictionary is in general from the end of the nineteenth century, when Crown rule took over from Company administration in such major areas as Nigeria, Kenya and Uganda, up to 1968, when the last of Britain's African territories became independent. In cases of the longer established settlements on the West Coast, some of which had had a British Governor since the first half of the nineteenth century, the starting date has been taken back a decade or two to the period immediately preceding the Partition of Africa. The data thus furnish a biographical profile of practically every Colonial Governor in Africa from the time the professionalisation of the British Colonial Service began to make its impact in the 1870s,[18] through its unification in the mid-1930s, to its demise in the late 1960s: in sum, a century of colonial pro-consulship.

While the term 'Governor' is used generically throughout to denote the Sovereign's personal representative and the senior administrator in each territory, there were numerous variations in the exact title. For instance, Nigeria experienced two periods, separated by nearly forty years, of a Governor-

Generalship; in Zanzibar, the title was always British Resident; in early Uganda and Kenya, it had been Commissioner; and in the High Commission Territories the office remained that of Resident Commissioner to the end. The Lieutenant-Governors of Nigeria and the Chief Commissioners in Nigeria and the Gold Coast have not been included, as these offices did not rate gubernatorial recognition: the acid test was whether they corresponded directly with the Secretary of State for the Colonies or through another official in the territory. The post of Lieutenant-Governor was superior to that of Chief Commissioner in that the latter received his commission not from the Crown but only from the Governor.[19] To this extent, the inclusion of the Resident Commissioners of the three High Commission Territories does constitute a partial anomaly, as up to 1964 they were technically subordinate first to the Governor-General of South Africa and then after 1931 to the High Commissioner in Pretoria. Their 'independent' geographical status has been held to justify their inclusion here. In most of the African territories, the rank of Governor was upgraded to that of Governor-General at independence and was often held for a few months by the final Colonial Governor as a mark of special recognition, eg Dorman in Sierra Leone, Turnbull in Tanganyika, Coutts in Uganda, Jones in Nyasaland. Where this kind of territorial Governor-Generalship was a purely political appointment, eg Listowel in Ghana, the holder is not included in this biographical dictionary.

Since the Dictionary is arranged in alphabetical order, a separate index of names is unnecessary. The Appendix comprises a masterlist by territories of all the Governors included in this Dictionary, showing the years of their administration and where necessary specifying the changes in title.

Twelve variables have been identified for the biographical entries. The categories of information selected can be looked on as key items for the standard needs of a dictionary of this nature as well as for a subsequent prosopographical study of the British Colonial Governor in Africa. Each is discussed in detail below. Not all the information is available for every entry; particularly for those born in the middle of the last century. Not every piece of available information has been included, eg the date of each posting or promotion in the 'long grade', the exact period for which retirement appointments were held, the actual years of schoolboy education. Nor in the analysis of the data that follows in Part III of this Introduction would it be impossible for the researcher with special interests to pursue some of it to greater depth, eg the frequency of colonial marriages to a widow, the occupation of fathers-in-law; or, more esoterically, the favoured names of wives and the fecundity of colonial governors-in-the-making. The variables and their interpretation have been selected on and confined to the criteria of principal relevance and potential career significance.

NAME: Where the names used in the *Colonial Office Lists* or within the Colonial Service differs from that given in *Who's Who*, attention is drawn to this by an asterisk followed by an explanatory note at the foot of the page. This usually relates to the linking of two surnames, eg Ainsworth Dickson, Hayes Sadler and Sharwood Smith, or Arden-Clarke, Beresford-Stooke and Brooke-Popham. On the Colonial Office files the hyphen was often ignored;[20] in a number of cases, it was added at a later stage in an officer's career. Where on being elevated to a peerage a Governor took a different name for his barony, this is indicated in the head entry, eg Sir Arthur Richards = Lord Milverton, Sir Edward Grigg = Lord Altrincham, Sir John Maffey = Lord Rugby. No such information is given where the name was continued in the barony, eg Lord Lugard, Lord Twining. Sometimes this would include an African reference, eg Lord Milverton of Lagos and Clifton and Lord Twining of Godalming and Tanganyika; but Lord Howick of Glendale and Lord Lugard of Abinger. Where a knighted Governor did not use his first name with his title, this is indicated by a bracket round it, eg Sir Edward Grigg but Sir (Frederick) Gordon Guggisberg. This distinction, clear in *Who's Who*, is not always made in the *Colonial Office Lists*.

In cases where a Governor habitually retained his armed forces rank, this is included in the head entry. Most of these were regular officers, eg to take the unusual parade of Kenya's Governors alone, Major-General Northey, Brigadier-General Byrne and Air Chief Marshal Brooke-Popham. Occasionally, a non-regular officer liked to keep his rank after World War I. As W. R. Crocker wryly observed of Nigeria in the 1920s, and as is confirmed by the Staff Lists, it became a mark of distinction among District Officers *not* to use the rank of captain![21] A special case was Grigg. As Military Secretary to the Prince of Wales at the end of his war service, he was entitled to wear the uniform of a lieutenant-colonel in the Grenadier Guards. This he hoped to continue wearing on his appointment to Kenya. But the Colonial Office ruled that only Governors who were also General Officers were entitled to wear military uniform: it would be improper for a Governor to be dressed as a mere lieutenant-colonel—and when he was Commander-in-Chief into the bargain. In the event, the King had a word with the Colonial Office; and Grigg duly appeared on Armistice Day and the King's Birthday parades wearing the uniform of a colonel in the Guards.[22]

SON OF (s/o): Where it is clear that a Governor was the first, second, third, etc. son, this is indicated. Wherever possible, the profession of his father as well as his geographical provenance is included. These, however, are items on which the Britisher is traditionally reticent (or indifferent)—a fact evidenced by the scant information he provides for himself in *Who's Who*—and on which the *Colonial Office Lists* are utterly silent.

DATE OF BIRTH (b.): This speaks for itself. Among older generations, it was not always customary to give more than the year. Such a restriction was consistently observed in the *Colonial Office Lists*.

DATE OF DEATH (d.): This, too, requires no comment. A blank here indicates that the biographee is still (1979) alive.

MARRIED (m.): Besides the date of marriage, the wife's given names and her maiden name (d/o, daughter of), her father's occupation is given where this has been traced; but once again, such information is not commonly included in *Who's Who*, while the *Colonial Office Lists* resolutely disdained any reference to marriage. Where she earned an honour in her own right, this is shown, eg Lady Chaplin, Lady Clifford, Lady Guggisberg, Lady Stanley. Where the wife was a widow, this is indicated, along with her deceased husband's occupation. Where the biographee made a second marriage, similar details are given but information on the date of the first wife's death has not been included.

Divorce was rare among Colonial Governors. On being received at Buckingham Palace to take up the Governorship of Kenya in 1925, Grigg recorded that 'the Queen said that no divorced person should be invited to Government House, and none was ever invited in our day'.[23] Until the 1960s at least, it was a factor to be taken into account at the Colonial Office when a name was under consideration for a colonial governorship.

EDUCATION: This shows the biographee's secondary school (nearly always a Public School) and, where applicable, his university. In the case of Oxford and Cambridge, the *alma mater* of under half the entries in the dictionary but over three-quarters of those who entered the Colonial Administrative Service after World War I, the name of the college is also given. In a few cases after 1926, a college attachment at these two universities refers to the one-year Tropical Africa (later Colonial Administrative) Service course and does not denote a three-year degree course there.

While it is not necessary to include in a biographical dictionary a lengthy account of the British educational system, a summary note may be helpful. In brief, a boy of the 'social class' from which the bulk of the Colonial Administrative Service was recruited—and hence virtually all of the Governors, with the exception of Sir William Macgregor, the only one from an unambiguously 'working class' background—would typically attend a Preparatory School from the age of seven to twelve or thirteen. He would then go on to a Public School, leaving it when he was eighteen or so to go up to a university. All of this education would have been on an essentially fee-paying basis. Sometimes a boy would be privately educated instead of attending a preparatory school, eg Clifford. On occasion, too, a young man might continue his education privately on the continent instead of attending a university, eg Dundas, Lawrance, Moor. No 'crammers', such as the famous Wren's or Davies's which specialized in candidates for the Indian Civil Service or the Foreign Service's remarkable Jeanne Huette,[24] featured in this system, as the Colonial Service relied on record and references and eschewed supplementary examinations. As Kenneth Bradley explains in accounting for his choice of the Colonial Service as a career:

When I came down from Oxford I knew what I did not want to do, and also knew I certainly did not wish to sit for another examination as long as I lived. This ruled out both the Indian and the Home Civil Services, and the Diplomatic.[25]

Naturally there is rivalry among the Public Schools for a place in the national order of merit, just as there is with say colleges in the Ivy League or the Big Ten. Not all of them would accept the conventional Big Five of Eton, Harrow, Winchester, Rugby and Westminster, but the naming of the following nine schools as the senior institutions received the confirmation of the authoritative Royal Commission on the Public Schools appointed under Lord Clarendon in the middle of the nineteenth century: Charterhouse, Eton, Harrow, Merchant Taylors, Rugby, St Paul's, Shrewsbury, Westminster and Winchester. It has not radically altered since the Clarendon Report was published in 1864. While it is wiser to leave the observers of British public life—and wiser still, their alumni—to judge whether a school is a first, second or even third class institution, the inclusion of a school in the Head Masters' Conference at once confers on it the influential status of Public School as conventionally understood in Britain. Today there are over 200 such H.M.C. schools.

For the Armed Forces, from which a good number of Colonial Governors were drawn, especially before the professionalisation of the Colonial Service began to bear fruit around the turn of the century, graduation from the Royal Military College at Sandhurst (for cavalry and infantry regiments) and the Royal Military Academy at Woolwich (for engineers and artillery),[26] ranked as comparable with a university education, while the Royal Naval Colleges at Dartmouth and Osborne were held to be the equivalent of a good Public School. For all their respective Indian Civil Ser-

17

vice and armed forces tradition, Haileybury and the Imperial Service College, Wellington College and Westward Ho! have for the past hundred years still been Public Schools first and hothouses for imperial service second: the concept of an exclusively Indian Civil Service school died with the closure of Addiscombe, the military college for the ensigns of the East India Company, and the broadening of Haileybury ('the East India College' for its Writers) into a normal Public School after 1857. Unlike France, the British Colonial Service never achieved the national recognition of havings its own *École Coloniale*.

For those who wish to follow up the links, cultivated or incidental, between school or university and Colonial Service recruitment, a painstaking opportunity presents itself in the scrutiny of old boy associations, eg *Eton College Register*, *Harrow List*, *The Wykehamist*, *Rugby School Who's Who*, and of the standard *The Historical Register of the University of Oxford* (1220–1900) with its four Supplements taking the data up to 1965, or the *Historical Register of the University of Cambridge* (1494–1910) with its nine supplements up to 1975. Another rewarding but still time-consuming source would be an examination of the periodic lists of individual college alumni, eg *Clare College List*, *Trinity College Record*, Sir Ivo Elliott's *The Balliol College Register* (1934) or else a determined perusal of the Class Lists published in the annual *Oxford University Calendar* published from 1810 onwards or in the corresponding Cambridge volume.

In many cases it has been possible to indicate the field in which the biographee graduated and the class of degree obtained (see below). In most English universities the B.A. is a three year course, and at Oxford and Cambridge nearly always an Honours degree. In Scottish universities, the Honours course is often a four year one, at the end of which the degree awarded can be the M.A. Conversely, at Oxford and Cambridge the M.A. is not a qualification earned by examination, rather is it automatically awarded to a graduate who has 'kept his name on the books' (ie paid his college dues) for seven years from the date of matriculation. After the inauguration of the Tropical Africa Service courses at Oxford and Cambridge in 1926, a Colonial Probationer might stay on for a fourth year

18

at his college; or be sent on the course at the other university; or spend the year at Oxford or Cambridge, having graduated at neither of these.

At the typical British university before World War II, the field in which one graduated was a single or double subject one, ie an undergraduate took a degree in History or Geography or Modern Languages and was examined in this subject only.[27] Typically, the B.A. is classified into First Class, Upper Second, Lower Second and Third Class. At Cambridge the Second Class is divided into a II/1 and a II/2, but at Oxford there is no further classification of the Second Class.[28] At both these universities a Pass degree signifies that Honours were not awarded. For the past fifty years or so, the breakdown of all undergraduates taking their final examination (Tripos at Cambridge, Schools at Oxford) in the humanities and social studies — the predominantly favoured disciplines of our corpus — shows, as a generalization, approximately 6% being placed in the First Class, 75% in the Second, 17% in the Third, and 2% being awarded a Pass degree or fail.[29] It was possible up to World War II, and not unusual through the 1920s, to spend a year or two at Oxford or Cambridge and then leave ('go down') without entering for the degree examination and without penalty or disgrace ('being sent down').

Where a post-graduate qualification was earned — still today a rarity in a British public service career, save for the technical staff of professional Ministries — this is noted here. This includes being called to the bar, before World War II an extra qualification earned by a number of colonial administrators who 'read for the bar' while they were in Africa and 'ate their dinners' during their leaves. The only doctorate among our corpus (Sillery) was gained after retirement from the Colonial Service. Election to a College Fellowship (as opposed to later election to an Honorary Fellowship) or the award of a Harkness Fellowship is also noted under this heading: both were a signal distinction among Colonial Service officers. From among our Governors, only Eliot and Hardinge achieved the former and Cohen and Loyd the latter.

Where a person was a Scholar of his school and a Scholar or an Exhibitioner of his college (the term indicates intellectual excellence tested by examination and not merely an awarded financial bursary), or a university Prizeman or Medallist, this is indicated. Where it is known that he represented his university at some sport (gaining a 'Blue' at Oxford and Cambridge), this is also recorded, eg Robertson at rugby, Bell at rifle shooting. While such prowess at games might be considered by Sir Ralph Furse and his Appointments secretariat at the Colonial Office as evidence in a would-be District Officer of possessing those quintessential but elusive traits of 'character', 'initiative' and 'leadership qualities', it was, in African service lore if not in practice, the Sudan Political Service rather than the Tropical African Services that was reputed to base its recruitment on the principle of staffing 'a Land of Blacks ruled by Blues'.[30]

CAREER: It may be helpful to place the Colonial Service in its correct setting within the spectrum of Britain's imperial civil services. As Dominions, Canada (after 1867), Australia and New Zealand (South Africa was *sui generis*) had, of course, no imperial service administering them, but in Whitehall their affairs were up to the mid-1960s looked after by a separate department of the Home Civil Service, the Dominions (after World War II, the Commonwealth Relations) Office. A separate service, the Indian Civil Service (I.C.S.) and a separate home ministry in London, the India Office, looked after India (but not Ceylon), Burma (but not Malaya) and, up to 1937, Aden. The literature on the I.C.S. is enormous. Mention may be made here of such important service histories as L. S. S. O'Malley's *The Indian Civil Service* (1931), Sir Edward Blunt's *The Indian Civil Service* (1937), B. B. Misra's *The Bureaucracy in India* (1877), and for many the noblest memorial of them all, Philip Woodruff's *The Men Who Made India*, a tribute in two volumes, *The Founders* (1953) and *The Guardians* (1954). Within India, the advisory administration of the Indian states and the political work of the Gulf and most of the North West Frontier lay with another service, the Indian Political Service (I.P.S.), recruited one-third from the I.C.S. and two-thirds from the Indian Army. It, too, has earned a general history, in Sir Terence Craig Coen's *The Indian Political Service* (1971). Though a reflection not strictly within the terms of reference of this paragraph, nobody working on the I.C.S. or I.P.S. could afford to ignore the Indian Army cadre; nor would he wish to overlook a recent and readable history, Philip Mason's *A Matter of Honour* (1974).

For historical reasons, the Anglo-Egyptian Condominium of the Sudan came under the Foreign, not the Colonial, Office, and was administered by a self-bounded service, the Sudan Civil Service, part of it being the Sudan Political Service. Strangely, for all its coherence, compactness and competence, this distinguished Service has yet to discover its historian. In his absence, much about the Sudan Political Service can be gleaned from such books as Reginald Davies, *The Camel's Back* (1957), H. C. Jackson, *Sudan Days and Ways* (1954), M. A. Nigumi, *A Great Trusteeship* (1958), and K. D. D. Henderson's great biographical portrait of a great Sudanese administrator, Sir Douglas Newbold, in *The Making of the Modern Sudan* (1953). Those wishing to study the service in greater biographical depth may refer to *Sudan Political Service, 1899–1956* (1962), popularly known as 'The Book of Snobs', a clinical listing humanly interpreted by Robert O. Collins in his article in *African Affairs*, July 1972, pp. 294–203. The Anglo-Egyptian Civil Service has received some attention, notably in Thomas Russell Pasha's *Egyptian Service* (1949) and, of course, in the biographical studies of such proconsuls as Cromer and Milner. The Anglo-Iraqi Political Service has been described, in somewhat uncomplimentary terms, by Sir Ronald Storrs in his memoirs, *Orientations* (1937), while the writings of Maurice Collis and George Orwell's puckish, semi-autobiographical *Burmese Days* (1934) have put the Burma Service on the literary as well as the imperial map.

The Colonial Service was none of these things. Up to the 1930s, each Colony under the jurisdiction of the Colonial Office had its own Colonial Service. Progressive unification of the various branches, above all the Administrative Service in 1932, led to the creation of the Colonial Service. The process was technically carried a stage further in 1954 with its reformulation as Her Majesty's Oversea Civil Service.[31] Within the old Colonial Service, the Far Eastern dependencies, comprising Ceylon, Straits Settlements, Federated Malay States and Hong Kong, occupied a special niche, and up to 1933/4 they alone recruited their Administrative Cadets by open competitive examination held along with that for applicants to the I.C.S. and the Administrative Branch of the Home Civil Service. The Malayan Civil Service retained its distinct designation of M.C.S. up to World War II. Several studies of post-war public administration in Malaya have provided insights into the pre-war M.C.S., for example R. O. Tilman, *Bureaucratic Transition in Malaya* (1964) and M. J. Esman, *Administration and Development in Malaysia* (1972). Useful, too, is the article on the M.C.S. by J. de Vere Allen in *Comparative Studies in Society and History*, April 1970. Currently (1978), Dr Robert Heussler is writing a history of the M.C.S.; unfortunately for the total Colonial Service historian, this will probably not go beyond the traumatic year of 1941.

At no time was the British Colonial Service the same service as the Colonial Office. This is contrary to the British Foreign Service, where the Foreign Office has always been staffed by diplomats temporarily reposted to London. The Colonial Office was part of the Home Civil Service—an office in its own right after its separation from the War Office in 1854—and as such recruited its Assistant Principals by competitive examination. It was one of the first departments to urge competition over patronage in the selection of its Clerks, so that by the 1880s it became, next to the prestigious Treasury, the most popular department of the post-Trevelyan reformed British Civil Service.[32] From the 1930s onwards, a handful of 'beachcombers', as they were known, could generally be found in the Colonial Office, officers on secondment from the Colonial Service for a year or two at a time. Governors who had had this experience include quite a fair proportion from our corpus. For a short time, between 1937 and 1945, the Colonial Office experimented by attaching a serving Colonial Governor to it in the rank of Assistant Under Secretary. Three Governors were involved: Moore, Burns and Battershill. But the scheme was discontinued for a number of reasons: in the explanation of one of the Governors selected, 'the Governors themselves were unable or unwilling to make the financial sacrifice involved'.[33] A reverse beachcombing scheme also operated whereby Colonial Office officials were seconded to a territory for two years. A conspicuous example of an official who so

22

loved the Service life that the Office nealy lost him was J. M. Martin's posting as District Officer to Malaya in 1931. Later he was to become Deputy Under Secretary at the Colonial Office.

On August 1, 1966 the Colonial Office was merged with the Commonwealth Relations Office, and on October 17, 1968 it disappeared altogether into the new Foreign and Commonwealth Office. A few residual functions were handled by the Ministry of Overseas Development. Good material on the working of the Colonial Office is to be found in D. M. Young, *The Colonial Office in the Early Nineteenth Century* (1961); Brian L. Blakeley, *The Colonial Office 1868–1892* (1972); Robert V. Kubicek, *The Administration of Imperialism: Joseph Chamberlain at the Colonial Office* (1969). For the more modern period, there are Sir George Fiddes, *The Dominions and Colonial Offices* (1926), H. L. Hall, *The Colonial Office* (1937), Sir Cosmo Parkinson, *The Colonial Office from Within* (1947) and Sir Charles Jeffries, *The Colonial Office* (1956). Sir John Shuckburgh's draft history of the Colonial Office during World War II was never published. J. M. Lee has an administrative study of the modern Colonial Office in manuscript form. While there is so far no history of the Colonial Service,[35] an idea of its organisation can be found in Sir Anton Bertram, *The Colonial Service* (1930) and in Sir Charles Jeffries, *The Colonial Empire and its Civil Service* (1938) and his *Whitehall and the Colonial Service* (1972); and of its ethos and style in such important studies as Robert Heussler, *Yesterday's Rulers: the Making of the British Colonial Service* (1963), Sir Charles Jeffries' *Partners for Progress* (1949), and Sir Ralph Furse, *Aucuparius: Recollections of a Recruiting Officer* (1962). The valuable insiders' memoirs are too numerous to list here.[36]

Where, as for the majority of the biographees, the person joined the Colonial Administrative Service soon after graduation, this is indicated by 'Cadet', followed by the territory of his initial posting. While in some colonies at some periods the new entrant was variously known as Assistant District Officer, Assistant District Commissioner, Assistant Resident, Assistant Collector, etc., the term Cadet, which enjoyed a long and respectable history in the Far East Service (see above), came into general usage throughout the Colonial Service after the formalization of the administrative training courses at Oxford and Cambridge in 1926 and the emergence of the unified Colonial Administrative Service six years later. In the event, the first years of a junior administrator's work and training on the job were similar in context and conception whatever his African colony or his temporary title.

The years as a Cadet were usually coterminous with a probationary period of two to three years from the date of sailing to take up his first appointment on completion of the Tropical African Services (after 1932, the Colonial Administrative Service, and from 1946 the Devonshire 'A') course at Oxford or Cambridge or, later, London. Once the Colonial Office had recruited and trained an administrator, he became the responsibility of 'his' Colonial government, either until he was transferred to another territory (usually in the context of promotion) or until he retired at the age of 45–55. Thereafter he came into the care of the Crown Agents for the Colonies for the payment of his pension.[37] In cases of dismissal, appeal lay to the Secretary of State, but the responsibility for a decision not to confirm an officer in his initial appointment was that of the colony's administration. If at the end of his probationary period the young official had passed his statutory examinations in law, language and the territory's Financial Instructions and General Orders, and was considered by his Provincial Commissioner to be likely to make a satisfactory officer, he would be confirmed in his appointment by the territorial government (not by the Colonial Office) as 'permanent and pensionable'. Now he was an Assistant District Officer (A.D.O.) or Commissioner (A.D.C.—not to be confused with the A.D.C. who was *Aide-de-camp* to His Excellency the Governor). Promotion to District Officer (D.O.) or District Commissioner (D.C.) might take another 4–14 years. That would take him to the end of the 'long grade'. Just a few officers spent their whole career, twenty years or more, as D.C. Most, however, advanced to the 'superscale' ranks of Senior D.C./D.O., and many to Resident or Provincial Commissioner, after 15–25 years' service. In each colony there was, too, a small establishment of 'staff grade' posts, Senior Provincial Commissioner/Senior Resident.

However, by this time the highflyers in the Service (which

by definition nearly all our corpus of Governors must have been) would have attracted the attention of their senior officers in the territory's Secretariat and hence the notice of the Personnel Division in the Colonial Office. Now began the unofficial but recognized 'course' of being groomed—it would rarely be in under 10–12 years—for high office. Typically this would take the form of being transferred away from one's first territory to become perhaps Colonial Secretary of a small island in the West Indies or Deputy Colonial Secretary in a larger territory. The final step might be as Chief Secretary of a major colony, with a chance to show one's mettle as Acting Governor, or as Governor of a small colony.[38] The Chief Secretaryship in Nairobi, Lagos and Dar es Salaam proved to be the testing-ground and stepping-stone for many a future Governor (eg respectively Coutts and Turnbull, Cameron and Benson, Hollis and Mitchell), just as the governorship of an island in the Pacific or Indian Ocean could be the precursor to a Governorship of a major African territory (eg Arden-Clarke, Twining, Crawford). Some, of course, plucked the plums by shorter or less conventional routes, like Grigg from Westminster, Northey and Brooke-Popham from the armed forces, or Hall, Creasy and Cohen from Whitehall, to take the post-1920 years alone.

Where the entry reads 'Provincial Commissioner', 'Colonial Secretary', etc. without the name of a territory following, it is to be taken as representing promotion within the same territory as the previous career entry. The name of a territory is shown only on first appointment or on subsequent transfer.

For the sake of convenience, the nomenclature of the territory follows that of its most widely accepted form during the colonial period, even though at an earlier or later period it may have been known by another name. Thus Nyasaland is preferred over the British Central Africa Protectorate of 1904 and over the Malawi of 1964. Similarly, a cadet posted to the British East Africa Protectorate in 1900 is given as Kenya, even though the name was not officially used until 1920, and British Somaliland, the Somaliland Protectorate or Somalia consistently appear here as Somaliland. Because of the difference —a constitutional rather than material one insofar as the structure of administration was concerned[39]—between Colony, Protectorate and Mandate, the generic term 'territory' has been preferred throughout this Introduction. A note of all the changes in territorial nomenclature appears in the Appendix.

With one exception, no attention has been paid in this biographical dictionary to acting ranks. The exception is to indicate where an official has had his first opportunity of being tried out by the Colonial Office in the capacity of acting for the Governor. This might be either while His Excellency was on leave or during the interregnum between the departure of one substantive Governor and the arrival of another. Clearly this moment carries a potential significance for career evaluation. Only the first occasion on which a person acted as Governor has been indicated, not subsequent occasions whether in the same territory or in another. While technically this appointment was styled 'Officer Administering the Government' (OAG), the shorthand of 'Acting Governor' has been adopted here; even when His Excellency's actual title was 'Commissioner' or 'High Commissioner' etc., rather than 'Governor'.

GOVERNORSHIPS: These are shown for each biographee in chronological order of appointment. Where the actual title of the position was other than Governor, though of gubernatorial equivalence within the Colonial Service, this is indicated in parenthesis, eg Commissioner (early Uganda and Kenya), Resident Commissioner (the three High Commission Territories), Resident (Zanzibar), High Commissioner (Palestine, Cyprus), Governor-General (Sudan, Nigeria 1914–19 and again from 1954, and most of the African territories immediately and after independence). The exact titles and the dates of their alteration are set out in the Appendix.

In by far the largest number of cases, a governorship was a colonial civil servant's final appointment: it was the post from which he retired. In the few cases where this was not the case and a man went on to another, non-Governor, Colonial Service appointment after holding a governorship—this is at its most conspicuous among the Resident Commissioners of the High Commission Territories—, for the sake of orderliness and career continuity the governorship has been included under the heading of 'Career' as well as shown under 'Governorships' eg Crawford, Gowers.

The usual term of a modern Colonial Governor was five years, with eligibility for re-appointment for a lesser period. The normal retiring age was fifty-five, or sixty in an earlier period. While a single governorship was common, a surprisingly large proportion of our African corpus held more than one governorship and a few of them three or four.

HONOURS: Only honours awarded by the British Sovereign have been included here. No attention has been paid, for instance, to the order of the Brilliant Star of Zanzibar nearly always awarded to the Resident there or to the King Leopold's personal decorations of early British administrators in Central Africa. Indian decorations, such as the Companion of the Indian Empire (CIE) and the Grand Cross of the Star of India (GCSI), are here found only among the Sudan's Governors-General: for bad or good, few colonial administrators and fewer Colonial Governors came to Africa with Indian experience.[40] With the exception of the military decorations of the Military Cross (MC), Distinguished Service Order (DSO) and Companion of the Bath (CB)—the first two often won by colonial administrators on active service with the King's African Rifles or Royal West African Frontier Forces in World Wars I and II—, the honours listed are all civil orders. (The Order of the British Empire carries a military as well as a civil division).

A partial explanation of the honours system insofar as it related to the Colonial Service will be in order. Outstanding work—and any attempt at definition would be fraught with difficulties—was generally rewarded by appointment to one of three orders of chivalry. The Order of St Michael and St George, founded in 1818 to bestow a token of royal appreciation on Maltese, Ionian and British officials who had served with distinction in the Mediterranean, was reorganized after the cession of the Ionian Islands to Greece in 1864 and became primarily an order to reward British citizens who had shown outstanding service in the colonies. A further change in 1879 extended this category to those who had performed meritorious service in foreign affairs. In essence, this has meant the

Colonial and the Foreign Services, though the Registry of the Order remained at the Colonial Office. By virtue of its sheer size, and of the existence of its levels of Officer and Member, the Order of the British Empire tended in the public eye to overshadow that of St Michael and St George as the Colonial Service Order *par excellence*, but at the levels of Knight Commander and of Companion there is no doubt that Fiddes' definition of the latter as 'pre-eminently the Colonial Order' remained accurate.[41]

In each order there are a finite number, a quota system, and a series of grades.[42] These grades are, in ascending order of merit within each order:

The Most Distinguished Order of St Michael and St George:	Companion (CMG), Knight Commander (KCMG), Knight Grand Cross (GCMG)
The Most Excellent Order of the British Empire:	Member (MBE), Officer (OBE), Commander (CBE), Knight Commander (KBE), Knight Grand Cross (GBE)

Promotion from one grade to another within the same order was frequent, not necessarily one step at a time: eg an officer holding the MBE might be advanced to CBE without the intermediary decoration of OBE. In this case, the superior grade supersedes the lower: such an officer would use only the initials 'CBE' after his name, not 'CBE, MBE'. Where an honour was bestowed by the sovereign from two orders, both feature after the recipient's name, in ranking and not chronological order: eg 'CMG, OBE'. However, Knighthoods awarded from different orders are *de rigueur* used concurrently, eg 'KCMG, KBE'.

One other style of knighthood sometimes awarded to Colonial Governors was the plain Knight Bachelor (Kt, sometimes Knt), not attached to any order. This was usually considered in the Colonial Service to constitute a less prestigious award than a KBE or KCMG. Knight Baronet (Bt), of course, while bearing the honorific Sir, is nowadays a purely hereditary knighthood. None of the Colonial Governors in this corpus had this title, though Clifford and Dundas were from within the British nobility.[43] It was rare for a Colonial

Governor to retire without a knighthood, most often the KCMG. Senior governorships nearly always carried advancement to a GCMG: exceptions were few. As decolonization progressed, such a distinction was also conferred on the final, and sometimes the penultimate, Governors of territories where previously the post had not customarily carried a GCMG, eg Uganda, Northern Rhodesia, Sierra Leone. In most cases a Colonial Governor was knighted, from within one order or another, before taking up office. Where this was not the case, as Sir Alan Burns once observed:

I have often thought that it would be wiser if the Secretary of State were to recommend to His Majesty that this Honour [a knighthood] should be awarded to the Governor of even a small colony *before* he assumes office, or at any rate at the first opportunity thereafter. Surprise is always expressed when each successive occasion on which such an Honour could be received [New Year and the Sovereign's Birthday] passes without the Governor being awarded what is generally regarded as a routine Honour, and this gives rise to speculation and affords the opportunity to agitators to ascribe the withholding of the Honour to Colonial Office dissatisfaction with the Governor's activities.[44]

The third order of chivalry (but ranking above the Order of the British Empire) frequently found among the honours of Colonial Governors was that of the Royal Victorian Order. Lying in the personal gift of the Sovereign and likewise consisting of a number of grades (five), it is awarded for services rendered personally to members of the Royal Family. In Colonial Service circles, especially during the reign of Queen Elizabeth II and again as an outcome of the royal visits to the Empire by her uncle the Prince of Wales in the 1920s, a KCVO might be conferred on a Colonial Governor who had hosted his royal visitor in Government House or a lesser grade of order, such as CVO or MVO, bestowed on an official who had played a particularly onerous part in arranging the royal visit.

Elevation to a peerage was a rarity for the African Colonial Governor. Only seven from out of our corpus of almost 200 received this signal distinction: Kitchener, Lugard, Grigg, Maffey, Richards, Twining and Baring. But of these, only the last three baronies were directly attributable to their African governorships: Lugard was not created a peer until 1928,

Grigg until 1945 and Maffey until 1947, all many years after their retirement from Africa, while Kitchener's honours were military and not administrative recognition of his services. For the Colonial Governors outside Africa, too, the list has been but little longer nor any more frequently related to work as a Governor: Foot and Grey are recent instances, neither being a colonial recognition. From a biographical viewpoint, the conferring of a barony often involves a change in name, and where this has occurred it has been indicated under Name and again under Honours (eg Sir Edward Grigg became Lord Altrincham; Sir Arthur Richards, Lord Milverton; Sir John Maffey, Lord Rugby).

Honorary degrees from a university, often the recipient's *alma mater*, and an Honorary Fellowship of a college, invariably his own, are shown here under Honours. So, too, are the one or two incidents of a Colonial Governor having been appointed, in his pre-gubernatorial career, as Page of Honour (Hardinge) or Extra ADC to the Sovereign (Northey). The conferring of Privy Counsellor (PC) was unknown among modern Colonial Governors: Lugard and Grigg were so recognized, but for their subsequent services, not for those related to their governorships.

CLUBS: Emphasizing the potential influence of the club exercized by proconsuls of another ilk, the writer recently noted of London's clubland: 'Here is a continuing context of power and policy-planning, all the more subtle because it is always personal and often unofficial, cutting across the customary channels of authority and frequently through the conventional corridors of power'.[45] The significance of the London Club, that not uniquely but typically British institution at home and overseas, has been undervalued by those studying the interaction of Britain's ruling elites. *Who's Who* is one of the few biographical works to take account of this social variable.

By tradition, the Athenaeum has been 'the' club for the governing elite. Right up to the 1960s the chances were high of discovering at least one Colonial Governor, and at times an excess of Excellencies, in its Coffee or Morning Room at any hour of the day between 10 a.m. and 10 p.m. Most of the other leading non-political London clubs have featured two or three Colonial Governors among their members, though the researcher will remark on the high number who have belonged to the East India and Sports. Recent amalgamations in Clubland have seen the Oxford and Cambridge merge with the United University, while the East India, Sports, and Devonshire has now been joined by the Public Schools.[46]

Outside London, Edinburgh's New Club, the Royal Yacht Club at Cowes and the Civil Service Club, Cape Town, have a distinction of their own. The Hawks' Club at Cambridge and Vincents' at Oxford invited to their membership those who had gained a blue; not, however, exclusively blues at Vincents', thereby recognizing a non-athletic social eminence which at Cambridge was catered for by the Pitt Club.

Many Colonial Governors belonged to one of two societies, the Royal African or the Royal Empire (later Royal Commonwealth, and earlier Royal Colonial Institute) Society. Because these are more of a society than a club, they are shown under Recreations.

The Corona Club, though not listed by many of our corpus, was open to all members of the Colonial Service. Founded by Joseph Chamberlain in 1900, it existed solely as an annual dining club (it also had its own tie, of English oakleaves in gold on a discreet blue background). The dinner constituted an occasion for several hundred civil servants from the Colonial Service, if they were on leave in June, and from the Colonial Office to gather together and be addressed by the Secretary of State for the Colonies. The top table, often festooned with up to thirty Colonial Governors and ex-Governors, in evening dress and wearing full decorations, was a gubernatorial scene to remember.

RECREATIONS: The entries are based almost entirely on those submitted by respondents for inclusion in *Who's Who*. They have been supplemented only where the writer has personal knowledge of a Governor's hobby or recreational pursuit. Where the *Who's Who* entry reads in what might appear to be a somewhat bizarre manner, the information is presented here as a direct quotation, eg 'gentle swimming and rough shooting', or simply 'various'.

Membership of a Society which for this corpus reflects more of a hobby than a profession is also included under this heading, eg the Royal Geographical, Royal Zoological, Royal Empire, Royal African Societies.

One notices the characteristic upper-middle class addiction to field sports, such as fishing and shooting of one kind or another, as well as to outdoor games like golf, tennis and squash. These lent themselves more easily than the team games of one's schooldays to the often restricted facilities of recreational life in the colonies.

RETIRED: The date given here is in nearly every instance that of the termination of the biographee's final governorship. In nine cases out of ten this was also the date of his retirement from the Colonial Service. Just occasionally, a person continued in his Colonial Service career after he had held a governorship, eg Norman-Walker. A similar exception was Sir Alan Burns' special posting in 1940 to a senior post in the Colonial Office between two of his governorships. In such cases, the governorship is also included under Career so as to ensure continuity and completeness under both heads. A number of those who were appointed to a colonial governorship direct from a career in the armed forces had previously retired, eg Tait, Kennedy, William-Powlett, Brooke-Popham, and this is made clear in the text.

Where a Governor resigned, eg, Battershill, Girouard, Lugard, or where he died in office, eg, Coryndon, Kittermaster, Panzera, this is indicated under this head. For some half-dozen Colonial Governors in this corpus it was a moot point, and one not entered into here, whether he resigned or was virtually dismissed.[47]

Perhaps even more so than in Club affiliation, the opportunities for continuing influence, often in an overseas context, created by retirement occupations is an aspect of proconsular activity which has yet to earn the attention it deserves. There need, of course, be nothing sinister in such an exploration of post-retirement undertakings. Directorships of companies with overseas involvement; chairmanships of national charitable organizations; council membership of schools, colleges and institutes; the presidentship of the Anglo-this or Anglo-that African Society—all of these have a place in the composite profile of the British Colonial Governor in retirement. Others retired into the kind of gentle obscurity they had often dreamed of. Yet others seem to have been on as many boards and committees as they were during office.[48] In no other aspect of the British Colonial Governor's career is there such diversity.

PUBLICATIONS: A perhaps unexpectedly high proportion of our corpus of British Colonial Governors have written one or more books. Most of these have focused on some theme in the territory where they served: history, anthropology, law, language, administration. A few of them have carried this recreation to a higher plane, their publications today ranking as significant contributions to the study of life in that territory. One or two others wrote professionally on items far removed from their colonial career, eg Twining on crown jewels, Eliot on Finnish grammar, Buddhism and sea-slugs. H. H. Johnston was a wide-ranging scholar, Lugard a prolific publisher, and Clifford a fiction-writer in a colonial class by himself.

While in general terms only the books written by the Governors have been listed here, several of them also contributed articles to the professional journals like the Journal of the Royal African Society (today *African Affairs*) or that of the International African Institute (*Africa*); and others to such Service or neo-service magazines as *Corona*, *United Empire*, *Crown Colonist* and *New Commonwealth*.

Where an autobiography exists, this is placed first. It is marked 'autob.'. This omnibus term allows for a full autobiography, a partial memoir, or just some degree of personal reminiscence. Other books by the Governors follow in chronological order.

SELECTED SUPPLEMENTARY SOURCES (SUPPLEMENTARY): This category of data is designed to represent something of a bonus for the researcher who wants to read further about the African career of a particular Governor. There are five principal kinds of source material. Not all of them exist for every biographee, and where there is a wealth of reference to their African career the total has, save in the case of the major Governors, had to be restricted to half a dozen or so published sources, listed in alphabetical order of author. Articles and theses are not normally included here. Any autobiography is, of course, listed under the previous head, Publications.

First, there are the straight biographies. Where these exist (and the total, though beginning to grow, remains distressingly small), they are given as the first entry. All the other types of allusions to the biographee's African assignment follow in alphabetical order of author, not in chronological order of publication.

Next, the standard regional histories expectedly furnish good accounts and analyses of a given governorship. Here pride of place goes to Volumes II (Harlow and Chilver, 1965) and III (Low and Smith, 1976) of the *Oxford History of East Africa*, and to Kenneth Ingham's *A History of East Africa* (1962). The comparable West Coast history, Ajayi and Crowder's *History of West Africa*, Vol. II (1974), is noticeably weak in its treatment of Colonial Governors. Closer attention to the gubernatorial record can rightly be expected from most of the leading histories of individual territories, eg Sir Alan Burns, *History of Nigeria* (1955); Christopher Fyfe, *A History of Sierra Leone* (1962); Harry A. Gailey, *History of the Gambia* (1964); Lewis Gann, *A History of Northern Rhodesia* (1964); David Kimble, *A Political History of Ghana* (1963); Judith Listowel, *The Making of Tanganyika* (1965); G. H. Mungeam, *British Rule in Kenya* (1966); Anthony Sillery, *The Bechuanaland Protectorate* (1952).

Thirdly, there are the reminiscences and memoirs of Colonial Service colleagues which can often be highly informative about the Governors under whom they have served.[49] Sometimes these may be incidental insights into fellow Governors, eg Mitchell and Grigg on Cameron, Burns on Clifford and Cameron, Cameron on Lugard and Clifford; or Franklin and Archer both on Storrs in single sentence cameos. Sometimes they may represent the view of Government House and its incumbents as seen by the District Commissioner in the field, a notable example being Robin Short's frank opinions of the three Governors under whom he served in Northern Rhodesia, or, in a more incidental way, those of

W. R. Crocker, Stanhope White and Ian Brook of their several gubernatorial masters in Nigeria. Or else such extra viewpoints may be gleaned from Colonial Office officials (Cosmo Parkinson, Jeffries); or from the Secretaries of State for the Colonies, some of whom are far more outspoken in memoir than they were in office (Amery, Lyttelton, Swinton); or, a source perhaps not immediately coming to mind, the records of politicians in Africa, specially informative being the memoirs of Blundell, Welensky, and Elspeth Huxley's biography of Lord Delamere. In general, the African viewpoint, such as Nkrumah on the Governors of the Gold Coast he knew or Nyerere and Ahmadu Bello on those with whom they worked, remains a conspicuous hiatus in the literature.

Fourthly, there are the travellers' tales—the traveller with an eye for human beings. Margery Perham's detailed diaries (two of which have now appeared, *African Apprenticeship* (1974) and *East African Journey* (1976), with that on Nigeria in the press), Elspeth Huxley's careful travelogue of East and of West Africa, *The Sorcerer's Apprentice* (1948) and *Four Guineas* (1954) respectively, and John Gunther's encyclopaedic travelogue, *Inside Africa* (1955), are leaders of this class of supplementary pictures of His Excellency at work—and play.[50]

Finally, there are the outsider academic studies of African administration, history, politics or the transfer of power, different enough from all the previous sources to justify separate categorization. Examples of this kind of scholarly analysis, often providing an insight into a Governor's policy or his handling of a problem, include Robert Heussler, *The British in Northern Nigeria* (1968), David Apter, *The Gold Coast in Transition* (1955) and again his *The Political Kingdom of Uganda* (1961), and Cranford Pratt, *Tanzania: The Critical Phase* (1976). It has not been possible to list here the doctoral theses or post-doctoral research on Colonial Governors currently in hand (still not as extensive as one could hope for), but for the guidance of the researcher attention may be drawn to such work as the unpublished theses of Richard Rathbone on Arden-Clarke, C. P. Youé on Coryndon, T. Fuller on Hesketh Bell; of C. Nordman on the West African Governors between 1938 and 1945, and Robert Baldock on the East

African Governors from 1918 to 1925; and such current (1978) biographical writing as R. E. Robinson on Cohen, A. J. Stockwell and H. A. Gailey on Clifford, Charles Douglas-Home on Baring, and R. A. Frost on Mitchell.

The final line of this entry, marked off by a single blank space so that it stands out for a quick reference, consists of three items of direct relevance and outstanding importance for further research. As far as is known, they have not been thus assembled before. These are (a) a reference to the date of the obituary notice in *The Times* (London); (b) a note of the existence of an entry in the *Dictionary of National Biography* (DNB); and (c) an indication of whether any of the biographee's papers are held in the Oxford Colonial Records Project (OCRP) major archive in the Rhodes House Library, Oxford University, and/or whether a tape-recording of an oral interview with him exists.[51] Each of these three sources requires further commentary.

Against *The Times* entries (and these have been traced for over ninety per cent of the Colonial Governors), the first date given is usually that of the obituary notice. These range in length from a single paragraph to several columns; even, in Lugard's case, to an accompanying editorial. A second date here refers either to further appreciations or to a notice of the funeral arrangements. Any subsequent notice, especially if it appeared some months after the obituary, is likely to refer to the deceased's will, but such a search could be a prolonged separate exercise and has not been purposely pursued in this dictionary unless probate was granted within the same calendar year.

For the *DNB* entries, earned by fewer than fifteen per cent of our corpus, reference is given to the Supplement number, eg 'DNB VI'. For the sole Governor Supp. who died before 1900 (Portal), the number of the volume in the original printing is given. Both of these figures, however, exclude the somewhat different case of the fifteen South African Governors, two-thirds of whom gained an entry in the DNB, four of them appearing in the original twenty-two volumes.

For the Oxford Colonial Records Project reference, 'OCRP' denotes the existence of manuscript material and

'OCRP/t' the existence of a tape-recorded interview. In the latter case, a transcript is also in existence. Some ninety oral interviews, ranging from two to twenty hours, were undertaken while the writer was Research Officer with the OCRP from 1967 to 1972. Of these, almost a quarter relate to Colonial Governors. The manuscript material may vary from a few letters to over a score of volumes of diaries, letters and private papers. Calendars have been prepared for some forty major collections and can be consulted at Oxford. Those who wish to examine the complete listing of all the African holdings collected under the OCRP up to 1971 are recommended to refer to the handbook by Louis Frewer, *Manuscript Collections of Africana in Rhodes House Library*, Oxford (1968), and its two *Supplements* (1971) and (1978, compiled by Wendy S. Byrne). The last-named *Supplement* contains a Name Index covering all three guides. Subsequent documentation is contained in the periodic *Checklists of Accessions* issued by Rhodes House Library. Not all the OCRP archive is yet open and *bona fide* researchers are advised to check with the Superintendent of Rhodes House Library in advance to establish whether the material they wish to consult is under any sort of donor's restriction. Valuable listings of further African manuscript material in Great Britain, including some Governors' papers, are in J. D. Pearson, ed. (1971), *A Guide to Manuscripts and Documents in the British Isles relating to Africa,* and D. H. Simpson (1975), *Manuscript Catalogue of the Library of the Royal Commonwealth Society*. Durham University houses the Sudan Archive and the Middle East Centre of St Antony's College, Oxford, has an important holding of further private papers, including those of several Colonial Governors. A catalogue is currently in hand.

Two points need to be made before concluding this discussion of the range of data included in this Biographical Dictionary. The first is that no specific reference has been made to a Governor's religious affiliation. This is in accordance not only with standard British biographical format and with the practice of the Colonial Office Personnel Division, but also with the British way of life where the public affirmation of a person's religion in no way holds the importance that it does in the United States. This may be explained in a number of ways, none of which calls for elaboration here. In the event, under five per cent of the 200 or so British Colonial Governors in Africa featured in this Biographical Dictionary were not members of the Church of England (Anglican) or the Church of Scotland (Presbyterian). In their count of a similar number of British Colonial Governors spread over a slightly shorter period (only sixty years) but a far wider geographical area (the whole of the British Empire), Nicolson and Hughes estimated that there were only six Roman Catholics and three Jews among them (they may indeed be in error over one of the latter, who, though of Jewish descent was, in fact, brought up in the Anglican faith). Typically and acceptedly in such a context, they decline to name any of them. The same discretion is observed here.

Secondly, in a book dealing with the Colonial Service, no explanation is required for the total absence of any reference to a biographee's political party affiliation or inclination. Colonial Governors, like all colonial civil servants, were assumed to be above party politics. It was an unchallenged fact of colonial life that every Colonial Service official was *ipso facto* disenfranchised for as long as he was a serving officer, by being debarred from voting in any parliamentary election in the British Isles, even if he happened to be on leave at the time. Nonetheless, for those appointed from outside the Colonial Service, such as politicians and retired service officers, political sympathies might inescapably represent a factor in their nomination; and even among career Governors, none could afford to treat the Secretary of State's directives with cavalier apoliticality for too long.[52] In contrast to the French experience, no Colonial Governor was expected to display any overt political party activity during the tenure of his governorship. Only two Colonial Governors seem to have stood for election to Parliament after retirement, Johnston and Young—both failed in their bid, Johnston twice.[53] One, Probyn, had even stood for Parliament before joining the Colonial Service. Unqualified political appointments, like Grigg, Malcolm Macdonald and Listowel, are naturally excluded from this statistic. Political party activity after retirement was, of course, a very different matter; as, among several, Molly Huggins, wife of Sir John Huggins, former Governor of

Jamaica, showed so sparkingly in her autobiography, *Too Much to Tell* (1967).

3 *Some conclusions from the data*

By way of concluding remarks, we may address ourselves to two reflections on the data presented in this Biographical Dictionary of the British Colonial Governor in Africa. First, what are the features of the composite profile of the British Colonial Governor? What sort of picture emerges, what kinds of patterns take shape, in the Colonial Governor's career? Secondly, what contribution can such a work offer to the kind of research in which the writer, along with other interested scholars, is presently engaged, a series of related studies leading eventually to a definitive history of the British Colonial Service?

For the purposes of etching in a composite profile of the British Colonial Governor in Africa, it is in order to set on one side the neo-gubernatorial posts such as the Lieutenant-Governorship of Nigeria's Northern, Western and Eastern Provinces, the Chief Commissionerships of the Gold Coast and the Resident-Commissionerships of the three High Commission territories (but including in our survey the comparable, yet independent, command of the British Resident-ship of Zanzibar). The four South African governorships, which came to an end in 1910, have also been excluded from the profile and tables which follow save where the incumbent also served in a 'straight' Colonial Service territory. Allowing, on the other hand, such changes of title as that from Commissioner to Governor in Kenya in 1906 or in Uganda in 1907, from Administrator to Governor in Tanganyika (1920) and that from High Commissioner to Governor in Southern (1906) and Northern (1908) Nigeria, one is presented with a final corpus of some 150 British Colonial Governors of Africa in the near century from the 1870s, in the case of Sierra Leone and the Gold Coast, to the independence of Nyasaland and The Gambia in 1965.★

★The appointment of Lord Soames as the last Governor of Zimbabwe-Rhodesia in December 1979 came too late for inclusion in the analysis of the data.

An important distinction that has to be made in composing this portrait of the British Colonial Governor in Africa is a generational one. Although the Colonial Service reaches back to the first half of the nineteenth century (the first set of Colonial Regulations was issued in 1837 and the first Colonial Office List was published in 1862) and its professionalization began in the last quarter of the same century, following on the rationalization of recruitment into the Home Civil Service initiated by the Northcote-Trevelyan reforms, it was not until towards the turn of the century that this phenomenon began to take effect at the top and gubernatorial levels. Even then, up to World War I there were still a lot of non-Colonial Service men appointed to colonial governorships. While the position improved yet further in the inter-war period, partly as a result of the dismay expressed by the Colonial Service at the two Colonial Conferences of 1927 and 1930 over the substantial loss of plum appointments to outsiders and partly as an outcome of the unambiguous undertaking of the Warren Fisher committee set up in 1929 to enquire into and recommend on the system of appointment to the Colonial Service, including the systematization of nominations to colonial governorships,[54] the greatest advance in the proportion of such governorships coming the way of Colonial Service officers instead of being offered to army officers, parliamentarians or Colonial Office officials, had to wait on another Colonial Service reform. This was the impact, working its way through to the top level, of the final professionalization of the Colonial Service introduced by the formalization of its training programme through an academic year—in the majority of cases an extra year—at the university following the establishment of the Tropical African Services course at Oxford and at Cambridge in 1926. For a summary of the provenance of African Colonial Governors, see Tables I and II.[55]

Nicolson and Hughes have recently made an informative study of the filial and educational (scholastic rather than university) background of a cohort of the two hundred or so British Colonial Governors who held office throughout the Empire between 1900 and 1960.[56] Their valuable article also examines in detail the various methods of entry into the Colonial Service. This has now been supplemented by a two-part study, undertaken by the writer and Dr Ivan Lloyd Phillips, of the inter-colony migration and promotion among the same cohort of British Colonial Governors.[57] From a comparative examination of these two important sources, together with a statistical study of the entries in the present volume, the following premises can be derived in respect of 'the' British Colonial Governor in Africa.

Table I: *The Nature of the Final Post held prior to Appointment to an African Governorship, 1900–1965*[*]

A. *Appointed from another Governorship*		
(cf. Table II, columns C1 and C2)		
in Africa	20	
in the West Indies/British Guiana/British Honduras	8	
in the Pacific/Indian/Atlantic Ocean	6	
in South East Asia/Far East	5	
in the Mediterranean/Aden	4	= 43
B. *Appointed from a Chief/Colonial Secretaryship*		
(cf. Table II, columns C3 and C4)		
in Africa	35	
outside Africa	9	= 44
C. *Appointed from other posts*		
Lieutenant-Governor/Chief Commissioner	9	
Deputy Governor	6	
Armed Forces	7	
Provincial Administration (in Africa)	5	
Chief Native Commissioner/Secretary for Native Affairs	1	
Administrator (West Indies)	3	
Provincial Administration (Malaya)	3	
Sudan Political Service	3	
Resident-Commissioner (Basutoland)	2	
British High Commission (South Africa)	2	
Colonial Office	2	
Foreign Office	2	
Politics	2	= 47
Total African governorships filled:		134‡

*Reproduced with the editor's permission from A. H. M. Kirk-Greene, 'The Progress of Pro-consuls: Migration and Advancement Among the Colonial Governors of British African Territories, 1900–1965', *Journal of Imperial and Commonwealth History*, Vol. VII, no. 2, January 1979.
‡22 Governors held more than one African governorship

The average tenure of office was about 4½ years. The four West African territories registered an average of 5¼ years, those of Central Africa only 4. The mean age of the British African Governor on appointment was about 50½, with that in the five East African territories being only just above 49 years of age and West Africa returning an average of 51. Normal retiring age was 55 years old.

Educational qualifications follow the pattern expectedly established by the Colonial Service 'generations' discussed above. Thus by the time those accepted for the Colonial Administrative Service from 1926 onwards had reached Government House, mostly in the 1950s and almost totally for the 1960s up to the moment of the appointment of the 'last'— and sometimes deliberately non-Colonial Service—Governor, it was unusual for the post-1950 Governor not to be a university graduate. Conversely, as Nicolson and Hughes have shown, the number of Governors who had been educated at Eton—perhaps the premier British Public School —declined considerably after the inter-war period. The last Etonian to hold high African office was Sir Mark Young, Governor of Tanganyika from 1938 to 1941, his brother Hubert having been Governor of Northern Rhodesia between 1934 and 1938. Eton's position was overtaken by Winchester in the post-World War I period. With only one African

---

Legend to Table II

A — Territory (grouped by regions)

B1 — Total governorships filled 1900–1965
B2 — Average length of governorship
B3 — Average age on appointment

C1 — Appointment from another Colonial governorship, in Africa
C2 — Appointment from another Colonial governorship, outside Africa
C3 — Appointment from Chief/Colonial Secretaryship, in Africa
C4 — Appointment from Chief/Colonial Secretaryship, outside Africa
C5 — Appointment from provincial administration
C6 — Appointment from another Colonial Service post
C7 — Appointment from within the same territory
C8 — Appointment from outside the Colonial Service

D1 — Having experience of the same territory
D2 — Having experience outside Africa
D3 — Having experience of provincial administration
D4 — Having experience of the Colonial Office

Table II: *Key Indices to the Appointment, Advancement and Migration of British Colonial Governors in Africa, 1900–1965*

A: Territory	B: Tenure and Age			C: Post held immediately prior to governership								D: Experience on appointment			
A	B1	B2	B3	C1	C2	C3	C4	C5	C6	C7	C8	D1	D2	D3	D4
Nigeria	8	6	54	3	4	1	0	0	0	0	(1)	3	8	6	1
Gold Coast	11	5¼	50	3	2	0	1	1	1	0	3	3	8	8	2
Sierra Leone	13	4¾	49	0	3	4	2	1	3	0	0	0	11	11	2
Gambia	14	4¾	51	0	3	4	2	0	5	0	0	0	9	13	0
West Africa	46	5¼	51	6	12	9	5	2	9	0	3 (+1)	6	36	38	5
N/S. Nigeria	10	4	46¼	3	0	1	0	1	2	3	3	3	6	6	0
Kenya	14	4½	52¾	5	2	0	0	1	0	0	6	1	12	4	2
Uganda	13	4¾	47¾	2	1	3	1	0	5	0	1	1	8	11	1
Tanganyika	9	4½	51	1	3	4	1	0	0	0	(1)	0	7	9	1
Somaliland	11	4½	44¼	0	0	3	0	4	3	6	1	7	4	10	0
Zanzibar	10	5	50½	1	1	5	1	0	2	1	0	1	4	8	1
East Africa	57	4½	49¼	9	7	15	3	5	10	7	8 (+1)	10	35	42	5
N. Rhodesia	9	3½	51	1	2	5	0	0	0	1	1	3	3	6	1
Nyasaland	12	4¾	50¼	1	2	5	1	0	2	1	1	5	6	9	0
Central Africa	21	4	50½	2	4	10	1	0	2	2	2	8	9	15	1
Totals	134★	4½	50¼	20	22	35	9	8	23	12	16 (+2)★★	27	86	101	11

★less 22 Governors holding more than one African governorship
★★includes two ex-Sudan appointments also included under C3

43

governorship to its credit before that (Thomson in Nigeria, 1925–31, and his not a Colonial Service appointment), out of the final total of eighteen governorships held by Etonian, Harrovian and Wykehamist career colonial officers Winchester could point to six of the last seven (the other was from Harrow), though only two of these posts were in Africa, Armitage in Nyasaland 1950–61 and Bell in Northern Nigeria 1957–61 (he, too, was not a career Colonial Service official but from the Sudan Political Service). It is the rest of the top Clarendon Schools (Rugby, Shrewsbury, Charterhouse, Westminster and St Paul's) and the leading non-Clarendon Public Schools, above all Cheltenham, Clifton and Marlborough, that provided the majority of British Colonial Governors after the Great War. In terms of total figures, 39 of the 169 British Colonial Governors whose education has been identified went to one of the Clarendon Schools (Charterhouse 9, Eton 8, Winchester 7, Rugy 6, Harrow and St Paul's 3 each, Shrewsbury 2 and Westminster 1), 80 to one or other of the 42 Public Schools belonging to the Head Masters' Conference (with as many as 10 from Cheltenham, 6 from Clifton, 5 each from Marlborough and Tonbridge), and 32 from 28 secondary schools which were not members of the HMC (including 3 from George Watson's, Edinburgh, alone).

Moving on from the Nicolson and Hughes figures on 'provenance' to those of career 'progress', what emerges conspicuously from an analysis of the data is the nature of the path to Government House, particularly in its penultimate stretch. The successful holding of the post of Chief or Colonial Secretary was a major step towards a likely governorship: approximately three out of every four African Governors had at one time or another served as Chief or Colonial Secretary. From our corpus of African Governors, as many as six out of the thirteen Governors of Sierra Leone after 1900, and another six out of the fourteen Governors of The Gambia over the same period, came to their governorship straight from a Chief/Colonial Secretaryship elsewhere. In Tanganyika and Northern Rhodesia the proportion was higher yet, registering five out of nine. The percentage is six out of ten for Zanzibar and five out of twelve for Nyasaland. Furthermore, a good number of other Governors who came into an African governorship had had previous experience of a Chief/Colonial Secretaryship in yet another colony.

Significantly, it was in the Second-Class rather than the First-Class governorships that this promotional pattern was most prominent. By contrast, In Kenya, no Governor was ever appointed direct from a Colonial Secretaryship. In Nigeria, only Robertson, the last Governor-General, was; and technically this is not quite correct, as he had in fact retired— from the Sudan Political Service, what is more—before being offered the governorship of Nigeria. In the Gold Coast, too, while the unusually young (46) and able Hugh Clifford was the only man who came to the governorship direct from the testing-ground of a Colonial Secretaryship, it was, after all, the highly responsible Colonial Secretaryship of Ceylon, the premier colony in the Empire. This was the beginning of the brilliant Clifford's four governorships spread over the next two decades.

One can also usefully examine the reverse position, the promise of certain Chief/Colonial Secretaryships as a launching-pad for a safe and near-certain landing in Government House. Among these, pride of place must go to Kenya. As many as eight African Governors had had their schooling as Chief Secretary in Kenya. Another four African Governors came each from being Chief Secretary in Tanganyika or Colonial Secretary of the Gold Coast, and three apiece from having held the same post in Northern Rhodesia and Nigeria. In the last-named connection, in the mid-1930s no less than six holders of the office of Chief Secretary, Lagos, were simultaneously serving as Governor of one colony or another, and a seventh was Assistant Under-Secretary of State for the Colonies (Cameron, Thomas, Grier, Jardine, Moore, Burns and Tomlinson). The same point could be made about the value of a training in the Secretariat at Dar-es-Salaam under Sir Donald Cameron. Outside Africa, the post of Colonial Secretary of the senior territories of Ceylon or of Palestine provided two African Governors each, while a spell as Colonial Secretary of one of the West Indian colonies—often Trinidad or Barbados in the African context—became to be looked on as a grooming for a governorship. It was Sir Alexander Grantham who, before deciding whether to accept the offer of the

Colonial Secretaryship of Bermuda, looked up the careers of previous holders of the post and with satisfaction noted that 'none had remained there for more than three years before being promoted to a higher post elsewhere'.[58]

Migration between colonial governorships is a much larger story than that being considered in this volume. Nevertheless, for the African Governors it is revealing to see in a summary way what kind of cross-fertilization there was between West and East or Central Africa. Among the top governorships, Cameron had been Governor of Tanganyika before returning to Nigeria, this time as Governor, while Bourdillon brought with him to Nigeria experience as Governor of Uganda. In Kenya, Girouard had been Governor of Northern Nigeria, and two other Governors of Kenya, Byrne and Moore, came with experience as Governor of Sierra Leone. Bell (H.H.) went to Northern Nigeria from the governorship of Uganda, Gowers to Uganda from the Lieutenant-Governorship of Northern Nigeria, Rankine was British Resident in Zanzibar when he was appointed Governor of Western Nigeria, and Shenton Thomas went to the Gold Coast after being Governor of Nyasaland. An even greater level of inter-African migration is found among the Chief/Colonial Secretaries in their penultimate moves towards a governorship. Cameron was Chief Secretary in Lagos and Jackson in Accra before their respective appointments as Governor of Tanganyika. In Northern Rhodesia, three of the nine Governors brought with them West African experience of a Chief/Colonial Secretaryship, Maybin and Benson both having done a stint in Lagos and Maxwell in Accra. The Gold Coast and Nigeria provided the same kind of experience for Shenton Thomas and Geoffrey Colby before their promotion to the governorship of Nyasaland. Kenya provided three Governors of The Gambia and two of Sierra Leone, as well as three to each of its neighbours, Somaliland and Uganda.

Two final touches may be made to our composite portrait of the African Governor. Rarely did he have any direct experience of work in the Colonial Office. Indeed, leaving aside the three special appointments between 1937 and 1945 of attaching a serving Governor to the Colonial Office (Moore, Burns, Battershill), the percentage has minimal significance.

Macpherson in Nigeria and Dorman in Sierra Leone are two of the few concerned. Similarly, the appointment of a Colonial Office official to a colonial governorship became a rarity after 1939. Creasy to the Gold Coast in 1948 and Hall, along with his immediate successor, Cohen, to Uganda in 1945 and 1952 respectively, are virtually the only examples. In strong contrast, most of the African Governors could point to — and they often profited from — substantial experience as District Officer or Provincial Commissioner.[59] This qualification was at its most conspicuous in Tanganyika, where it was an asset possessed by every single one of the territory's Governors; in Uganda (all the Governors but two, both of them Colonial Office officials); and to an only slightly lesser extent in Nyasaland, Northern Rhodesia, Sierra Leone and The Gambia.

And so, with tentative strokes, one may paint in the final face on our portrait of the British Colonial Governor of Africa in the twentieth century. The pattern assumes greater clarity after the 1920s.[60] Now the British Colonial Governor of an African territory probably came from a middle class background,[61] good family stock, a professional family but probably not landed gentry, and was often the younger son — and often a vicar's one, too.[62] He had been to one of the major-minor English public schools (the chances of it being Cheltenham were high) and taken a degree at Oxford or Cambridge, sometimes a Second or frequently a Third. Whereas in the earlier years this might have been a first Class degree in Classics or the no less rigorous discipline of gaining admission into and passing successfully out of the Royal Military College at Sandhurst or the Royal Military Academy at Woolwich, later it tended to become more diversified, with more degrees gained in say Modern History at Oxford, English at Cambridge, and on occasion Law or Anthropology, or maybe in Geography or Modern Languages at a Scottish or provincial university[63] in all probability our 'typical' Governor had attended the special Colonial Service training course at either Oxford or Cambridge. In nearly every case he was a member of the Colonial Administrative Service.

After a career of some fifteen to twenty years in the provincial administration, more often than not in the colony of his first posting (especially if that were an African territory), there would probably be promotion on transfer, to a Chief or Colonial Secretaryship. This, along with a CMG, could typically come round about the age of 40–45. A governorship of a smaller territory might well follow, or the Chief Secretaryship of a larger one against the pending chance of the governorship of a major colony. Such a career summit might come along around the age of 50, with sometimes a second governorship to follow or, just occasionally (even outside the special demands of wartime), a current governorship extended for a couple of years.

While there was not too much diversity among the London clubs to which a Colonial Governor belonged, with the Athenaeum looming prominent and the East India and Sports attracting a lot of them, too, retirement occupations and hobbies run the whole gamut from public service to private seclusion, and so destroy any attempt to construct a stereotype at this level. As regards honours, an overwhelming majority of the African Colonial Governors were awarded the KCMG, generally on appointment if they did not already hold a knighthood. The exceptions to a knighthood among African Colonial Governors are few, conspicuous, and generally controversial. Most had already earned some civil decoration during their Colonial Service career, usually the CMG and sometimes the OBE or MBE in junior days. For major colonies like Nigeria and Kenya the work of the Governor was nearly always recognized by his being created a GCMG, but for most of the African colonies this was true only for Governors at the close of the colonial period: Tanganyika, Uganda, Northern Rhodesia, Gold Coast, Sierra Leone, Nyasaland, The Gambia are all cases in point. Once again, it is the exceptions to this convention that are the more noticeable.

Such is the identikit of the 'typical' twentieth century British Colonial Governor in Africa as it is built up from the evidence presented in this Biographical Dictionary—always granted that there might be no such creature as a 'typical' Colonial Service Governor.[64]

Turning now to the outer question raised (p. 39), a number of possibilities present themselves on how this Biographical Dictionary can represent a contribution to British history, in particular British imperial history.

The data assembled under the first five heads of each bio-graphical entry offer a fresh and valuable insight into British social history. For the first time it is possible to consult in a single source comparative data on the family connections, marriage patterns and educational provenance of the whole of that segment of Britain's ruling élite represented by a century of African Colonial Governors. At this stage of the research there is little reason to believe that the other half of the corpus (the work is already in hand), the Colonial Governors of Britain's territories outside Africa, eg the Far East, West Indies, etc., will reveal significant variations from these find-ings. The African sample is extensive enough (covering every territory under the aegis of the Colonial Office) and extended enough (spanning one hundred years, virtually the whole lifetime of the Colonial Service between its professionalization in the 1860s to its demise in the 1960s) to justify certain social conclusions about the British Colonial Governor being drawn from the data now assembled. Some of these have already been examined in detail above.

Beyond this dimension of British social history, the data lends itself to important interpretations on a number of matters within an exclusively Colonial Service context. Some of these, too, have been analysed and commented on above. However, a note of caution must be sounded over the hand-ling of this kind of Service data.

While one may chart, compute and comment on careers, the ultimate variables involved in promotion to a colonial gover-norship are too subtle to respond unerringly to the cold, inhuman methods of mathematical regression. 'Only those within the Colonial Service can quite realise what it is to feel that you have got your governorship at last', commented one of their number. 'It is the crown of your service, and you have the feeling that, no matter what comes, your career has been to a great extent successful'.[65] Nomination to one of the dozen African governorships in the gift of the Secretary of State for the Colonies was too susceptible to that quite unquantifiable variant of chance, of being, in Colonial Service terms, the right man for the right post at the right time—or rather, of being thought in the Colonial Office, far more impartial than partisan, to be the right man—to allow infallible conclusions to be drawn from even impeccable data. Whatever conclusions are derived about the British Colonial Governor in Africa from the data in this Biographical Dictionary—and much of value may legitimately be so drawn—the wise student will interpret them as trends, at most as hypotheses, and not as laboratory theorems or guaranteed formulae for advancement to a colonial governorship in Africa. While the holding of a high educational qualification, the award of an honour early in one's career, or a 'beachcombing' secondment to the Colonial Office may well have subsequently constituted *one* of the influences in the Colonial Office's selection of a Governor, it was no more than one factor. Rarely can it be proved to the point of total unexceptionability to have constituted *the* decisive factor. In the Colonial Service it was nearly always a matter of quality over qualification, of practical experience and proven record over paper education. The desiderata of 'character', 'leadership' and 'responsibility', unswervingly dear to the key Colonial Service recruiting branch directed for over quarter of a century by one who deserves to be recognized as the maker of the modern Colonial Service, Sir Ralph Furse, do not lend themselves to either easy identification or simple statistical proof.

Beyond these uses of the material, there are further projects which can now suggest themselves. It might be revealing to construct a comparative profile for the Governors of the Indian Provinces and Presidencies. How did their background, social upbringing, educational record, career patterns and rewards differ? And what of their participation in public life after retirement, their contribution to the literature on Indian history, culture or administration? Nor would it be without profit to undertake a similar study of Colonial and Chief Secretaries, so often, as chief executive officer to the Governor, the senior administrator of a territory in all but name and, in so many instances, the 'man–most–likely–to' when the next colonial governorship falls vacant. Chief Justices, Lieutenant-Governors and Chief Commissioners are further top categories of colonial office for analysis by means of collective biography.

Then there are the most comparable of all, the Colonial Governors of the non-African territories of the British

Empire, in the Far East, the Pacific, the Atlantic, the Mediterranean and the West Indies. Many of Britain's most distinguished Colonial Governors feature in this list. Some of them had considerable African experience without achieving an African governorship, men like Foot, Grantham, Grey, Luke, Maddocks, Stanley (R.); others made their careers and their names in a single region only, such as Grimble in the Western Pacific or Swettenham in South-East Asia; yet others, Burdon and Stubbs, made their way to the top by other routes. The possible value of having been awarded a Far Eastern Cadetship or having been selected for service in Palestine are other factors that need to be assessed in the context of a high-flyer's career. For all of these, and their fellow Colonial Governors, a companion Biographical Dictionary such as that currently in hand must commend itself as a source essay in prosopography for the putative historian of the Colonial Service.

For just because a colonial governorship represented the summit of a Colonial Service career, and because, as the years went by, more and more of the Governors were appointed from within the Colonial Service until in the peak period of say 1935–1960 the proportion approached ninety per cent (always excepting the curious Kenya list, with only one Colonial Service appointment—and that not a career one—among all the Governors between the two World Wars), the data now gathered will assume primary importance in the next stage of the writer's current research programme, namely a historical profile of the District Officer in Africa.

As what is believed to be the first published prosopographical enquiry into a well-defined and supra-territorial sector of the Colonial Service, this Biographical Dictionary of the British Colonial Governor in Africa may have as many undisclosed weaknesses as it hopefully has surface strengths. In any event, the research for it and its formulation will have an indubitable influence on the writer's—and hopefully others'—successor projects on the history and nature of the British Colonial Service. If one has started at the top, that is no more than where every Administrative Cadet worth his salt saw himself ending. Just   Napoleon's soldiers were encouraged to sense a Marshal's baton in their knapsacks, so most of Furse's Administrative Cadets believed they had a Royal

Warrant sewn into the lining of their solar topee and could visualize a Governor's plumes waving in the wind . . . at least until some down-to-earth senior officer shattered the dream early on in their career, for the ultimate benefit of all concerned, Africans and aliens, administrators and administered, alike!

In a work which has required extensive reading and research, has called for wide discussion and co-operation, and has demanded a lot of patience from many more than the author alone, the list of those who have earned profound thanks is likely to be a long one. Grateful acknowledgement to the Staff of the Hoover Institution, Stanford; of Rhodes House Library, Oxford; and of the former Colonial Office Library, London, will take care of the biggest debts of scholarly gratitude. Among individuals, Professor Peter Duignan and Dr Lewis Gann of the Hoover Institute have been inspiring enthusiasts to work with. Thanks to a grant from the Modern History Faculty Board, Oxford University, David Prysor-Jones, B.Phil., then my graduate research assistant and later Assistant Editor of *West Africa*, was enabled to undertake valuable spade work on the initial card index. My wife has been everything the fortunate scholar's helpmeet can be. Finally, I am deeply grateful to the British Academy, the Hoover Institution, Stanford, and to the Warden and Fellows of St Antony's College, Oxford, for their financial support and continuing hospitality during the writing of this book. Corrections and additions to what is recognized as being a biographically incomplete text will be welcomed.

A. H. M. Kirk-Greene

Stanford 1976–
Oxford 1978

NOTES

1 A. H. M. Kirk-Greene, 'The British Colonial Governor in Africa: Research and Resources', paper presented to the African Studies Association Conference, San Francisco, 1975; 'The Pro-

gress of Proconsuls: Advancement and Migration among British Colonial Governors in Africa, 1900–1965', *Journal of Imperial and Commonwealth History*, VII, 2, 1979, 180–212; 'The Governors-General of Canada, 1867–1952: A Collective Profile', *Journal of Canadian Studies*, Winter 1978, 35–57.

2 Although the total of governorships filled during the period exceeded two hundred, approximately ten per cent of the incumbents were appointed to more than one African governorship. A complete history of appointments, in chronological order for each African territory, is given in the Appendix.

3 Robert Heussler, *Yesterday's Rulers*, 1963, 3. Cf. Brian V. Blakeley, *The Colonial Office, 1869–1872*, 1972, 127.

4 Lawrence Stone, 'Prosopography', in Felix Gilbert and Stephen R. Graubard, eds., *Historical Studies Today*, 1972. I am grateful to Dr Kristin Mann of Stanford University for drawing my attention to this chapter. A relevant, interesting publication which might lend itself to such an approach is J. C. Sainty, *Colonial Office Officials, 1794–1870*, 1976.

5 For a brief discussion of these sources, see pp. 10–11.

6 Information kindly supplied by Mr F. E. Page, Archivist of the Crown Agents for the Colonies.

7 I am grateful to Mr F. E. Sitch of the Ministry of Overseas Development for enabling me to consult this list.

8 Copy consulted by courtesy of His Excellency the Governor of the Gilbert and Ellice Islands.

9 Cf. H. Hannam, 'African Material in the Library of the Foreign and Commonwealth Office', *Africa Research and Documentation*, 8/9, 1975, 22.

10 Sir Charles Jeffries, *Whitehall and the Colonial Service: an administrative memoir, 1939–1956*, 1972, 108. See also A. H. M. Kirk-Greene, 'The Thin White Line: the Size of the British Colonial Service in Africa', paper presented to the African Studies Association of the United Kingdom Conference, Oxford, 1978.

11 Sir Anton Bertram, *The Colonial Service*, 1930, 14.

12 *Obituaries from the Times, 1961–1970*, Newspaper Archive Developments Ltd., Reading, compiled by Frank C. Roberts, 1975. A second volume, covering 1971–1975, is in press. This in its turn promises to be further supplemented by the project of the Dolphin Press, whose first annual volume of *The British National Obituary* is scheduled to appear shortly.

13 Since this essay was written, a further source for biographical data on the East and West African Governors after World War I has become available. This is the valuable thesis by Dr Robert Baldock, 'Colonial Governors and the Colonial Office: a Study

of British Policy in Tropical Africa, 1918–1925' (Bristol University unpublished Ph.D., 1978). The Coryndon material in this has been substantially advanced in another dissertation, Dr Christopher P. Youé, 'The African Career of Robert T. Coryndon: Personality and Policy in British Colonial Rule' (Dalhousie University unpublished Ph.D., 1978).

14 Henige, *Colonial Governors*, p. x.

15 Although Christopher Fyfe's otherwise encyclopaedic *A History of Sierra Leone* (1962) does not carry such a list, it ranks as the only book to contain in its Index the gubernatorial entry 'Governors: excursuses on'!

16 See A. H. M. Kirk-Greene, 'Governors and Governorship in British Africa', in Peter Duignan and Lewis H. Gann, *The African Proconsul*, 1978, Table VI.

17 A list in which Zanzibar was regularly included, subject to the fine print caveat of 'Does not rank as a governor for pension purposes'. On the implications of the legislation for Colonial Governors, see Brian V. Blakeley, 'Pensions and Professionalism: The Colonial Governors (Pensions) Acts and the British Colonial Service, 1865–1911', *Journal of Imperial and Commonwealth History*, IV, 2, January 1976, 138–53.

18 Cf. Brian V. Blakeley, *The Colonial Office*, 122.

19 Among Sir Donald Cameron's several blows at the prestige of his senior officials while he was Governor of Nigeria (1931–35) was his successful downgrading of his two Lieutenant-Governors to the rank of Chief Commissioner.

20 To the author's disgust, his name on the Colonial Office files was always (and quite wrongly) catalogued under 'G.,A.H.M.K-'.

21 W. R. Crocker, *Nigeria: A Critique of British Colonial Administration*, 1936, 200.

22 Lord Altrincham, *Kenya's Opportunity*, 1955, 72–3.

23 Ibid., 74.

24 See A. Duff Cooper, *Old Men Forget*, 1953, 40–41, and Harold Nicolson, *Some People*, 1927.

25 Kenneth Bradley, *Once A District Officer*, 1936, 25.

26 'Sappers' who became Colonial Governors at this time are conspicuous by their number and quality. They include Chancellor, Girouard, Guggisberg, McCallum, Nathan and Young (H).

27 A feature—and major attraction—of the new universities of the 1960s was a far greater flexibility in the combination of subjects allowed for joint Honours, especially on the liberal arts side.

28 Generally speaking, a II/1 is an acceptable degree to qualify for graduate study. By the 1930s, the Colonial Office was able to

stipulate in its regulations that 'whilst a university degree is not an absolutely indispensable qualification, the candidates selected for Administrative appointments in the last few years have nearly all been in possession of a degree, usually with Honours . . . There is no reason to anticipate that at future selections the standard in this respect will be any less high'. Later, a Second was looked on as the norm.

29 In 1977, the following statistics obtained at Oxford. Out of 2,570 candidates taking their finals for the award of the BA ('Schools'), 13% were awarded a First, 71.7% a Second, 13.5% a Third, 1.4% a Pass, and 0.4% a Fail. Although the proportion of Firsts awarded has increased in recent years (while recruitment for the Colonial Administrative Service on permanent and pensionable terms may be considered to have largely ceased by 1960), the general pattern established is applicable to the peak periods of recruitment to the Colonial Administrative Service, 1926–9, 1935–8 and again from 1945 to 1950.

30 Two examples will suffice. The first is taken from Lord Vansittart's Foreword to H. C. Jackson's autobiographical *Sudan Days and Ways*, 1954: 'The author was selected with seven others. Look at their credentials! A former Rugby football captain of Oxford and Scotland; an ex-captain of the Cambridge University cricket team; a member of the Oxford University Soccer XI; a rowing trials man; a member of the Oxford and Middlesex County cricket teams; and a Somerset County Rugby footballer. This was a typical intake' (vii). Collie Knox, who accompanied Archer on his transfer from Uganda to the Sudan as Private Secretary, in his diary noted 'Everywhere we went, the world of athletics was upheld. To a large extent the governing of the Sudan is in the hands of Old Blues'—*It Might Have Been You*, 1958, 205.

31 Although the title originally proposed in the White Paper, 'Reorganization of the Colonial Service' (Col. No. 306, 1954), was 'Her Majesty's Oversea Civil Service', in deference—*pace* Sir Charles Jeffries—to the shift in Colonial Office usage of 'overseas' from adverb to adjective, the title was officially changed two years later to 'Overseas'—see Jeffries, *Whitehall and Colonial Service*, 7.

32 Cf. Blakeley, *The Colonial Office*, ix and 13, note 44.

33 Sir Alan Burns, *Colonial Civil Servant*, 1949, 161.

34 Interview, Sir John Martin, Oxford, 6 December 1976.

35 Cf. John S. Galbraith's judgement that 'The development of the Colonial Service has not yet received the attention of a careful historian'—'The Empire since 1783' in Robin W. Winks, ed.,

The Historiography of the British Empire Commonwealth, 1966, 52. Margery Perham highlighted the same gap when she wrote: 'An immense literature has been written about British colonial policy and administration, and surprisingly little about the men who expressed policy in administration'—Introduction to Robert Heussler, *Yesterday's Rulers*, 1963.

36 Mention may be made in this context of A. H. M. Kirk-Greene's bibliographical survey, 'The British Colonial Governor in the Literature', *African Research and Documentation*, XII, 1977, 10–13.

37 On the Crown Agents, see in particular A. W. Abbott, *A Short History of the Crown Agents and their Office* 1959, privately printed, and Richard M. Kesner, 'Builders of Empire: The Role of the Crown Agents in Imperial Development, 1880–1914', *Journal of Imperial and Commonwealth History*, V, 1977, 310–30.

38 On the critical importance of the post of Chief/Colonial Secretary as a stepping-stone to a governorship, see Kirk-Greene, 'Progress of Consuls', Table V.

39 For a concise explication of the legal classification of the kinds of dependency, see M. Wright, *British Colonial Constitutions*, 1952, Chapter I.

40 Lee, *Colonial Development*, gives a figure of sixty-seven officers who in 1947 transferred from the defunct I.C.S. into the Colonial Administrative Service. On African Governors from India, see O'Malley, *Indian Civil Service*, 259 ff.

41 Sir George V. Fiddes, *The Dominions and Colonial Offices*, 1926, 65.

42 In 1924, for example, the GCMG was restricted to 100, of which 30 were assignable for service overseas. The figures for the KCMG and CMG were respectively 300 (90) and 725 (217). On quotas, Sir Geoffrey Archer has recorded how he, as Governor-General of the Sudan, and the High Commissioner, Lord Lloyd, had jointly sought from the Foreign Office an increase in the number of awards available for Sudanese service. 'The list submitted, as arranged between us, had been for one KCMG, one CMG, two CBEs, and several OBEs and MBEs. As it turned out, all that was granted was one KCMG'—Archer, *Personal and Historical Memoirs*, 241. In *Titles and Forms of Address* (9th edition, 1955), there is an exhaustive table at p. 144 showing the correct order of the fifty-two degrees of honour and decorations likely to be awarded in imperial circles, ranging from VC to ED and including every level of all the Orders discussed here.

43 In Uganda in the 1950s, two hereditary knights baronet were serving simultaneously in subordinate positions: Sir George Duntz, Bt, was an administrator while Sir Archibald Dunbar,

Bt, was an agricultural officer. In Northern Nigeria, the Residents before World War I included the Honourable David Carnegie and the Honourable H. B. Hermon-Hodge.

44 Burns, *Colonial Civil Servant*, 147.

45 Kirk-Greene, 'The Governors-General of Canada', 46. Cf. C. P. Snow's observation that 'In English prosperous life the clubs a man belonged to told one something . . . If one could read the fine print, those details had a certain eloquence, just as accents had'—*In Their Wisdom*, 1974, 168.

46 Those who wish to read more about the origins, ethos, customs and anecdotes of London's clubland may refer to Major Arthur Griffiths, *Clubs and Clubmen*, 1907; Ralph Nevill, *London Clubs*, 1911; T. H. S. Escott, *Club Makers and Club Members*, 1914; Charles Patrick Graves, *Leather Armchairs*, 1963; P. K. Hiller, 'The English Gentlemen's Club', *This England*, Winter 1976, 26–8; 'Can Clubs Survive the Cold?', *The Times*, 2 November 1976; and Anthony Lejeune and Malcolm Lewis, *The Gentlemen's Clubs of London*, 1979. Individual Club histories also exist, eg H. S. Eccles and Earl Spencer's history of Brooks's written for its bicentenary in 1964. In their respective heydays, essentially 'clubbable men' like Lord Mountbatten and Sir Harold Macmillan are reputed to have belonged to fourteen and seven clubs respectively.

47 Kenya (Eliot, Girouard, Northey, Renison) and the Sudan (Wingate, Archer) seem to have been two of the most 'accident-prone' territories for Governors.

48 As John Buchan noted of the retired proconsul, 'He becomes the quarry of a thousand organizations in quest of a president or an apologist'—*Lord Minto*, 1924, 209.

49 Cf. A. H. M. Kirk-Greene, 'More Memoirs as a Source for a Service History', *Journal of Administration Overseas*, XV, October 1976, 235–40.

50 For a comment on this, see the review article, 'Miss Perham Remembers', *West Africa*, 21 November 1977, 2352–4.

51 For an account of the OCRP, see J. J. Tawney, 'The Oxford Colonial Records Project', *African Affairs*, LXVII, 269, October 1968, 345–50; and, more fully, Patricia Pugh's account in the *Journal of the Society of Archivists*, VI, II, 1978, 78–86.

52 Table I in Harry S. Gailey, *Sir Donald Cameron, Colonial Governor*, 1974, 135, is interesting. It is, however, incomplete—for instance, Coryndon is unexpectedly omitted from the Kenyan governorships.

53 At least two former colonial administrators are currently (1978) Members of Parliament, Sir George Sinclair and Ivor Stanbrook,

and several others have either recently stood or are about to stand for election.

54 See Cmd. 2883 and 2884 (1927); Cmd. 3628 and 3629 (1930); and Cmd. 3554 (1930), the Warren Fisher Report.

55 Reproduced with permission from Kirk-Greene, 'Progress of Proconsuls', Table III.

56 Nicolson and Hughes, 'Provenance of Proconsuls', 1975.

57 For Part I, see Kirk-Greene, 'Progress of Proconsuls', 1979.

58 Sir Alexander Grantham, *Via Ports*, 1965, 19.

59 It was the view of at least one Colonial Governor coming in from the outside—in this case, the Foreign Service—that such an upbringing was almost essential: 'Nobody can really know about the Colonial Service unless he has sweated all the way up the ladder; unless, in particular, he has been a District Commissioner or the equivalent, and has thus acquired that "D.C. outlook" which is like the Ark of the Covenant or the corporate essence of the Service'—Sir Charles Johnston, *The View from Steamer Point*, 1964, 191.

60 For the period up to World War I, see P. Duignan and L. Gann, *The Rulers of British Africa*, 1979, Chapter 5.

61 Cf. K. G. Bradley, *Once a District Officer*, 1966, 4 and 9.

62 Robert Collins has calculated that as many as one third of the 400 men who joined the Sudan Political Service were sons of clergy-men—'The Sudan Political Service', 301. As Table V in Kirk-Greene, 'On Governorship and Governing' discloses, the Colonial Service, too, could point to a high percentage of clergy-men's sons. There was a similar situation in the ICS, especially before the 1920s—cf. S. M. Misra, *The Bureaucracy in India*, 1977.

63 For an elaboration of this, see A. H. M. Kirk-Greene, 'Scholastic Attainment and Scholarly Achievement in Britain's Imperial Services: The Case of the African Governors', paper presented to the Canadian Association of African Studies Conference, Guelph, 1980.

64 Such a close observer as Margery Perham was of the same opinion about the Colonial Service in general: 'There is no type British colonial servant, only a bewildering variety'—*African Apprenticeship*, 1974, 232.

65 Sir Ralph Williams, *How I Became a Governor*, 1913, 345.

A BIOGRAPHICAL DICTIONARY OF THE BRITISH COLONIAL GOVERNOR

Volume 1: Africa

AINSWORTH DICKSON, Thomas★

s/o. Francis Dickson and Bonella Ainsworth, Lancashire
b. 28 July 1881, Lancashire **d.** 1 April 1935
m. —
ch. —

Education: St Paul's School
privately in Europe

Career: 1909 Customs Assistant, Kenya
1911 Assistant District Commissioner
1914 War Service, East Africa
1916 Mission to Algeria and Tunisia
1919 District Commissioner
1921 Provincial Commissioner

Governorships: Swaziland 1928–35 (Resident
Commissioner)

Honours: MC 1916; CMG 1930

Clubs: Royal Empire Society

Recreations: travel in Middle East and North Africa

Retired: died in office

Publications: —

Supplementary: —

Obit. 2 April, 13d

★Given in the *Colonial Office Lists* as Dickson, T. A. but as Ainsworth
Dickson, T., in *Who's Who*.

ARCHER, Geoffrey (Francis)

s/o. (2nd) Bradley Archer, Hyde Park, London, and
  nephew of F. J. Jackson, Governor of Uganda

b. 1882   **d.** 1 May 1964

m. Olive Mary, d/o Colonel Charles Bulkeley Godman,
  1916

ch. —

Education: —

Career: 1902 Assistant Collector, East African Protectorate
  (Cadet, Kenya)
  1907 District Commissioner
  1911 in charge, Northern Frontier District, Kenya
  1912 Acting Commissioner, Somaliland
  1913 Deputy Commissioner

Governorships: Somaliland 1914–22 (Commissioner to
  1919)
  Uganda 1922–24
  Sudan 1924–26 (resigned)

Honours: CMG 1913; KCMG 1920

Clubs: —

Recreations: ornithology, tennis, golf

Retired: 1926, resigned

Publications: *Personal and Historical Memoirs of an East
  African Administrator*, 1964, autobiog.; *The Birds of
  Somaliland and the Gulf of Aden*, 1938 (with Eva Godman)

Supplementary: James Barber, *Imperial Frontier*, 1968;
  H. F. P. Battersby, *Richard Corfield of Somaliland*, 1914;
  Collie Knox, *It Might Have Been You*, 1938; Douglas
  Jardine, *The Mad Mullah of Somaliland*, 1923; J. R. P.
  Postlethwaite, *I Look Back*, 1947.

  Obit. 4 May, 18a

ARDEN-CLARKE, Charles (Noble)*

s/o. (1st) The Reverend C. W. A. Clarke,
Bournemouth, missionary in South India
b. 25 July 1898, Bournemouth **d.** 16 December 1962
m. Georgina Dora Reid
ch. 1s 2d

Education: Rossall School

Career: 1917 war service, France and Russia
1920 Cadet, Northern Nigeria
1934 Principal Assistant Secretary, Nigeria
1936 Secretary to the Government, Bechuanaland

Governorships: Bechuanaland 1937–42 (Resident
Commissioner)
Basutoland 1942–46 (Resident
Commissioner)
Sarawak 1946–49
Gold Coast 1949–57 (Governor-General
1957)

Honours: CMG 1941; Kt. 1946; KCMG 1948; GCMG 1952

Clubs: Athenaeum

Recreations: gardening; philately

Retired: 1957
Chairman, Royal African Society, 1959; Chairman, Royal
Commonwealth Society for the Blind, 1959; Member,
Monckton Commission on Central Africa, 1960.

Publications: —

Supplementary: Dennis Austin, *Politics in Ghana*, 1964;
F. M. Bourret, *Ghana: the Road to Independence*, 1960;
C. Douglas-Home, *The Last Proconsul*, 1978; Hugh
Boustead, *The Wind of Morning*, 1971; Elspeth Huxley,
Four Guineas, 1954; Kwame Nkrumah, *Autobiography*,
1957; Sir James Robertson, *Transition in Africa*, 1974;
Richard P. Stevens, *Lesotho, Botswana and Swaziland*, 1967;
West Africa, August 13, 1949

Obit. 18 Dec., 13a

*Name changed from Clarke to Arden-Clarke by deed poll, and in *Colonial Office List* from 1951.

ARMITAGE, Cecil (Hamilton), Captain

s/o. S. H. T. Armitage, MD
b. 8 October 1869   **d.** 10 March 1933
m. —
ch. —

Education: —

Career: 1889 commissioned into South Wales Borderers
1894 Assistant Inspector, Gold Coast
Constabulary
1895 Ashanti expedition
1899 Private Secretary to Governor of the Gold
Coast
1900 Ashanti campaign; Acting Resident, Kumasi
1901 Travelling Commissioner, Gold Coast
1910 Chief Commissioner, Northern Territories

Governorships: The Gambia 1920–27

Honours: DSO 1901; CMG 1911; KBE 1926
Silver Medallist, Zoological Society

Clubs: East India and Sports

Recreations: Fellow, Royal Zoological Society

Retired: 1927

Publications: *The Ashanti Campaign of 1900*, 1901 (with A. F. Montanaro).

Supplementary: Harry A. Gailey, *A History of the Gambia*, 1964

Obit. 13 March, 9a, 14c; 14, 11d; 16, 17b

ARMITAGE, Robert (Perceval)

s/o. F. Armitage, CIE, Inspector-General of Police, Madras
b. 21 December 1906   **d.** —
m. Gwladys Lyona, d/o Lieutenant-Colonel H. M.
     Meyler, CBE, DSO, MC, 1930
ch. 2s

Education: Winchester College
           New College, Oxford   History, Class II, 1928

Career: 1929   Cadet, Kenya
           1947   Administrative Secretary
           1948   Financial Secretary, Gold Coast
           1951   Minister of Finance

Governorships: Cyprus 1954–55
                    Nyasaland 1956–61

Honours: MBE 1944; CMG 1951; KCMG 1954

Clubs: Royal Commonwealth Society

Recreations: golf, gardening

Retired: 1961
     Trustee, Beit Trust, 1963

Publications: —

Supplementary: Harry Franklin, *Unholy Wedlock*, 1963;
     Robert I. Rotberg, *The Rise of Nationalism in Central Africa*,
     1965; Sir Roy Welensky, *4000 Days*, 1964; *West Africa*,
     May 9, 1953.

ARROWSMITH, Edwin (Porter)

s/o. Edwin Arrowsmith
b. 23 May 1909   **d.** —
m. Cloudagh, d/o W. G. Connor, MD
ch. 2d

Education: Cheltenham College,
Trinity College, Oxford   History, Class III, 1932

Career: 1932 Cadet, Bechuanaland
1940 Commissioner, Turks and Caicos Islands
1946 Administrator, Dominica

Governorships: Basutoland 1952–56 (Resident
Commissioner)
Falkland Islands 1957–64
British Antarctic Territory 1962–64 (High
Commissioner)

Honours: CMG 1950; KCMG 1959

Clubs: Flyfishers'; Hurlingham; Royal Commonwealth
Society

Recreations: fly-fishing;
President, Flyfishers' Club

Retired: 1964 (resigned 1938)
Director, Overseas Services Resettlement Bureau, 1965;
Chairman, Royal Commonwealth Society for Blind, 1970

Publications: —

Supplementary: Sir Ralph Furse, *Aucuparius*, 1962; Sir
Harry Luke, *Cities and Men*, III, 1956

BARING, Evelyn, Hon. (Lord Howick)

s/o.   Earl of Cromer and Lady Katharine Thynne, d/o
          Marquess of Bath
b.   29 September 1903   **d.**   10 March 1973
m.   Lady Mary Cecil Grey, d/o Earl Grey
ch.   1s 2d

Education: Winchester College
                New College, Oxford   History, Class I, 1924

Career: 1926 entered Indian Civil Service
             1929 Secretary to Agent of Government of India in
                   South Africa
             1934 retired

Governorships: Southern Rhodesia 1942–44
                    High Commissioner in South Africa
                       1944–51
                    Kenya 1952–59

Honours: KCMG 1942; KCVO 1947; GCMG 1955
              Queen's Commendation for Brave Conduct 1959
              Elevated to peerage as Baron Howick of Glendale, 1960

Clubs: —

Recreations: —

Retired: 1959 (1934 from Indian Civil Service)
              Vice-President, Liverpool School of Tropical Medicine,
              1967; Member, Times Trust; Chairman, Commonwealth
              Development Corporation, 1960; Director, Swan Hunter;
              Chairman, Nature Conservancy, 1960; Chairman, British
              North American Committee, 1970

Publications: —

Supplementary: C. Douglas-Home, *The Last Proconsul*,
                    1978, biog.; George Bennett, *Kenya*, 1963; Michael
                    Blundell, *So Rough A Wind*, 1964; A. V. Clayton and
                    D. Savage, *Government and Labour* in Kenya, 1974;

D. A. Low and Alison Smith, *History of East Africa*, III, 1976; Nicholas Monsarrat, *Life is a Four Letter Word*, II, 1970; M. P. K. Sorrenson, *Land Reform in the Kikuyu Country*, 1967.

Obit. 11 March, 2h; 12, 14f; 15, 18b, 18g; 16, 18h; 17, 16g; 21, 17h   OCRP/t

BARKLY, Henry

s/o. Aeneas Barkly, Ross-shire, West India Merchant

b. 24 February 1815   **d.** 20 October 1898

m. 1st Elizabeth Helen, d/o John Timins, Hilfield, 1840
2nd Anne Marie, d/o General Sir Thomas Pratt, KCB,
     Bruce Castle, Rowland Hill, 1860

ch. 2s

Education: Bruce Castle, Tottenham

Career: 1845 MP, Leominster

Governorships: British Guiana 1848–1853
                 Jamaica 1853–1856
                 Victoria 1856–1863
                 Mauritius 1863–1870
                 Cape Colony 1870–1877

Honours: KCB 1853

Clubs: Carlton

Recreations: —

Retired: 1877
Member, Royal Commission on Defence of British
Possessions and Commerce Overseas, 1879; FRS; FRGS;
President, Bristol Archaelogical Society; Committee,
London Library

Publications: —

Supplementary: Mona Macmillan, *Sir Henry Barkly,
Mediator and Moderator*, 1970, biog.; T. R. Davenport,
South Africa: A Modern History, 1978; C. J. F. Muller, *Five
Hundred Years: A History of South Africa*, 1969; E. A.
Walker, *A History of Southern Africa*, 1959, and ed.,
Cambridge History of the British Empire, VIII, 1963

Obit. Oct. 22; 26; 27   DNB XXII

BATTERSHILL, William (Denis)

s/o. —

b.   29 June 1896   **d.**   11 August 1959

m.   Joan Elizabeth, d/o Major-General Sir John Gellibrand, 1924

ch.   2d

Education: King's College, Worcester

Career: 1914 war service, India and Iraq
               1920 Cadet, Ceylon Civil Service
               1928 Assistant Colonial Secretary, Jamaica
               1935 Colonial Secretary, Cyprus
               1936 Acting Governor
               1937 Chief Secretary, Palestine

Governorships: Cyprus 1939–41
                       Colonial Office 1941–45 (Deputy Under-Secretary)
                       Tanganyika 1945–49 (resigned)

Honours: CMG 1938; KCMG 1941

Clubs: East India and Sports

Recreations: fishing, riding

Retired: 1949, to Kyrenia, Cyprus (resigned)

Publications: —

Supplementary: Judith Listowel, *The Making of Tanganyika*, 1965

    Obit. 12 August, 10d

BEETHAM, Edward (Betham)

s/o. Dr. Beetham, MD, Knaresborough

b. 19 February 1905   **d.** March 1979

m. Eileen Joy Parkinson, 1933

ch. 1d

Education: Charterhouse School
Lincoln College, Oxford   Law, Class III, 1926

Career: 1928 Cadet, Kenya
          1938 Colonial Office
          1938 District Commissioner, Sierra Leone
          1940 Chief Assistant Colonial Secretary

Governorships: Swaziland 1946–50 (Resident
          Commissioner)
          Bechuanaland 1950–53 (Resident
          Commissioner)
          Windward Islands 1953–55
          Trinidad and Tobago 1955–60

Honours: OBE 1946; CVO 1947; CMG 1950; KCMG 1955

Clubs: Army and Navy; Phyllis Court, Henley-on-Thames

Recreations: golf

Retired: 1960
Chairman, Texaco Ltd., United Kingdom, 1963;
Chairman, Norbury Insulation Group Ltd.; Director,
Barclay's Bank DCO

Publications: —

Supplementary: Molly Huggins, *Too Much To Tell*, 1967

BELFIELD, Henry (Conway)

s/o. (1st) John Belfield, JP, Devon, and Eliza, d/o Captain
G. Bridges, R.N.

b.   29 November 1855   **d.**   8 January 1923

m.   Florence, d/o the Reverend James Rathbone

ch. 1s 2d

Education: Rugby School
Oriel College, Oxford   History, Class IV,
1877
Called to the Bar, Inner Temple

Career: 1880 practised law
1884 entered Colonial Legal Service
1888 Commissioner of Lands, Selangor
1891 Senior Magistrate, Perak
1896 Commissioner of Lands and Mines, Malaya
1901 Resident
1912 Special Commissioner on Land Tenure, Gold
Coast

Governorships: Kenya 1912–19

Honours: CMG 1909; KCMG 1914

Clubs: Junior Carlton; Bachelors'; Ranelagh

Recreations: shooting, fishing, reading, Malay language

Retired: 1918

Publications: *Handbook of the Federated Malay States*

Supplementary: A. V. Clayton and D. Savage, *Govern-
ment and Labour in Kenya*, 1974; R. G. Gregory, *India and
East Africa*, 1971; Vincent Harlow and E. M. Chilver,
History of East Africa, II, 1965; M. F. Hill, *Permanent Way*,
I, 1950; Elspeth Huxley, *White Man's Country*, 1935;
W. McGregor Ross, *Kenya From Within*, 1927; M. P. K.
Sorrenson, *Origins of European Settlement in Kenya*, 1968;
Robert L. Tignor, *The Colonial Transformation of Kenya*,
1976.

Obit. 9 Jan. 10f; 1 March 15f

BELL, Gawain (Westray)

s/o. William Westray Bell
b. 21 January 1909   **d.** —
m. Silvia, d/o Major Adrian Cornwell-Clyne
ch. 3d

Education: Winchester College
Hertford College, Oxford   History Class II,
     1930; shooting blue

Career: 1931 Sudan Political Service
       1938 seconded to Colonial Service, Palestine
       1941 war service, Middle East (Arab Legion)
       1945 District Commissioner, Sudan
       1949 Deputy Sudan Agent, Cairo
       1953 Deputy Civil Secretary, Sudan
       1954 Permanent Secretary
       1955 Political Agent, Kuwait

Governorships: Northern Nigeria 1957–61

Honours: MBE 1942; CBE 1955; KCMG 1957

Clubs: Athenaeum; Bath

Recreations: walking, riding, skiing, shooting, rifle
shooting

Retired: 1962
Secretary-General, Council Middle East Trade, 1963;
Constitutional Adviser, Federation of Southern Arabia,
1965; Secretary-General, South Pacific Commission,
1966; Governing Body, School of Oriental and African
Studies, London University, 1970; Executive Committee,
Leprosy Relief Association

Publications: —

Supplementary: Sir Ahmadu Bello, *My Life*, 1962;
K. D. D. Henderson, *The Making of the Modern Sudan*,
1953; Sir James Robertson, *Transition in Africa*, 1974; Sir
Bryan Sharwood Smith, *But Always As Friends*, 1969

OCRP/t

73

BELL, (Henry) Hesketh (Joudou)

s/o. Henry A. J. Bell
b. December 1864, West Indies **d.** 1 August 1952
m. —
ch. —

Education: privately in Brussels and Paris

Career: 1882 clerical grade, Barbados
1883 Treasury Department, Grenada
1890 Supervisor of Customs, Gold Coast
1891 Senior Assistant Treasurer
1892 District Commissioner, Accra
1894 Receiver-General, Bahamas
1899 Administrator, Dominica
1904 Acting Governor, Leeward Islands

Governorships: Uganda 1906–09 (Commissioner to 1907)
Northern Nigeria 1909–12
Leeward Islands 1912–15
Mauritius 1916–24

Honours: CMG 1903; KCMG 1908; GCMG 1925

Clubs: Athenaeum; Bath; West Indian

Recreations: —

Retired: 1925, to Cannes, France; 1939, to Bahamas

Publications: *Glimpses of a Governor's Life*, 1946, autobiog. (covering 1899–1909 only); *Love in Black*, 1911; *Witchcraft in the West Indies*, 1889; *Foreign Systems of Colonial Administration in the Far East*, 1928; *Witches and Fishes*, 1948; *Obeah*

Supplementary: Sir Geoffrey Archer, *Personal and Historical Memoirs*, 1964; James Barber, *Imperial Frontier*, 1968; Sonia Graham, *Government and Mission Education in Northern Nigeria*, 1966; R. G. Gregory, *India and East Africa*, 1971; Vincent Harlow and E. M. Chilver, *History of East Africa*, II, 1965; Robert Heussler, *The British in Northern Nigeria*, 1968; Kenneth Ingham, *A History of East Africa*,

1962; Kenneth Ingham, *The Making of Modern Uganda*, 1958; E. D. Morel, *Nigeria: its People and its Problems*, 1911; J. R. P. Postlethwaite, *I Look Back*, 1947

Obit. 5 Aug, 6d; 8, 6d; 14, 6e   DNB Supp. VII

BENSON, Arthur (Edward Trevor)

s/o. The Reverend Arthur H. Benson, Staffordshire,
formerly of County Limerick and St Saviour's,
Johannesburg

b. 21 December 1907   **d.** —

m. Daphne Mary Joyce, d/o E. H. M. Fynn, Southern
Rhodesia, 1933

ch. 2d

Education: Wolverhampton School
Exeter College, Oxford   Classics, Class II,
1929

Career: 1932 Cadet, Northern Rhodesia
1939 Colonial Office
1940 War Cabinet Office
1943 Colonial Office
1944 Secretariat, Northern Rhodesia
1946 Administrative Secretary, Uganda
1949 Chief Secretary, Central African Council
1951 Chief Secretary, Nigeria
1952 Acting Governor

Governorships: Northern Rhodesia, 1954–59

Honours: CMG 1952; KCMG 1954; GCMG 1959
Honorary Fellow, Exeter College, Oxford 1963

Clubs: Leander

Recreations: fishing, shooting

Retired: 1959
JP, Devon, 1962

Publications: —

Supplementary: Harry Franklin, *Unholy Wedlock*, 1963;
Sir Ralph Furse, *Aucuparius*, 1962; David C. Mulford,
Zambia: the Politics of Independence, 1967; Kenneth Kaunda
Zambia Shall Be Free, 1962; Robert I. Rotberg, *The Rise of
Nationalism in Central Africa*, 1965; Robin Short, *African
Sunset*, 1973; Sir Roy Welensky, *4000 Days*, 1964

OCRP

BERESFORD-STOOKE, George★

s/o.   The Reverend C. A. Stooke, Bath
b.   3 January 1897   **d.** —
m.   Creenagh, d/o Sir Henry Richards, Chief Justice, North
      Western Provinces, India, 1931
ch.   1s 1d

Education: King Edward VI School, Bath

Career: 1914 war service, Royal Navy
      1920 Cadet, Sarawak
      1925 District Officer, Kenya
      1933 Assistant Treasurer, Mauritius
      1936 Deputy Treasurer, Kenya
      1938 Deputy Chief Secretary
      1940 Chief Secretary, Zanzibar
      1942 Chief Secretary, Northern Rhodesia

Governorships: Sierra Leone 1948–53

Honours: CMG 1943; KCMG 1948

Clubs: Athenaeum

Recreations: —

Retired: 1959
   Second Crown Agent, 1953; Overseas Commander, Boy
   Scouts Association, 1954; Member, Kenya Camps
   Commission, 1959; Gentleman Usher of the Blue Rod in
   the Order of St Michael and St George, 1959; President,
   Anglo-Sierra Leone Society, 1962; Vice-Chairman,
   International African Institute

Publications: —

Supplementary: Elspeth Huxley, *Four Guineas*, 1954

★The name was changed, in the *Colonial Office Lists*, from G. B. Stooke after
  1948. *Who's Who* adheres to an entry under Stooke but retains the hyphen.

BERKELEY, Ernest (James Lennox)

s/o. George R. Lennox Berkeley
b. 31 May 1857   **d.** 24 October 1932
m. Nelly, d/o Sir James Harris, Foreign Office
ch. 1s 1d

Education: Royal Academy, Gosport
                Royal Military College, Sandhurst

Career: 1876 commissioned into 57th Foot
             1877 transferred to 60th Rifles
             1885 Vice-Consul, East Coast Africa
             1891 Consul, Zanzibar
             1892 Administrator, British East Africa Co.
             1895 Commissioner, Uganda
             1899 Consul-General, Tunis

Governorships: Uganda 1895–99 (Commissioner)

Honours: CB 1897; KCMG 1921

Clubs: Travellers'

Recreations: Fellow, Royal Geographical Society

Retired: 1920 (from the army 1877)

Publications: —

Supplementary: James Barber, *Imperial Frontier*, 1967;
    M. F. Hill, *Permanent Way*, I, 1950; C. W. Hobley, *Kenya:
    from Chartered Company to Crown Colony*, 1929; Kenneth
    Ingham, *The Making of Modern Uganda*, 1958; H. Moyse-
    Bartlett, *The King's African Rifles*, 1956; Margery Perham
    and Mary Bull, *The Diaries of Lord Lugard*, 1959

BLOOD, Hilary (Rudolph Robert)

s/o. (1st) Canon A. F. Blood, Kilmarnock, Scotland
b. 1893   **d.** 20 June 1967
m. Alison Farie, d/o Boyd Anderson, Ayr, Scotland
ch. 1s 2d

Education: Irvine Royal Academy
Glasgow University

Career: 1914 war service, Royal Scots Fusiliers
1920 Cadet, Ceylon
1926 District Judge
1930 Colonial Secretary, Grenada; Acting
Governor, Windward Islands
1934 Colonial Secretary, Sierra Leone

Governorships: The Gambia 1942–47
Barbados 1947–49
Mauritius 1949–53

Honours: CMG 1934; KCMG 1944; GBE 1953
Hon. LL.D., Glasgow 1944

Clubs: Athenaeum; Pilgrims'; Royal Commonwealth
Society

Recreations: bridge, sailing

Retired: 1961
Constitutional Commissioner, British Honduras, 1959;
Constitutional Commissioner, Zanzibar, 1960;
Chairman, Constitutional Commission, Malta, 1960;
Chairman, Royal Commonwealth Society for the Blind,
1962; Chairman, Royal Society of Arts, 1963; Vice-
President, Royal Commonwealth Society, 1963

Publications: —

Supplementary: —

Obit. 21 June, 10g; 29, 12h

BOURDILLON, Bernard (Henry)

s/o. (1st) The Reverend Bernard Keene Bourdillon, Emu
Bay, Tasmania, and Laura Elizabeth, d/o Richard
Townsend, Cork, Ireland.

b. 3 December 1883, Tasmania   **d.** 6 February 1948

m. Violet Grace, d/o The Reverend H. G. Billingshurst,
Sussex, 1909

ch. 3s

Education: Tonbridge School (scholar)
St John's College, Oxford (scholar)   Classics,
Class II, 1906

Career: 1908 entered Indian Civil Service
1915 Registrar, High Court, Allahabad
1918 Judicial Assistant, Persian Gulf
1919 Settlement Officer, Baghdad
1920 Seconded to Iraq Political Service
1921 Political Secretary to High Commissioner,
Iraq
1922 Secretary to the High Commissioner
1929 Colonial Secretary, Ceylon
1930 Acting Governor
1931 Chief Secretary

Governorships: Uganda 1932–35
Nigeria 1935–42
Sudan 1940 (Governor–General designate)

Honours: CMG 1924; KBE 1931; KCMG 1934; GCMG
1937
Hon. Fellow, St John's College, Oxford, 1943

Clubs: East India and Sports

Recreations: photography, ornithology, polo

Retired: 1943
Director, Barclay's Bank DCO; Director, Barclay's
Overseas Development Corporation; Chairman, Orion
Property Trust; Chairman, British Empire Leprosy Relief
Association; Member, Colonial Economic Development

Council; Council Member, Royal Zoological Society;
Council Member, Royal African Society

Publications: *The Future of the Colonial Empire*, 1945

Supplementary: Sir Alexander Grantham, *Via Ports*, 1965;
James S. Coleman, *Nigeria: Background to Nationalism*,
1958; Vincent Harlow and E. M. Chilver, *History of East
Africa*, II, 1965; K. D. D. Henderson, *The Making of the
Modern Sudan*, 1953; Robert Heussler, *The British in
Northern Nigeria*, 1968; Kenneth Ingham, *The Making of
Modern Uganda*, 1958; Margery Perham, *Lugard*, II, 1960;
Sir Bryan Sharwood Smith, *But Always as Friends*, 1969

Obit. 7 Feb., 6e; 12, 6b, 6f; 17, 7c   DNB Supp. VI

BOWRING, Charles (Calvert)

s/o. J. C. Bowring

b. 20 November 1872   **d.** 13 June 1945

m. Ethel Dorothy, d/o G. K. Watts, Commissioner of Public Works, East Africa, 1909

ch. 4s 3d

Education: Clifton College

Career: 1890 entered Colonial Audit Branch
1892 Auditor, Hong Kong
1895 Auditor, Nyasaland
1899 Auditor, Uganda Railway
1901 Treasurer, Kenya
1911 Chief Secretary
1912 Acting Governor

Governorships: Nyasaland 1923–29

Honours: CMG 1908; KBE 1919; KCMG 1925

Clubs: East India and Sports

Recreations: —

Retired: 1929
JP, Bedford

Publications: —

Supplementary: M. F. Hill, *Permanent Way*, I, 1950; Elspeth Huxley, *White Man's Country*, 1935; G. H. Mungeam, *British Rule in Kenya*, 1966; W. McGregor Ross, *Kenya From Within*, 1927; Robert L. Tignor, *The Colonial Transformation of Kenya*, 1976

Obit. 16 June, 8f

BROOKE-POPHAM, (Henry) Robert (Moore), Air Chief Marshal*

s/o.   Henry Brooke, Wetheringsett Manor, Suffolk, and
         Dulcibella, d/o The Reverend Robert Moore
b.   18 September 1878, Suffolk   **d.**   20 October 1953
m.   Opal Mary, d/o Edgar Hugonin, 1926
ch.   1s 1d

Education: Haileybury College
                Royal Military College, Sandhurst
                Staff College, 1910

Career: 1898 commissioned into Oxfordshire Light
                    Infantry
            1912 joined Royal Flying Corps
            1919 Director of Research, Air Ministry
            1921 Commandant, Royal Air Force Staff College
            1926 Air Officer Commanding, Air Defence
            1928 Air Officer Commanding, Iraq Command
            1931 Commandant, Imperial Defence College
            1935 Inspector-General, Royal Air Force
            1936 Air Officer Commanding-in-Chief, Middle
                    East

Governorships: Kenya 1937–39

Honours: DSO 1915; AFC 1918; CMG 1918; CB 1919;
            KCB 1927; GCVO 1935; Principal ADC to the King, 1933

Clubs: Army and Navy; Royal Air Force

Recreations: hunting
            Fellow, Royal Aeronautical Society

Retired: 1937, from Royal Air Force; rejoined 1939,
            retired 1942. Commander-in-Chief, Far East, 1940;
            President, Navy Army and Air Force Institute (NAAFI),
            1944; Inspector-General, Air Training Corps

Publications: —

*The Popham was added in 1904. The *Colonial Office Lists* index the name
under P. *Who's Who* carried a hyphenated entry under Popham, Brooke.

83

Supplementary: Lord Altrincham, *Kenya's Opportunity*, 1955; George Bennett, *Kenya*, 1963; A. V. Clayton and D. Savage, *Government and Labour in Kenya*, 1974; J. G. Farrell, *The Singapore Grip*, 1978; M. F. Hill, *Permanent Way*, I, 1950; Robert L. Tignor, *The Colonial Transformation of Kenya*, 1976

Obit. 21 Oct., 11a, 11b; 24, 8b; 18 Nov., 10d.
                                        DNB Supp. VII   OCRP

BRUTON, Charles Lamb

s/o. Henry William Bruton, Bewick House, Gloucestershire
b. 6 April 1890   **d.** 26 March 1969
m. Mona Mary, d/o L. W. Webster, 1926
ch. —

Education: Radley College
Keble College, Oxford

Career: 1913 Private Secretary to the Bishop of Stepney
1914 Cadet, Uganda
1924 District Commissioner
1935 Senior District Commissioner
1936 Provincial Commissioner

Governorships: Swaziland 1937–42 (Resident Commissioner)

Honours: OBE

Clubs: MCC; Vincent's

Recreations: cricket (played for Gloucestershire, 1922)

Retired: 1947
Commissioner, East African Refugee Association, 1942

Publications: —

Supplementary: —

BULWER, Henry (Ernest Gascoyne), General

s/o. (y) W. E. Lytton Bulwer of Heydon, Norfolk, and
Emily, d/o General Gascoyne, M.P.

b. 11 December 1836   **d.** 30 September 1914

m. —

ch. —

Education: Charterhouse School,
Trinity College, Cambridge

Career: 1860 Resident, Ionian Islands
1865 Private Secretary, Ambassador at
Constantinople
1866 Treasurer, Trinidad
1867 Acting Governor, Dominica
1871 Consul-General, Borneo
1875 Lieutenant-Governor, Natal

Governorships: Labuan 1871–1875
Natal 1882–1885
Cyprus 1885–1892 (High Commissioner)

Honours: KC 1874; GCMG 1883

Clubs: Athenaeum; United University

Recreations: —

Retired: 1892

Publications: —

Supplementary: E. H. Brookes and C. Webb, *A History of
Natal*, 1965; D. Schreuder, *Gladstone and Kruger*, 1969;
E. A. Walker, *A History of Southern Africa*, 1959, and ed.,
Cambridge History of the British Empire, VIII, 1963

Obit. 3 Oct.; 5 Dec.   OCRP

BURNS, Alan (Cuthbert Maxwell)

s/o. James Burns, Treasurer of St Christopher-Nevis, West
      Indies

b. 9 November 1887   **d.** —

m. Kathleen Hardtman, 1914

ch. 2d

Education: St Edmund's College, Ware

Career: 1905 Clerk, Treasury and Customs Department,
               St Kitts
          1910 Magistrate, Anguilla
          1912 Supervisor of Customs, Nigeria
          1914 Assistant Secretary
          1915 war service, West African Frontier Force
          1924 Colonial Secretary, Bahamas; Acting
               Governor
          1929 Deputy Chief Secretary, Nigeria
          1934 Governor, British Honduras
          1940 Assistant Under-Secretary, Colonial Office
          1942 Acting Governor, Nigeria

Governorships: British Honduras 1934–40
                 Gold Coast 1941–47

Honours: CMG 1927; KCMG 1936; GCMG 1946

Clubs: Athenaeum

Recreations: —

Retired: 1956
    Permanent British Representative, UN Trusteeship
    Council, 1947; Chairman, Commission of Inquiry into
    Land and Population, Fiji, 1959

Publications: *Colonial Civil Servant*, 1949, autobiog.;
    Nigeria Handbook, 1917; *History of Nigeria*, 1929; *Colour
    Prejudice*, 1948; *History of the British West Indies*, 1954; *In
    Defence of Colonies*, 1957; *Fiji*, 1963

Supplementary: K. G. Bradley, *Once A District Officer*,
    1966; F. M. Bourret, *Ghana: the Road to Independence*, 1960;
    Sir Alexander Grantham, *Via Ports*, 1965; K. D. D.
    Henderson, *The Making of the Modern Sudan*, 1953

OCRP/t

BYATT, Horace (Archer)

s/o. (1st) Horace Byatt, Midhurst, Sussex
b. 22 March 1875   **d.** 8 April 1933
m. Olga, d/o J. Arthur Campbell, Argyll, Scotland, 1924
ch. 3s

Education: Lincoln College, Oxford (Exhibitioner)
Classics, Class IV, 1898

Career: 1899 Assistant Collector, Nyasaland
1905 Assistant Political Officer, Somaliland
1906 Secretary to the Administration
1910 Acting Administrator
1914 Colonial Secretary, Gibraltar
1915 Lieutenant-Governor, Malta
1916 Administrator, German East Africa

Governorships: Somaliland 1911–14 (Administrator)
Tanganyika 1920–24 (provisionally from 1916)
Trinidad and Tobago 1924–29

Honours: CMG 1912; KCMG 1918; GCMG 1930

Clubs: Carlton; East India and Sports

Recreations: shooting, fly-fishing

Retired: 1929
JP, Hertfordshire

Publications: —

Supplementary: Gilchrist Alexander, *Tanganyika Memories*, 1936; H. F. P. Battersby, *Richard Corfield of Somaliland*, 1914; Sir Ralph Furse, *Aucuparius*, 1962; Prosser Gifford and Roger Louis, *Britain and Germany in Africa*, 1967; Vincent Harlow and E. M. Chilver, *History of East Africa*, II, 1965; M. F. Hill, *Permanent Way*, II, 1958; Kenneth Ingham, *A History of East Africa*, 1962; Douglas Jardine, *The Mad Mullah of Somaliland*, 1923; Judith Listowel, *The Making of Tanganyika*, 1965; Walter Morris-Hale, *British Administration in Tanganyika*, 1969

Obit. 10 April, 12 f, 14d; 2 May 20c

BYRNE, Joseph (Aloysius), Brigadier-General

s/o. J. Byrne, DL, Londonderry, Northern Ireland
b. 2 October 1874 **d.** 13 November 1942
m. Marjorie, d/o Allan F. Joseph, Cairo, 1908
ch. 1d

Education: St George's College, Weybridge
Maison de Melle, Belgium
Called to the Bar, Lincoln's Inn, 1922

Career: 1893 commissioned into Royal Inniskilling
Fusiliers
1899 South African war
1903 Central Judicial (Claims) Commission,
Pretoria
1916 Inspector-General, Royal Irish Constabulary

Governorships: Seychelles 1922–26
Sierra Leone 1927–30
Kenya 1931–36

Honours: CB 1916; KBE 1918; KCMG 1928; CGMG 1934

Clubs: United Service

Recreations: fishing, shooting, golf

Retired: 1936 (resigned R.U.C., 1920)

Publications: —

Supplementary: Lord Altrincham, *Kenya's Opportunity*,
1955; George Bennett, *Kenya*, 1963; A. V. Clayton and D.
Savage, *Government and Labour in Kenya*, 1974; Robert G.
Gregory, *India and East Africa*, 1971; Vincent Harlow and
E. M. Chilver, *History of East Africa*, II, 1965; M. F. Hill,
Permanent Way, I, 1950; Sir Harry Luke, *Cities and Men*, III,
1956

Obit. 14 Nov. 6f; 20, 7h

CAMERON, Donald (Charles)

s/o.   Donald Charles Cameron, sugar planter, Demerara, British Guiana, and Mary Emily d/o Michael Brassington, Dublin

b.   3 June 1872, British Guiana   **d.**   8 January 1948

m.   Gertrude, d/o Duncan Gittens, sugar planter, Oldbury, Barbados, 1903

ch.   1s

Education: Rathmines School, Dublin

Career: 1890   entered British Guiana Civil Service (Inland Revenue)
1899   Second-class Clerk, Secretariat
1901   Private Secretary to the Governor
1902   Private Secretary to Governor of Newfoundland
1904   Assistant Colonial Secretary, Mauritius
1908   Assistant Secretary, Southern Nigeria
1910   Provincial Commissioner
1914   Central Secretary, Nigeria
1921   Chief Secretary; Acting Governor

Governorships: Tanganyika 1924–31
Nigeria 1931–35

Honours: CMG 1918; KBE 1922; KCMG 1926; GCMG 1932
Hon. LL.D., Cambridge, 1937

Clubs: East India and Sports

Recreations: —

Retired: 1935
Member, Education Advisory Committee, Colonial Office; Vice-Chairman, Governing Body Imperial College of Agriculture

Publications: *My Tanganyika Service and Some Nigeria*, 1939, autobiog.; *Principles of Native Administration and their Application*, 1930 (Dar es Salaam) and 1934 (Lagos)

Supplementary: Harry A. Gailey, *Sir Donald Cameron: Colonial Governor*, 1974, biog.; Lord Altrincham, *Kenya's Opportunity*, 1955; Ralph A. Austen, *Northwest Tanzania under German and British Rule*, 1968; B. T. G. Chidzero, *Tanganyika and International Trusteeship*, 1961; Prosser Gifford and Roger Louis, *Britain and Germany in Africa*, 1967; Vincent Harlow and E. M. Chilver, *History of East Africa*, II, 1965; Robert Heussler, *The British in Northern Nigeria*, 1968; Kenneth Ingham, *A History of East Africa*, 1962; Judith Listowel, *The Making of Tanganyika*, 1965; D. A. Low and Alison Smith, *The History of East Africa*, III, 1976; Sir Philip Mitchell, *African Afterthoughts*, 1954; Walter Morris-Hale, *British Administration in Tanganyika*, 1969; I. F. Nicolson, *The Administration of Nigeria*, 1969; Margery Perham, *East African Journey*, 1976; J. Clagett Taylor, *The Political Development of Tanganyika*, 1963

Obit. 10 Jan. 6g; 16, 7c; 20, 6c   DNB Supp. VI

CAMERON, Edward (John)

s/o. (4th) John C. Cameron, MD, Deputy Surgeon-General, and Julia, d/o J. Mooyaart, Auditor-General, Ceylon

b. 14 May 1858   **d.** 20 July 1947

m. Eva Selwyn, d/o Robert Isaacs, LL.D., New South Wales

ch. 1s 2d

Education: Shrewsbury School
Clifton College
Merton College, Oxford

Career: 1882 Private Secretary to Governor of the Bahamas
1884 Treasurer, Sierra Leone
1885 Colonial Secretary
1887 President, Virgin Islands
1893 Commissioner, Turks and Caicos Islands
1901 Administrator, St Vincent
1909 Administrator, St Lucia; Acting Governor, Windward Islands

Governorships: The Gambia 1914–20

Honours: CMG 1905; KCMG 1916

Clubs: —

Recreations: 'sundry'

Retired: 1920

Publications: —

Supplementary: —

Obit. 26 July, 4f; 28, 7e

CARDEW, Frederic, Colonel

s/o. —

b.   27 September 1839   **d.** 6 July 1921

m.   1st Clara, d/o J. D. Newton, Plymouth, 1865
      2nd Katharine, d/o J. Savill and widow of Colonel Kent
         Jones, 1887

ch. 3s

Education: Royal Military College, Sandhurst

Career: 1858 commissioned into Bengal Army
         1863 North West Frontier operations
         1873 Deputy Assistant Quarter-Master General,
              Aldershot
         1879 Zulu war
         1881 Transvaal campaign
         1882 Assistant Military Secretary, China
         1884 Sub-Commissioner, Zululand
         1890 Resident Commissioner
         1896 Consul for Liberia

Governorships: Sierra Leone 1894–1900

Honours: CMG 1884; KCMG 1897

Clubs: United Service

Recreations: —

Retired: (from army 1890)

Publications: —

Supplementary: Christopher Fyfe, *A History of Sierra
Leone*, 1962; John Hargreaves, *A Life of Sir Samuel Lewis,*
1958; Margery Perham and Mary Bull, *Diaries of Lord
Lugard*, 1963

Obit. 9 July, 15b; 12, 13e; 17 Sept. 11b

CARTER, Gilbert (Thomas)

s/o. —
b. 1849   **d.** 1927
m. —
ch. —

Education: —

Career: 1864 entered Royal Navy
1870 Paymaster, Colonial Steamer *Sherbro*, Sierra
       Leone
1873 Ashanti campaign
1875 Private Secretary to Governor of Leeward
       Islands
1879 Collector of Customs, Gold Coast
1882 Treasurer, The Gambia
1863 Acting Governor

Governorships: The Gambia 1888–90 (Administrator)
Lagos 1890–96
Bahamas 1898–1904
Barbados 1904–10

Honours: CMG 1890; KMCG 1893

Clubs: —

Recreations: —

Retired: 1910

Publications: —

Supplementary: Sir Alan Burns, *History of Nigeria*, 1969;
Arthur N. Cook, *British Enterprise in Nigeria*, 1943;
Michael Crowder, *The Story of Nigeria*, 1973; Harry A.
Gailey, *A History of the Gambia*, 1964; Sir William Geary,
Nigeria Under British Rule, 1927; Samuel Johnson, *The
History of the Yorubas*, 1921; Margery Perham and Mary
Bull, *Diaries of Lord Lugard*, 1963; Ellen Thorp, *Ladder of
Bones*, 1956

CHANCELLOR, John (Robert), Lieutenant-Colonel

s/o.   (2nd) E. Chancellor, Juniper Green, Midlothian, Scotland

b.   20 October 1870   d.   31 July 1952

m.   Elsie, d/o G. Rodie Thompson, JP, DL, Ascot, 1903

ch.   2s 1d

Education: Royal Military Academy, Woolwich
Staff College, 1902

Career: 1890   commissioned into Royal Engineers
1896   Dongola expedition
1897   North West Frontier operations
1903   Intelligence Department, War Office
1906   Secretary, Colonial Defence Committee
1909   Assistant Secretary, Imperial Conference on Defence

Governorships: Mauritius 1911–15
Trinidad and Tobago 1916–21
Southern Rhodesia 1923–28
Palestine 1928–31

Honours: DSO 1898; CMG 1909; KCMG 1913; GCMG 1922; GCVO 1924; GBE 1947

Clubs: Army and Navy; Travellers'

Recreations: —

Retired: 1931
Chairman, Agricultural Marketing Facilities Executive Committee; Chairman, Livestock Commission; Chairman, International Conference on Locusts, 1934; President, Trustee Saving Banks Association, 1951; Vice-Chairman, British Council, 1940; Member, Colonial Empire Marketing Board; Member, Colonial Development Advisory Committee; Vice-President, Royal Empire Society; Council, Royal African Society; Director, British South Africa Co.

Publications: —

Supplementary: N. and H. Bentwick, *Mandate Memories*, 1965; Albert M. Hyamson, *Palestine Under the Mandate*, 1950

OCRP

CHAPLIN, Alan Geoffrey Turnstal

s/o. Albert Chaplin, London, and Hester Potts, Newcastle
b. 27 September 1908,   **d.** 20 April 1967
        South Africa
m. 1st Amy Elizabeth Collier, 1939
        2nd Patty Dent Allen, 1962
ch. 2s

Education: Michaelhouse School, Natal

Career: 1926 Basutoland Mounted Police
            1928 transferred to Basutoland Administration
            1937 Assistant District Commissioner
            1940 Representative, High Commission
                  Territories in South Africa
            1944 Assistant Administrative Secretary, High
                  Commission Territories
            1948 Colonial Office
            1950 Development Commissioner, British
                  Honduras
            1954 Colonial Secretary, Bermuda
            1955 Acting Governor

Governorships: Basutoland 1956–61 (Resident
                    Commissioner)

Honours: CMG 1956

Clubs: Royal Bermuda Yacht

Recreations: tennis, riding, bridge

Retired: 1962

Publications: —

Supplementary: Richard P. Stevens, *Lesotho, Botswana and Swaziland*, 1967

CHAPLIN, (Francis) Drummond (Percy)

s/o. Major Percy Chaplin, 6oth Rifles
b. 10 August 1866   **d.** 16 November 1933
m. Margaret Seton,CBE, d/o William Seton Smith, 1895
ch. —

Education: Harrow School
University College, Oxford   Classics, Class II
Called to the Bar, Lincoln's Inn, 1891

Career: 1891 practised law
1897 *The Times* correspondent, Johannesburg
1899 *Morning Post* correspondent, St Petersburg
1900 Manager, Consolidated Goldfields Co, Johannesburg
1905 President, Transvaal Chamber of Mines
1907 Member, Transvaal Legislative Assembly
1910 Member, House of Assembly, Union of South Africa

Governorships: Southern Rhodesia 1914–23 (Administrator)
Northern Rhodesia 1921–23 (Administrator)

Honours: KCMG 1917; GBE 1923

Clubs: Bachelors'; United University; Arthur's; MCC; Civil Service, Cape Town

Recreations: golf, tennis

Retired: 1923 (resigned), to South Africa
Member, House of Assembly, Union of South Africa, 1924; Director, British South Africa Co

Publications: —

Supplementary: L. H. Gann, *A History of Northern Rhodesia*, 1964, *A History of Southern Rhodesia*, 1965

Obit. 17 Nov. 14c, 20a; 14, 20b; 18, 7c; 22, 19a; 23, 17d

CLARKE, Marshal (James), Lieutenant-Colonel

s/o. —
b. 1841   **d.** 1 April 1909
m. Annie, d/o Major-General Lloyd, 1880
ch. 2s 1d

Education: —

Career: Commissioned into Royal Artillery
     1874 Resident Magistrate, Natal
     1876 ADC to Sir Thomas Shepstone, Special
        Commissioner
     1877 Special Commissioner, Lydenburg
     1881 Resident Magistrate, Basutoland
     1882 Commissioner, Cape Police
     1884 Resident Commissioner, Basutoland
     1893 Acting Administrator, Zululand
     1898 Resident Commissioner in Southern
        Rhodesia

Governorships: Basutoland 1884–93 (Resident
     Commissioner)

Honours: CMG 1880; KCMG 1886

Clubs: —

Recreations: —

Retired: 1905 (from army 1883)

Publications: —

Supplementary: —

CLIFFORD, Hugh (Charles)

s/o. (1st) Major-General Hon. Sir Henry Clifford, VC, KCMG, CB, and Josephine, d/o Joseph Anstice, Professor of Mathematics, London, and Madeley Wood, Salop., and grandson of 7th Baron Clifford of Chudleigh.

b. 5 March 1886, London   **d.** 18 December 1941

m. 1st Minna, d/o Gilbert à Becket, 1896
2nd Elizabeth Lydia Rosabelle, OBE, d/o Edna Bonham and widow of Henry Philip Ducarel de la Pasture, 1910

ch. 1s 2d

Education: privately, at Woburn Park
gained Queen's Cadetship to Sandhurst, 1883

Career: 1883 Cadet, Malaya
1887 Agent, Pahang
1894 Commissioner, Cocos-Keeling Islands
1896 Resident, Pahang
1900 Governor (North Borneo Co.), North Borneo and Labuan
1901 reappointed Resident, Pahang
1903 Colonial Secretary, Trinidad and Tobago
1904 Acting Governor
1907 Colonial Secretary, Ceylon

Governorships: [North Borneo and Labuan 1900 (resigned)]
Gold Coast 1912–19
Nigeria 1919–25
Ceylon 1925–27 (resigned)
Malaya 1927–29 (resigned)

Honours: CMG 1900; KCMG 1909; GCMG 1921; GBE 1925

Clubs: Athenaeum; St George's Hill Golf

Recreations: reading, writing, golf, shooting, swimming, flying, tennis, bridge. Fellow, Royal Geographical Society

Retired: 1929 (resigned)

Publications: Over twenty publications, including joint authorship of a dictionary of Malay, a translation of the penal code into Malay, and the introduction to W. Walton Claridge, *A History of the Gold Coast and Ashanti*, 1915; *The German Colonies*, 1918; *The Gold Coast Regiment in the East African Campaign*, 1920; and such novels as *Court and Kampong*, 1897; *Bush-Whacking*, 1901; *Malayan Monochromes*, 1913; *Sketches in Brown Humanity*, 1898; *In Days that Are Dead*, 1926; *A Prince of Malaya*, 1926.

Supplementary: Harry A. Gailey in P. Duignan and L. H. Gann, eds., *The African Proconsul*, 1978, biog.; Laura Boyle, *A District Officer's Wife*, 1968; J. de Vere Allen, "Two Imperialists", *Jo. Mal. Br. Roy. As. Soc.*, 1954; Sir Alan Burns, *Colonial Civil Servant*, 1949; Molly Huggins, *Too Much To Tell*, 1967; H. A. J. Hulugalle, *British Governors of Ceylon*, 1963; David Kimble, *A Political History of Ghana*, I, 1963; I. F. Nicolson, *The Administration of Nigeria*, 1969; Leonard Woolf, *Growing*, 1961; R. E. Wraith, *Guggisberg*, 1967

Obit. 20 Dec. 6f   DNB Supp. VI   OCRP

CODRINGTON, Robert Edward

s/o. —

b. 6 January 1869,   **d.** 16 December 1908
       Gloucestershire

m. —

ch. —

Education: Marlborough College

Career: 1890 visited Virginia, USA
            1893 Sergeant-Major, Bechuanaland Border Police
            1895 Collector of Revenue, Nyasaland
            1898 Deputy Administrator, North-East Rhodesia

Governorships: North-Eastern Rhodesia 1898–1907
            (Administrator)
            North-Western Rhodesia 1907–1908
            (Administrator died in office)

Honours: —

Clubs: —

Recreations: —

Retired: —

Publications: —

Supplementary: L. F. G. Anthony, *North of the Zambezi*, 1953; L. H. Gann, *History of Northern Rhodesia*, 1964; Robert I. Rotberg, *The Rise of Nationalism in Central Africa*, 1965

COHEN, Andrew (Benjamin)

s/o.   W. S. Cohen, Berkhamsted, Hertfordshire,
Director of the Economic Board for Palestine,
and Mattie Cobb, Headmistress of Roedean
and Principal of Newnham College, Cambridge

b.   October 1909   **d.**   17 June 1968
m.   Mrs Helen Donington, 1944
ch.   1s

Education: Malvern College
Trinity College, Cambridge   Classics,
Class I, 1931
Harkness (Commonwealth Fund)
Fellow, 1939

Career: 1932 Home Civil Service, Inland Revenue
1933 transferred to Colonial Office
1940 seconded to Malta
1943 Assistant Secretary, Colonial Office
1947 Assistant Under-Secretary, Africa
Division
1952 Governor of Uganda
1957 Permanent British Representative,
UN Trusteeship Council
1961 Director-General, Department of
Technical Co-operation, London
1964 Permanent Secretary, Ministry of
Overseas Development

Governorships: Uganda 1952–57

Honours: OBE 1942; CMG 1948; KCMG 1952;
KCVO 1954
Hon. LL.D., Belfast

Clubs: Athenaeum

Recreations: —

Retired: died in office, 1968

Publications: *British Policy in Changing Africa*, 1959

Supplementary: Ronald Robinson in P. Duignan and
L. H. Gann, eds., *The African Proconsul*, 1978, biog.;
David Apter, *The Political Kingdom in Uganda*, 1961; Darrel
Bates, *A Gust of Plumes*, 1972; Lord Chandos, *An
Unexpected View from the Summit*, 1963; John Gunther,
Inside Africa, 1955; Kenneth Ingham, *The Making of Modern
Uganda*, 1958; D. A. Low and Cranford Pratt, *Buganda and
British Overrule*, 1960; D. A. Low and Alison Smith,
History of East Africa, III, 1976; Sir Bryan Sharwood Smith,
But Always as Friends, 1969; Don Taylor, *The British in
Africa*, 1962; Sir Roy Welensky, *4000 Days*, 1964; *West
Africa*, 30 November, 1948; 13 October 1951

Obit. 19 June 10f; 20, 12h; 24, 10g; 25, 12h

COLBY, Geoffrey (Francis Taylor)

s/o. (1st) Francis Colby, FRCS
b. 26 March 1901   **d.** 22 December 1958
m. Lilian Florence Illingworth, 1931
ch. 2d

Education: Charterhouse School
Clare College, Cambridge (Scholar)   Natural
Sciences, Class III, 1922

Career: 1925 Cadet, Nigeria
1939 Principal Assistant Secretary
1943 Director of Supplies, Lagos
1945 Administrative Secretary

Governorships: Nyasaland 1948–56

Honours: CMG 1947; KCMG 1949

Clubs: Royal Societies

Recreations: golf, fishing

Retired: 1956

Publications: —

Supplementary: Robert I. Rotberg, *The Rise of Nationalism in Central Africa*, 1965

Obit. 24 Dec. 9a

COLVILLE, Henry (Edward), Major–General★

s/o. Colonel C. R. Colvile★ Lullington, MP, and Hon. Katharine Russell, d/o Baroness de Clifford

b. 10 July 1852, Leicestershire **d.** 25 November 1907

m. 1st Alice, d/o Hon. R. Daly
2nd Zélie Isabelle, d/o M. Richard de Préville, Basses Pyrénées, France, 1886

ch. 1s

Education: Eton College

Career: 1870 commissioned into Grenadier Guards
1880 A.D.C. to General Officer Commanding, Cape
1883 Eastern Sudan expedition, Intelligence Department
1884 Nile expedition, DAAG Intelligence
1885 Chief of Intelligence Department, Frontier Force
1893 Intelligence Department, Namkan expedition, Burma
1894 Unyoro expedition, Uganda
1898 promoted Major–General
1899 Brigade Commander, Gibraltar
1900 Divisional Commander, South African War

Governorships: Uganda 1893–95 (Commissioner)

Honours: CB 1885; KCMG 1895

Clubs: Guards'; Travellers'; Automobile; Aero; Royal Yacht Squadron, Cowes

Recreations: photography, gardening, yachting

Retired: 1895 (from Uganda); 1901 (from army)

Publications: *The Accursed Land,* 1884
History of the Sudan Campaign, 1889

★These are the forms used by *Who's Who.* However, some authorities use Colvile for the Governor too, e.g. the standard *History of East Africa*

The Land of the Nile Springs, 1895
Various campaign histories

Supplementary: H. Moyse–Bartlett, *The King's African Rifles*, 1956; M. F. Hill, *Permanent Way*, I, 1950; H. B. Thomas, *Uganda*, 1935

Obit. 26 Nov. 12e; 27, 10b; 30, 10b   DNB Supp. II

CORDEAUX, Harry (Edward Spiller), Major

s/o. Edward Cordeaux, Indian Civil Service
b. 15 November 1870   **d.** 2 July 1943
m. Maud, d/o Hon. George Wentworth-Fitzwilliam and
       widow of Hon. Cospatrick T. Dundas
ch. —

Education: Cheltenham College
              St John's College, Cambridge (Scholar)
                 Classics, Class III, 1892

Career: 1894 commissioned into Indian Army
            1896 Indian Staff Corps
            1898 Assistant Resident, Aden
            1899 Assistant Resident, Somaliland
            1902 Sub-Commissioner
            1903 Acting Commissioner
            1904 Deputy Commissioner

Governorships: Somaliland 1906–10 (Commissioner)
                   Uganda 1910 (never assumed office)
                   St Helena 1912–20
                   Bahamas 1920–26

Honours: CMG 1902; CB 1904; KCMG 1921

Clubs: United Service

Recreations: field sports, oriental languages

Retired: 1926

Publications: —

Supplementary: H. F. P. Battersby, *Richard Corfield of Somaliland*, 1914; Sir Alan Burns, *Colonial Civil Servant*, 1949; Douglas Jardine, *The Mad Mullah of Somaliland*, 1923; H. Moyse-Bartlett, *The King's African Rifles*, 1956

Obit. 3 July 7d; 9 Aug. 6c

CORYNDON, Robert (Thorne)

s/o. Selby Coryndon, Solicitor, Plymouth and Kimberley, Cape Colony, and Emily, d/o Charles Heney Caldecott, Grahamstown, South Africa

b. 2 April 1870, Queenstown, **d.** 10 February 1925 Cape Colony

m. Phyllis Mary, d/o J. C. Worthington, Lowestoft, Suffolk

ch. 3s 1d

Education: Cheltenham College
St Andrew's College, Grahamstown

Career: 1889 Bechuanaland Border Police
1890 Mashonaland Campaign
1893 Matabelle War
1896 Private Secretary to Cecil Rhodes
1897 British South Africa Company Representative, Barotseland
1914 Chairman, Southern Rhodesia Native Reserve Commission

Governorships: North-Western Rhodesia 1900–07
Swaziland 1907–16 (Resident Commissioner)
Basutoland 1916–17 (Resident Commissioner)
Uganda 1918–22
Kenya 1922–25

Honours: CMG 1911; KCMG 1919

Clubs: Travellers'; Athenaeum

Recreations: big game hunting

Retired: died in office, 1925

Publications: —

Supplementary: P. Duignan in P. Duignan and L. H. Gann, eds., *The African Proconsul*, 1978, biog.; George Bennett, *Kenya*, 1963; Majorie Ruth Dilley, *British Policy in Kenya Colony*, 1937; R. G. Gregory, *India and East*

Africa, 1971; Lord Altrincham, *Kenya's Opportunity*, 1955; Vincent Harlow and E. M. Chilver, *History of East Africa*, II, 1965; M. F. Hill, *Permanent Way*, I 1950; Elspeth Huxley, *White Man's Country*, 1935; Kenneth Ingham, *A History of East Africa*, 1962; W. McGregor Ross, *Kenya From Within*, 1927; A. J. Wills, *An Introduction to the History of Central Africa*, 1973

Obit. 11 Feb. 12d, 14d; 12, 11c

DNB Supp. IV   OCRP

COUTTS, Walter (Fleming)

s/o.   The Reverend John Coutts, DD, Crieff, Scotland
b.   30 November 1912,   **d.** —
           Aberdeen
m.   Janet Jamieson, d/o A. C. Jamieson, Welwyn,
           Hertfordshire
ch.   1s 1d

Education: Glasgow Academy
                 St Andrew's University
                 St John's College, Cambridge

Career: 1936 Cadet, Kenya
              1947 District Commissioner
              1948 Administrator, St Vincent
              1955 Special Commissioner for African Elections,
                    Kenya
              1956 Minister for Education, Labour and Lands
              1958 Chief Secretary

Governorships: Uganda 1961–63 (Governor-General
                     from 1962)

Honours: MBE 1949; CMG 1953; Kt 1961; KCMG 1961;
GCMG 1962

Clubs: —

Recreations: fishing, golf

Retired: 1963

Publications: —

Supplementary: Sir Michael Blundell, *So Rough a Wind*,
1964

OCRP/t

CRAWFORD, Frederick

s/o.   James Mansfield Crawford, MD, Hull

b.   9 March 1906   **d.**   28 May 1978

m.   1st Mamie Alice, d/o John Harold Green, London and
Cape Town, 1936

2nd Clio, widow of Vasso Georgiadis, Uganda, and d/o
J. Colocotronis, Athens, 1962

ch.   2s

Education: Hymer's College

Balliol College, Oxford   English Class III,
1928

Career: 1929 Cadet, Tanganyika

1941 District Officer

1942 seconded to East African Governors'
Conference, Nairobi

1944 Executive Officer, Economic Central Board,
Tanganyika

1945 seconded to East African Governors'
Conference, Nairobi

1947 Economic Secretary, Northern Rhodesia

1948 Director of Development

1951 Governor of Seychelles

1953 Deputy Governor, Kenya

Governorships: Seychelles 1951–53

Uganda 1957–61

Honours: OBE 1945; CMG 1951; KCMG 1953;
GCMG 1961

Clubs: Brooks's; Royal and Ancient, St Andrews

Recreations: fishing, golf

Retired: 1961, to Salisbury, Rhodesia
Resident Director, Anglo-American Co. of South Africa

Publications: —

Supplementary: Sir Michael Blundell, *So Rough A Wind*,
1964; D. A. Low and Alison Smith, *History of East Africa*,
III, 1976

Obit. 29 May, 10e

CREASY, Gerald (Hallen)

s/o. (2nd) Leonard and Ellen Maud Creasy
b. 1 November 1897   **d.**
m. Helen Duff, d/o Reginald B. Jacomb
ch. 1s 1d

Education: Rugby School
King's College, Cambridge (Scholar)

Career:
1916 war service
1920 Colonial Office
1925 Private Secretary to Parliamentary Under-Secretary for Dominions
1927 Deputy Secretary, Colonial Office Conference
1928 accompanied Secretary of State for Colonies to Ceylon and Malaya
1929 Secretary, Colonial Agricultural Council
1935 accompanied Secretary of State for Colonies to West Africa
1937 Principal Private Secretary to Secretary of State for Colonies
1943 Assistant Under Secretary, Colonial Office
1945 Chief Secretary, West African Council

Governorships: Gold Coast 1948–49
Malta 1949–54

Honours: OBE 1937; CMG 1943; KCMG 1946; KCVO 1954
Hon. LL.D., Malta

Clubs: —

Recreations: —

Retired: 1954

Publications: —

Supplementary: Dennis Austin, *Politics in Ghana*, 1964; Elspeth Huxley, *Four Guineas*, 1954

CROOKS, John J., Major

s/o. —
b.   Ireland   **d.** —
m. —
ch. —

Education: —

Career: 1873 joined the Commissariat
               1873 Military clerk, War Office
               1874 Ashanti war
               1877 Assistant Treasurer, Sierra Leone
               1879 Assistant Secretary
               1880 ADC to the Governor
               1885 Clerk of Executive Council
               1888 Assistant Colonial Secretary
               1889 Colonial Treasurer; Deputy Governor
               1890 Judge, Supreme Court
               1891 Colonial Secretary

Governorships: Sierra Leone 1891–95 (Administrator)

Honours: —

Clubs: —

Recreations: —

Retired: 1895 (from the army, 1886)

Publications: *A Short History of Sierra Leone*, 1900
A History of the Colony of Sierra Leone, 1903
Historical Records of the Royal African Corps, 1925

Supplementary: Christopher Fyfe, *A History of Sierra Leone*, 1962; John Hargreaves, *A Life of Sir Samuel Lewis*, 1958

DANIEL, Rowland Mortimer, Lieutenant-Colonel

s/o. —
b. 1873   **d.** —
m. —
ch. —

Education: St Edmund's School, Canterbury

Career: 1893 commissioned into Glamorgan artillery militia
1898 Sub-Inspector, Bechuanaland Border Police
1899 South African war
1903 Assistant Resident Magistrate, Bechuanaland
1907 Assistant Commissioner
1914 war service, France
1923 Assistant Resident Commissioner
1926 Acting Governor

Governorships: Bechuanaland 1928–30 (Resident Commissioner)

Honours: CBE 1927

Clubs: —

Recreations: —

Retired: 1930

Publications: —

Supplementary: —

DENHAM, Edward (Brandis)

s/o. (1st) Charles Denham
b. 1876   **d.** 2 June 1938
m. Maude, d/o J. Bromhead Butt
ch. 1s 1d

Education: Malvern College
         Merton College, Oxford (Exhibitioner)
         History, Class II, 1898

Career: 1899 Cadet, Ceylon
         1905 Private Secretary to the Governor
         1908 District Judge
         1909 Private Secretary to the Governor
         1913 Colonial Office
         1914 Principal Assistant Colonial Secretary
         1916 Director of Education
         1920 Colonial Secretary, Mauritius
         1921 Acting Governor
         1923 Colonial Secretary, Kenya

Governorships: The Gambia 1928–30
         British Guiana 1930–34
         Jamaica 1934–38

Honours: CMG 1922; KBE 1927; KCMG 1931;
GCMG 1935

Clubs: Athenaeum; Oxford and Cambridge; West Indian

Recreations: field sports

Retired: died in office, 1938

Publications: *Rubber in the East*
Ceylon at the Census of 1911

Supplementary: George Bennett, *Keyna*, 1963;
A. V. Clayton and D. Savage, *Government and Labour in Kenya*, 1974; W. McGregor Ross, *Kenya From Within*, 1927; R. E. Wraith, *Guggisberg*, 1967

Obit. 3 June, 16b, 8c; 4, 11b; 7, 12f; 14, 11d   OCRP

DENTON, George (Chardin)

s/o. (2nd) The Reverend R. A. Denton, Dorset, and Mary
Wroughton, Adwick Hall, Doncaster

b. 22 June 1851   **d.** 9 Jan. 1928

m. Jean Margaret Alan, d/o Alan Stevenson, FRS,
Edinburgh, 1879

ch. 1d

Education: Rugby School

Career: 1869 commissioned into 57th Regiment
1880 entered Colonial Service as Chief of Police,
St Vincent
1886 Colonial Secretary
1888 Colonial Secretary, Lagos
1889 Acting Governor

Governorships: The Gambia 1900–11 (Administrator to
1901)

Honours: CMG 1891; KCMG 1900

Clubs: Windham; Naval and Military

Recreations: hunting, shooting, fishing. Fellow, Royal
Geographical Society; Fellow, Zoological Society

Retired: 1911

Publications: —

Supplementary: —

Obit. 10 Jan. 14c, 19b

DORMAN, Maurice (Henry)

s/o. John Ehrenfried and Madeleine Louise Dorman
b. 7 August 1912   **d.** —
m. Florence Churchward Smich, 1937
ch. 1s 3d

Education: Sedbergh School
Magdalene College, Cambridge   History,
Class II/2, 1934

Career: 1935 Cadet, Tanganyika
1940 Clerk of Councils
1945 Assistant to the Lieutenant-Governor, Malta
1947 Principal Assistant Secretary, Palestine
1948 Colonial Office
1950 Director, Social Welfare, Gold Coast
1952 Colonial Secretary, Trinidad and Tobago
1954 Acting Governor

Governorships: Sierra Leone 1956–62 (Governor-General
from 1961)
Malta 1962–71 (Governor-General from
1964)

Honours: CMG 1955; KCMG 1957; GCMG 1961;
GCVO 1961
Hon. DCL, Durham 1962; Hon. LL.D., Malta 1964

Clubs: Athenaeum; Casino Maltese, Valletta

Recreations: sailing, squash, golf

Retired: 1962
Director, MLH Consultants, 1971; Chairman, Swindon
Hospital Management Committee, 1972; Deputy
Chairman, Pearce Commission on Rhodesia, 1971;
Trustee, Imperial War Museum, 1972; Almoner,
Venerable Order of St John, 1972

Publications: —

Supplementary: Sir James Robertson, *Transition in Africa*,
1972; *West Africa*, 18 August, 1956; 25 March, 1961

OCRP/t

DUNDAS, Charles (Cecil Farquharson), Honourable

s/o. (5th) Viscount Melville

b. 6 June 1884, Stettin   **d.** 10 February 1956

m. Anne, d/o The Reverend S. Cox Hay, DD, New York, 1920

ch. —

Education: privately, in Europe

Career: 1903 clerk with Elder Dempster Shipping Co., Hamburg
1908 Cadet, Kenya
1914 District Commissioner
1916 Political Officer, German East Africa
1920 Senior District Commissioner, Tanganyika
1924 Assistant Chief Secretary
1926 Secretary for Native Affairs
1929 Colonial Secretary, Bahamas; Acting Governor
1931 Deputy Governor
1934 Chief Secretary, Northern Rhodesia

Governorships: Bahamas 1937–40
Uganda 1940–44

Honours: OBE 1923; CMG 1934; KCMG 1938

Clubs: —

Recreations: —

Retired: 1945

Publications: *African Crossroads*, 1955, autobiog.
Kilimanjaro and its People, 1924
The Ideal of the African Citizen, 1925

Supplementary: David Apter, *The Political Kingdom in Uganda*, 1961; Vincent Harlow and E. M. Chilver, *History of East Africa*, II, 1965; K. D. D. Henderson, *The Making of the Modern Sudan*, 1953; Kenneth Ingham, *The Making of Modern Uganda*, 1958; Kenneth Ingham, *A History of East*

Africa, 1962; D. A. Low and Cranford Pratt, *Buganda and British Overrule*, 1960; Walter Morris-Hale, *British Administration in Tanganyika*, 1969; G. H. Mungeam, *British Rule in Kenya*, 1966; Kathleen M. Stahl, *History of the Chagga People of Kilimanjaro*, 1964; Ralph A. Austen, *Northwest Tanzania under German and British Rule*, 1968

Obit. 11 Feb. 9c; 16, 10b   OCRP

EGERTON, Walter

s/o. —

b. 1858   **d.** 22 March 1947

m. Ada Maud, OBE, d/o The Reverend George Lloyd
Nash and widow of Charles Walter Sneyd-
Kynnersley, CMG, Malaya, 1905

ch. —

Education: Tonbridge School

Career: 1880 Cadet, Malaya
1883 Collector
1897 Magistrate
1902 Resident

Governorships: Southern Nigeria 1903–12 (High
Commissioner to 1906)
British Guiana 1912–17

Honours: CMG 1901; KCMG 1905
Hon. LL.D., Edinburgh

Clubs: Junior Carlton; Royal Automobile

Recreations: —

Retired: 1917
Member, Malta Royal Commission, 1931

Publications: —

Supplementary: A. E. Afigbo, *The Warrant Chiefs of
South-East Nigeria*, 1972; E. D. Morel, *Nigeria: its People
and Problems*, 1911; I. F. Nicolson, *The Administration of
Nigeria*, 1969

Obit. 24 March 9e

ELIOT, Charles (Norton Edgecumbe)

s/o. (1st) The Reverend Edward Eliot, BCL, curate of
Sibford Gower, Oxon, and Elizabeth Harriet Wyatt,
d/o The Reverend Charles Watling, Worcestershire

b. 8 January 1862, Oxfordshire   **d.** 16 March 1931

m. —

ch. —

Education: Cheltenham College
Balliol College, Oxford (Scholar)   Classics,
Class I, 1884; Hertford Scholar 1881; Boden
Sanskrit Scholar 1883; Ireland Scholar 1883;
Craven Scholar 1884; Derby Scholar 1886
Fellow, Trinity College, Oxford

Career:
   1887   entered Diplomatic Service
   1892   Morocco
   1893   Constantinople
   1895   Bulgaria
   1898   Washington, DC
   1899   High Commissioner, Samoa
   1900   Commissioner, British East Africa
           Protectorate
   1905   Vice-Chancellor, Sheffield University
   1912   Vice-Chancellor, Hong Kong University
   1918   High Commissioner, Siberia
   1919   Ambassador, Tokyo

Governorships: Kenya 1900–04 (Commissioner; resigned)

Honours: CB 1898; KCMG 1900; PC 1919; GCMG 1923
Hon. D.Litt., Oxford 1923; Hon. LL.D., Edinburgh
1905; Hon. DCL. Durham 1908, Hong Kong 1924,
Sheffield 1926; Hon. Fellow Trinity College, Oxford

Clubs: St James; Travellers'

Recreations: marine biology, languages, ancient and
modern

Retired: 1926 (resigned 1904)

Publications: *The East Africa Protectorate*, 1905, autobiog.;

A Finnish Grammar, 1900; *Turkey in Europe*, 1900; *Hinduism and Buddhism*, 1921; *Letters from the far East*, 1967; *Japanese Buddhism*, 1935

Supplementary: Sir Geoffrey Archer, *Personal and Historical Memoirs*, 1964; George Bennett, *Kenya*, 1963; Robert G. Gregory, *India and East Africa*, 1971; M. F. Hill, *Permanent Way*, I, 1950; C. W. Hobley, *Kenya: from Chartered Company to Crown Colony*, 1929; Elspeth Huxley, *White Man's Country*, 1935; Vincent Harlow and E. M. Chilver, *History of East Africa*, II, 1965; R. Meinertzhagen, *Kenya Diary*, 1957; G. H. Mungeam, *British Rule in Kenya*, 1966; Sir Harold Parletts, *In Piam Memoriam*, affixed to Eliot, *Japanese Buddhism*, 1935; W. McGregor Ross, *Kenya From Within*, 1927; M. P. K. Sorrenson, *Origins of European Settlement in Kenya*, 1968

Obit. 17 Nov. 14b, 16c; 21, 11g   DNB Supp. V

ELLENBERGER, Jules

s/o. (5th) The Reverend D. F. Ellenberger, Paris Evangelical
Mission Society, Basutoland

b. 16 January 1871   **d.** 1973

m. Fanny Sarah, d/o Eugene Casalis, MD, Paris, 1895

ch. 1s

Education: Lovedale, South Africa
Lycée St Louis, Paris

Career: 1890 Clerk to Assistant Commissioner,
Bechuanaland
1893 Interpreter, Bechuanaland Concessions
Commission
1894 Interpreter, Shippard Boundary Commission
1898 Assistant Resident Magistrate, Bechuanaland
1899 South African war
1902 Assistant Commissioner, Bechuanaland
1908 Special Commissioner
1916 Secretary to the Government
1920 Acting Governor

Governorships: Bechuanaland 1923–27 (Resident
Commissioner)

Honours: ISO 1922; CMG 1925

Clubs: —

Recreations: —

Retired: 1927, to Southern Rhodesia
Representative for Bechuanaland, Anglo–Caprivi
boundary adjudication, 1930; Chief Cordon Officer, Foot
and Mouth Disease, Bechuanaland, 1933

Publications: —

Supplementary: A. Sillery, *The Bechuanaland Protectorate*,
1952

OCRP

FAWCUS, (Robert) Peter

s/o. A. F. Fawcus, OBE
b.   30 September 1915   **d.** —
m.   Isabel Constance Ethelston, 1943
ch. 1s 1d

Education: Charterhouse School
          Clare College, Cambridge   Law, Class II,
              1937

Career: 1939 war service, Royal Naval Volunteer Reserve
          1946 Assistant District Officer, Basutoland
          1950 Secretariat, High Commission Territories
          1954 Secretary to the Government, Bechuanaland

Governorships: Bechuanaland 1959–65 (Resident
              Commissioner; Commissioner from
              1963)

Honours: OBE 1957; CMG 1960; KBE 1964

Clubs: —

Recreations: —

Retired: 1965

Publications: —

Supplementary: Richard. P. Stevens, *Lesotho, Botswana
    and Swaziland*, 1967

FEATHERSTONE, Eric Kellett

s/o. (2nd) The Reverend Thomas Featherstone, Carlisle
b. 22 July 1896   **d.** 3 August 1965
m. —
ch. —

Education: Carlisle Grammar School
Queen's College, Oxford (Exhibitioner)

Career: 1915 war service
1921 Cadet, Northern Nigeria
1939 Resident
1942 Commissioner, Swaziland
1947 Senior Resident, Northern Nigeria
1950 Commissioner for Nigeria in the United
Kingdom

Governorships: Swaziland 1942–46 (Resident
Commissioner)

Honours: CMG 1944

Clubs: Oxford and Cambridge

Recreations: —

Retired: 1955

Publications: —

Supplementary: *West Africa*, 29 July 1950
Obit. 5 Aug. 12f

FLEMING, Francis

s/o. James Fleming, QC, and Julia, d/o Major John Canning
b. 1842 **d.** 4 December 1922
m. Constance Mary, d/o M. D. Kavanagh, LL.B., and
  Hon. Mrs Kavanagh, 1892
ch. —

Education: Downside College
  Called to the Bar, Middle Temple, 1866

Career: 1869 Crown Solicitor, Mauritius
  1872 District Magistrate
  1876 District Judge, Jamaica
  1878 Attorney-General, Barbados
  1880 Private Secretary to Governor of Cape
    Colony
  1881 Puisne Judge, British Guiana
  1884 Attorney General, Ceylon
  1886 Colonial Secretary, Mauritus
  1887 Acting Governor
  1889 Colonial Secretary, Hong Kong

Governorships: Sierra Leone 1892–94
  Leeward Islands 1895–1901

Honours: CMG 1887; KCMG 1892

Clubs: —

Recreations: —

Retired: 1901
  Poor Law Guardian, Parish of St Mary Abbot's,
  Kensington; Member, Distressed Colonial Seamen
  Committee, 1909

Publications: —

Supplementary: Christopher Fyfe, *A History of Sierra
  Leone*, 1962

  Obit. 5 Dec. 15c

FORSYTH THOMPSON, Aubrey Denzil★

s/o.   Ernest Alfred Thompson
b.   3 October 1897   **d.** —
m.   Kathleen Esther Murray, 1924
ch.   1s 1d

Education: Weenen College, Natal
New College, Oxford

Career: 1917 war service, France
1921 Cadet, Uganda
1933 District Officer
1937 Assistant Resident Commissioner,
Bechuanaland

Governorships: Bechuanaland 1942–47 (Resident
Commissioner)
Basutoland 1947–52 (Resident
Commissioner)

Honours: CBE 1941; CMG 1944; CVO 1947

Clubs: —

Recreations: gardening

Retired: 1952, to Swaziland

Publications: —

Supplementary: —

FRERE, (Henry) Bartle (Edward)

s/o.   (6th) Edward Frere and Mary Anne, d/o James Greene, M.P.

b.   29 March 1815   **d.**   29 May 1884

m.   Catherine, d/o Sir George Arthur, Governor of Bombay, 1884

ch.   1s 4d

Education: Bath Grammar School
                 Haileybury College

Career: 1834   Writer, Bombay Civil Service
              1842   Private Secretary, Governor of Bombay
              1850   Chief Commissioner, Sind
              1872   on special duty, Commissioner to Zanzibar
              1875   accompanied Prince of Wales to Egypt and India

Governorships: Bombay 1862–1867
                     Cape Colony 1877–1880

Honours: GCSI 1867; baronetcy 1876; GCB 1876

Clubs: —

Recreations: —

Retired: from the Indian Civil Service, 1867
Hon. D.C.L. Oxford 1868; Hon. LL.D. Cambridge 1874; Hon. LL.D. Edinburgh 1884; President, Royal Asiatic Society 1872; President, Royal Geographical Society, 1873

Publications: —

Supplementary: John Martineau, *Sir Bartle Frere*, 1895, biog.; C. J. F. Muller, *Five Hundred Years: A History of South Africa*, 1969; D. Schreuder, *Gladstone and Kruger*, 1969; Freda Troup, *South Africa: An Historical Introduction*, 1972; E. A. Walker, *A History of Southern Africa*, 1959; E. A. Walker, ed., *Cambridge History of British Empire*, VIII, 1963; M. Wilson and L. M. Thompson, *The Oxford History of South Africa*, II, 1971; Philip Woodruff, *The Guardians*, 1954

Obit. 30 May   DNB IV   OCRP

GALWAY, Henry (Lionel), Lieutenant-Colonel★

s/o. Lieutenant-General Sir T. L. Gallwey, KCMG, Royal Engineers

b. 25 September 1859   **d.** 17 June 1949

m. Marie Carola, GBE, d/o Rt. Hon. Sir Rowland Blennerhasset, Bt., and widow of Baron Raphael D'Erlanger, 1913

ch. —

Education: Cheltenham College
Royal Military College, Sandhurst

Career: 1878 commissioned into 30th Regiment
1882 ADC and Private Secretary to Governor of Bermuda
1891 Deputy Commissioner, Oil Rivers Protectorate
1894 Benin expedition
1899 Divisional Commissioner, Niger Coast Protectorate
1900 Acting Governor, Southern Nigeria
1901 Chief Political Officer, Aro expedition

Governorships: St Helena 1902–11
The Gambia 1911–14
South Australia 1914–20

Honours: DSO 1896; CMG 1899; KCMG 1910
Hon. Colonel, 27th Australian Infantry, 1921

Clubs: Naval and Military; MCC; Pitt

Recreations: —

Retired: 1920

Publications: —

Supplementary: Arthur N. Cook, *British Enterprise in Nigeria*, 1942; Margery Perham and Mary Bull, *Diaries of Lord Lugard*, 1963; Ellen Thorp, *Ladder of Bones*, 1957

Obit. 20 June 7d

★Name changed from Gallwey to Galway in 1911.

GARRAWAY, Edward (Charles Frederick), Lieutenant-Colonel

s/o. (1st) Colonel Charles Sutton Garraway, Waterford, Ireland

b. 10 March 1865   **d.** 27 June 1932

m. Winifred Mary, d/o J. H. Harvey, JP, Hampshire

ch. 2d

Education: Waterford Diocesan School
Trinity College, Dublin   Medicine
Royal College of Surgeons, Ireland

Career:
- 1888 District Surgeon, Cape Colony
- 1891 District Surgeon, Bechuanaland
- 1892 Surgeon, Bechuanaland Border Police
- 1893 Matabele war
- 1899 South African war
- 1901 Divisional Medical Officer, South African Constabulary
- 1905 Principal Medical Officer
- 1908 Military Secretary, South Africa
- 1910 Military Secretary to the Governor-General
- 1914 Special Commissioner, Native Reserves, Southern Rhodesia

Governorships: Bechuanaland 1916–17 (Resident Commissioner)
Basutoland 1917–26 (Resident Commissioner)

Honours: CMG 1911; KCMG 1922

Clubs: Farmers', Dublin

Recreations: 'outdoor'

Retired: 1926

Publications: —

Supplementary: —

GIBBS, Humphrey (Vicary)

s/o. (3rd) Baron Hunsdon
b. 22 November 1902   **d.** —
m. Molly, DBE, d/o John Peel Nelson, 1934
ch. 5s

Education: Eton College
Trinity College, Cambridge

Career: 1928 farming in Southern Rhodesia

Governorships: Southern Rhodesia 1959–69

Honours: OBE 1959; KCMG 1960; KCVO 1965; GCVO 1969; PC 1969. Hon. LL.D., Birmingham; Hon. DCL, East Anglia

Clubs: Athenaeum; Bulawayo; Salisbury

Recreations: —

Retired: 1969

Publications: —

Supplementary: —

GILES, Alexander (Falconer)

s/o. A. F. Giles, LL.D.

b. 1915   **d.** —

m. Mrs M. Watson, d/o Lieutenant-Colonel
      R. F. D. Burnett and widow of Lieutenant-Colonel
      J. L. Watson

ch. 2s 1d

Education: Edinburgh Academy
                 Edinburgh University
                 Balliol College, Oxford   History, Class II,
                     1939
                 President of the Union, Oxford, 1939

Career: 1940 war service, Royal West African Frontier
                   Force
             1947 Cadet, Tanganyika
             1955 Administrator, St Vincent

Governorships: Basutoland 1962–66 (Resident
                     Commissioner; British Representative
                     from 1965)

Honours: MBE 1946; CMG 1960; KBE 1965

Clubs: United Service

Recreations: 'The printed word, gentle swimming,
rough shooting.'

Retired: 1966
Chairman, Victoria League, Scotland, 1968; Chairman,
Scottish Council, Royal Overseas League, 1968; Director
Toc H., 1968

Publications: —

Supplementary: —

GIROUARD, (Edouard) Percy (Cranwill), Colonel

s/o.   Hon. Désiré Girouard, Judge, Montreal, and Essie, d/o
       Joseph Cranwill
b.   26 January 1867   **d.**   26 September 1932
m.   Mary Gwendolen, d/o Hon. Sir Richard Solomon,
       1903
ch.   1s

Education: Royal Military College, Ontario

Career: 1886 Engineer, Canadian Pacific Railway
            1888 commissioned into Royal Engineers
            1890 Railway Traffic Manager, Woolwich
                     Arsenal, England
            1895 Dongola expedition, Sudan
            1896 Director, Sudan Railways
            1898 President, Egyptian Railways
            1899 Director, South African Railways
            1902 Commissioner, Transvaal and Orange River
                     Colonies (resigned 1904)
            1906 Assistant Quarter-Master General, Western
                     Command, Chester, England

Governorships: Northern Nigeria 1907–09 (High
                     Commissioner till 1908)
               Kenya 1909–12 (resigned)

Honours: DSO 1896; KCMG 1900

Clubs: Army and Navy; Brooks's

Recreations: —

Retired: 1912 (resigned)
Director, Armstrong Vickers Co.; Director-General,
Munitions Supply (resigned 1916)

Publications: *History of the Railways during the War in South
Africa*, 1903; Introduction to M. S. Kisch, *Letters and
Sketches from Northern Nigeria*, 1910

Supplementary: George Bennett, *Kenya*, 1963;
Kenneth Robinson and A. F. Madden, *Essays in Imperial Government*, 1963; A. V. Clayton and D. Savage, *Government and Labour in Kenya*, 1974; Sonia F. Graham, *Government and Mission Education in Northern Nigeria*, 1966; Vincent Harlow and E. M. Chilver, *History of East Africa*, II, 1965; Robert Heussler, *The British in Northern Nigeria*, 1968; M. F. Hill, *Permanent Way*, I, 1950; Elspeth Huxley, *White Man's Country*, 1935; G. H. Mungeam, *British Rule in Kenya*, 1966; C. W. J. Orr, *The Making of Northern Nigeria*, 1911; M. P. K. Sorrenson, *Origins of European Settlement in Kenya*, 1968; *Dictionary of South African Biography*, I, 1968

Obit. 27 Sept. 9a, 18b; 29, 13b   DNB Supp. V

GLENDAY, Vincent (Goncalves)

s/o. Alexander Glenday
b. 11 February 1891   **d.** 30 April 1970
m. Elizabeth Mary, d/o Sir Jacob Barth, CBE, Chief
      Justice of Kenya, 1939
ch. 3s

Education: St Bees School
              Wadham College, Oxford   Geology, Class II,
               1913; Diploma in Forestry

Career: 1913   Cadet, Kenya
            1920   District Commissioner, Somaliland
            1926   District Commissioner, Kenya
            1927   Mission to Abyssinia
            1934   in charge, Northern Frontier District, Kenya
            1939   Governor of Somaliland
            1942   Colonial Office
            1944   British Agent, East Aden

Governorships: Somaliland 1939–41
                      Zanzibar 1946–51 (Resident)

Honours: OBE 1929; CMG 1937; KCMG 1942

Clubs: —

Recreations: fishing, shooting, cricket, golf
Fellow, Geological Society

Retired: 1951
Speaker, East African Central Legislature, 1953–61
retired to South Africa

Publications: —

Supplementary: Sir Ralph Furse, *Aucuparius*, 1962;
H. Moyse-Bartlett, *The King's African Rifles*, 1956

Obit. 2 May 10g; 5, 12g

GOODE, Richard (Allmond Jeffrey)

s/o. (1st) Reverend T. A. Goode

b. 30th April 1873,   **d.**   25 May 1953
Newfoundland

m. Agnes, d/o Thomas Codrington, civil engineer

ch. 3s

Education: Fettes College, Edinburgh

Career: 1900 Secretary to the Administration, North-
Eastern Rhodesia
1908 Secretary to the Administration, North-
Western Rhodesia
1911 Secretary to the Administration, Northern
Rhodesia
1920 Deputy Administrator
1924 Chief Secretary
1926 Acting Governor
1927 Commissioner for Railways

Governorships: Northern Rhodesia 1923–24
(Administrator)

Honours: CBE 1918; CMG 1924; Kt. 1928

Clubs: Union; West Indian; Civil Service, Cape Town

Recreations: golf, fishing

Retired: 1936, to South Africa
Vice-President, South African Red Cross Association

Publications: —

Supplementary: —

GOOLD-ADAMS, Hamilton (John), Major

s/o. R. W. Goold-Adams
b. 27 June 1858 **d.** 12 April 1920
m. Elsie, d/o Charles Riordan, Montreal, 1911
ch. 1s 1d

Education: —

Career: 1878 commissioned into Royal Scots
1885 Troop Commander, Bechuanaland Border
Police
1888 Commanded Field Force
1893 Commanded Matabele campaign
1897 Commissioner
1899 South African war
1901 Lieutenant-Governor, Orange River

Governorships: Bechuanaland 1897–1901 (Resident
Commissioner)
Orange River 1907–10
Cyprus 1911–14 (High Commissioner)
Queensland 1914–20

Honours: CMG 1894; CB 1898; KCMG 1902; GCMG 1907

Clubs: Army and Navy

Recreations: —

Retired: died in office, 1920 (retired from army, 1895)

Publications: —

Supplementary: Hugh M. Hole, *The Passing of the Black
Kings*, 1932, *The Making of Rhodesia*, 1926; A. Sillery, *The
Bechuanaland Protectorate*, 1952; Sir Harry Luke, *Cities and
Men*, II, 1953; A. J. Wills, *An Introduction to the History of
Central Africa*, 1973

Obit. 16 April 13c; 17, 13f

GOULDSBURY, Valesius Skipton, Brigade-Surgeon

s/o. —
b. —   **d.** —
m. —
ch. —

Education: —

Career: Army Surgeon

Governorships: The Gambia 1877–84 (Administrator)
St Lucia 1891–97

Honours: CMG 1876

Clubs: —

Recreations: —

Retired: —

Publications: —

Supplementary: —

GOWERS, William (Frederick)

s/o. Sir William Gowers, MD, FRCS
b. 1875   **d.** 7 October 1954
m. Winifred Price, d/o William Paul, North Lynn
ch. —

Education: Rugby School
Trinity College, Cambridge   Classics, Class I, 1898
called to the Bar, Inner Temple

Career: 1899 British South Africa Company
1900 Assistant Native Commissioner, Matabeleland
1902 Third Class Resident, Northern Nigeria
1906 Second Class Resident
1910 First Class Resident
1921 Lieutenant-Governor, Northern Nigeria
1925 Governor of Uganda
1932 Senior Crown Agent for the Colonies, London

Governorships: Uganda 1925–32

Honours: CMG 1919; KCMG 1926

Clubs: Bath; Brooks's; MCC

Recreations: 'various'

Retired: 1938
Member, Governing Body School of Oriental and African Studies, London University, 1933; Vice-President, Fauna Preservation Society; Deputy Chairman, Cereals Control Board, 1939; Civil Defence Liaison Officer, Southern Command, 1940

Publications: —

Supplementary: Lord Altrincham, *Kenya's Opportunity*, 1955; Robert G. Gregory, *India and East Africa*, 1971; Robert Heussler, *The British in Northern Nigeria*, 1965; Kenneth Ingham, *The Making of Modern Uganda*, 1958;

Margery Perham, *Lugard*, II, 1960, *East African Journey*, 1976; J. R. P. Postlethwaite, *I Look Back*, 1947

Obit. 8 Oct. 11c; 12, 10b   OCRP

GRIFFITH, William (Brandford)

s/o. —
b. —   **d.** —
m. —
ch. —

Education: —

Career: 1861 Member, Legislative Assembly, Barbados
               1863 Auditor-General
               1874 Colonial Secretary
               1879 Lieutenant-Governor, Gold Coast

Governorships: Lagos 1880–86 (Administrator)
                      Gold Coast 1885–95

Honours: CMG 1879; KCMG 1887

Clubs: —

Recreations: —

Retired: 1895

Publications: —

Supplementary: W. Walton Claridge, *A History of the Gold Coast and Ashanti*, 1915

GRIGG, Edward (William Macleay), Lieutenant-Colonel (Lord Altrincham)

s/o. Henry Bidewell Grigg, Indian Civil Service, and
Elizabeth, d/o Sir Edward Dean-Thomson, Colonial
Secretary, New South Wales

b. 8 September 1879, Madras   **d.** 1 December 1955

m. Hon. Joan Alice Dickson-Poynder, d/o Lord Islington,
PC, GCMG, GBE, Governor of New Zealand

ch. 2s 1d

Education: Winchester College (Scholar)
New College, Oxford (Scholar) Classics,
Class III, 1902; Gainsford Greek Verse
Prizewinner

Career:
1903 editorial staff, *The Times*
1905 Assistant Editor, *Outlook*
1908 rejoined *The Times*, as head of colonial
department
1913 Joint Editor, *Round Table*
1914 served with Grenadier Guards
1919 Military Secretary to Prince of Wales in
Canada, Australia, New Zealand
1921 Private Secretary to Lloyd George
1922 elected MP (National Liberal) for Oldham
1923 Secretary, Rhodes Trust, Oxford

Governorships: Kenya 1925–31

Honours: MC 1917; DSO 1918; CVO 1919;
CMG 1919; KCVO 1920; KCMG 1928; PC 1944
Elevated to peerage as Baron Altrincham of Tormarton,
1945

Clubs: Guards'; Beefsteak

Recreations: —

Retired: 1931
Chairman, Milk Reorganisation Commission, 1932; MP
(National Conservative), Altrincham, 1933;
Parliamentary Under-Secretary for War, 1940; Resident

Minister Middle East, 1944; Editor, *National Review*, 1948; Deputy-Lieutenant, Gloucestershire, 1950.

Publications: *Kenya's Opportunity*, 1955, autobiog.; *The Greatest Experiment in History*, 1924; *Speeches by His Excellency Lt-Col. Sir Edward Grigg, 1925–30*, n.d; *The Faith of an Englishman*, 1936; *The British Commonwealth*, 1943; *British Foreign Policy*, 1944

Supplementary: George Bennett, *Kenya*, 1963; A. V. Clayton and D. S. Savage, *Government and Labour in Kenya*, 1974; Marjorie Ruth Dilley, *British Policy in Kenya Colony*, 1937; Robert G. Gregory, *India and East Africa*, 1971; Vincent Harlow and E. M. Chilver, *History of East Africa*, II, 1965; M. F. Hill, *Permanent Way*, I, 1950; Sir Philip Mitchell, *African Afterthoughts*, 1954; Margery Perham, *East African Journey*, 1976; Robert L. Tignor, *The Colonial Transformation of Kenya*, 1976; *National and English Review*, January 1956

Obit. 2 Dec. 13c; 5, 10b; 12, 13a; 15, 12c

DNB Supp. VII

GUGGISBERG, (Frederick) Gordon, Brigadier-General

s/o. (1st) Frederick Guggisberg, Galt, Ontario, Canada, merchant, and Dora Louise Wilson, United States of America

b. 20 July 1869, Toronto   **d.** 21 April 1930

m. 1st Ethel Hamilton Way, 1895
2nd Decima Moore, CBE, 1905

ch. —

Education: Burney's School, Hampshire
Royal Military Academy, Woolwich

Career: 1889 commissioned into Royal Engineers
1893 posted to Singapore
1897 Instructor, Royal Military Academy, Woolwich
1902 Assistant Director of Surveys, Gold Coast
1904 Director of Surveys
1908 reposted to military duties, Chatham, Kent
1910 Director of Surveys, Southern Nigeria
1913 Surveyor-General, Nigeria
1915 Director of Public Works, Gold Coast; war service, France

Governorships: Gold Coast 1919–27
British Guiana 1928–29

Honours: DSO 1918; CMG 1908; KCMG 1922

Clubs: Army and Navy

Recreations: —

Retired: 1929 (resigned); retired from army, 1919

Publications: *We Two in West Africa* (with Decima Moore), 1909, autobiog.; *The Shop: the Story of the Royal Military Academy*, 1900; *Modern Warfare*, 1903; *Handbook of the Southern Nigeria Survey*, 1911; *The Keystone*, 1924; *The Future of the Negro* (with A. G. Fraser), 1929

Supplementary: Ronald E. Wraith, *Guggisberg*, biog.,

1967; F. M. Bourret, *Ghana: the Road to Independence*, 1960; David Kimble, *A Political History of Ghana*, I, 1963; *Royal Engineers' Journal*, March 1931

Obit. 22 April 17d; 25, 14c; 26, 9g; 5 May 19b; 18 June, 16f
DNB Supp. IV

HALL, Douglas (Basil)

s/o. Captain Lionel Erskine Hall and Jane Reynolds
b. 1 February 1909   **d.** —
m. Rachel Marion Gartside-Tippinge
ch. 1s 2d

Education: Radley College
              Keble College, Oxford

Career: 1930 Cadet, Northern Rhodesia
          1950 Senior District Officer
          1953 Provincial Commissioner
          1954 Administrative Secretary
          1956 Secretary for Native Affairs

Governorships: Somaliland 1959–60

Honours: CMG 1958; KCMG 1959
          Succeeded cousin to baronetcy, 1979

Clubs: —

Recreations: vintage cars

Retired: 1960 JP, Devon

Publications: —

Supplementary: Robert Short, *African Sunset*, 1973

HALL, John (Hathorn)

s/o. —
b.   19 June 1894   **d.**   17 June 1979
m.   Torfrida Trevenen Mills
ch.   2d

Education: St Paul's School
Lincoln College, Oxford

Career: 1914 war service, France
1919 entered Egyptian Civil Service, Ministry of
Finance
1921 Assistant Principal, Colonial Office
1922 Principal
1932 seconded to Foreign Office
1933 Chief Secretary, Palestine

Governorships: Zanzibar 1937–40 (Resident)
Aden 1940–44
Uganda 1944–51

Honours: MC; DSO 1919; OBE 1931; CMG 1935; KCMG
1941; GCMG 1950

Clubs: Athenaeum; Hurlingham

Recreations: —

Retired: 1951
Director, Midland Bank; Director, Brixton Estate Ltd;
Director, Midland Bank Executive and Trustee Co;
Chairman, Clerical Medical and General Life Assurance
Society; Chairman, General Reversionary and Investment
Co; Hon. President, Limmer and Trinidad Asphalt Co

Publications: —

Supplementary: David Apter, *The Political Kingdom in
Uganda*, 1961; R. J. Gavin, *Aden Under British Rule*, 1975;
Vincent Harlow and E. M. Chilver, *History of East Africa*,
1965, II; Kenneth Ingham, *The Making of Modern Uganda*,
1958; D. A. Low and Alison Smith, *History of East Africa*,
III, 1976

Obit. 23 Nov.

HALL, Robert (de Zouche)

s/o. Arthur William Hall, Liverpool
b. 27 April 1904   **d.** —
m. Lorna Dorothy Markham, 1932
ch. 1s 1d

Education: Willaston School
Liverpool University
Caius College, Cambridge   Anthropology,
Class I, 1926

Career: 1926 Cadet, Tanganyika
1938 District Officer
1947 Provincial Commissioner
1950 Member for Local Government

Governorships: Sierra Leone 1953–56

Honours: CMG 1952; KCMG 1953

Clubs: —

Recreations: Fellow, Society of Antiquaries

Retired: 1956
Hon. Secretary, Vernacular Architecture Group, 1959
(President 1972); Chairman, Governing Body County
Museum, Somerset, 1961; Member, Hospital
Management Committee, Sandhill Park, 1961 (Chairman
1965); JP, Somerset

Publications: —

Supplementary: Margery Perham, *East African Journey*,
1976; *West Africa*, 21 February 1953

OCRP

HARDINGE, Arthur (Henry)

s/o. (1st) General the Hon. Sir A. E. Hardinge, KCB

b. 12 October 1859 **d.** 27 December 1933

m. Alexandra Mina, d/o Major-General Sir Arthur Ellis, 1899

ch. 1d

Education: Eton College
Balliol College, Oxford   History, Class I
Fellow of All Souls College, Oxford, 1881

Career: Page of Honour to the Queen
1880 entered Diplomatic Service
1885 Secretary to Marquess of Salisbury
1890 accompanied the Czarewitch to India
1891 Acting Consul-General, Cairo
1894 Consul-General, Zanzibar
1896 Consul-General, British East Africa
Protectorate
1900 Minister, Teheran
1906 Minister, Brussels
1911 Minister, Lisbon
1913 Ambassador, Madrid

Governorships: Kenya 1896–1900 (Commissioner)

Honours: CB 1895; KCMG 1897; KCB 1904; GCMG 1910; PC 1913

Clubs: Travellers'; St James's; Marlborough

Recreations: —

Retired: 1920

Publications: *A Diplomatist in Europe*, 1927, autobiog.; *A Diplomatist in the East*, 1928, autobiog.

Supplementary: Vincent Harlow and E. M. Chilver, *History of East Africa*, II, 1965; M. F. Hill, *Permanent Way*, I, 1950; C. W. Hobley, *Kenya: from Chartered Company to Crown Colony*, 1929; G. H. Mungeam, *British Rule in Kenya*, 1966; Margarery Perham, *Lugard*, I, 1956; M. P. K. Sorrenson, *Origins of European Settlement in Kenya*, 1928

Obit. 29 Dec. 10c, 15a

HAVELOCK, Arthur (Elibank)

s/o. (5th) Lieutenant-Colonel William Havelock, Knight of
Hanover, and Caroline, d/o Major Acton Chaplin,
Aylesbury.

b. 7 May 1844   **d.** 25 June 1908
m. Anne Grace, d/o Sir William Norris, 1871
ch. 1d

Education: Lee School, Blackheath
Royal Military Academy, Sandhurst

Career: 1862 commissioned into 32nd Cornwall Light
Infantry
1866 stationed at Gibraltar
1867 stationed at Mauritius
1868 stationed at the Cape
1872 Paymaster, Mauritius
1873 Private Secretary, Governor of Mauritius
1874 temporary Chief Civil Commissioner,
Seychelles
1875 Colonial Secretary, Fiji
1877 President of Nevis
1878 Acting Governor, St Lucia
1879 Chief Civil Commissioner, Seychelles

Governorships: Sierra Leone 1881–1884
Trinidad 1885
Natal 1886–1889
Ceylon 1890–1895
Madras 1895–1900
Tasmania 1901–1904

Honours: CMG 1880; KCMG 1884; GCMG 1895;
GCIE 1896; GCSI 1901

Clubs: Junior Carlton; United Service; Hurlingham

Recreations: —

Retired: from army, 1877; resigned 1904

Publications: —

Supplementary: E. H. Brookes and C. Webb, *A History of Natal*, 1965; H. A. J. Hulugalle, *British Governors of Ceylon*, 1963; C. J. F. Muller, *Five Hundred Years: A History of South Africa*, 1969; E. A. Walker, *A History of Southern Africa*, 1959

Obit. 26 June; 12 Aug.   DNB Supp. II

HAY, James (Shaw)

s/o. Colonel Thomas Pasley Hay
b. 25 October 1839   **d.** —
m. 1st Jane, d/o John Morin, Dumfries
     2nd Frances Marie, d/o Jacques Polatza, Brussels
     3rd Isabella, d/o G. F. Cockburn, 1894
ch. —

Education: —

Career: 1857   commissioned into 89th Foot
            1858   served in Indian Mutiny
            1875   District Commissioner, Accra
            1877   Inspector-General, Gold Coast Constabulary
            1878   Assistant Colonial Secretary
            1880   Inspector-General of Police, Mauritius

Governorships: The Gambia 1885–87 (Administrator)
                   Sierra Leone 1888–91
                   Barbados 1892–1900

Honours: CMG 1887; KCMG 1889

Clubs: United Service

Recreations: —

Retired: —

Publications: —

Supplementary: Christopher Fyfe, *A History of Sierra Leone*, 1962

HELM, Alexander (Knox)

s/o. William Hunter Helm, Dumfries, Scotland, and
Annie Clark

b. 24 March 1893 **d.** 7 March 1964

m. 1st Grace Little, 1922
2nd Isabel, d/o Walter G. Marsh, JP Cardiff, 1931

ch. 1s 2d

Education: Dumfries Academy
King's College, Cambridge

Career: 1912 entered Foreign Office
1917 war service, Palestine
1919 entered Levant Consular Service; Vice-
Consul, Constantinople
1927 Vice-Consul, Ankara
1930 transferred to Foreign Office
1937 Consul, Addis Ababa
1939 Counsellor, Washington DC
1947 Minister, Budapest
1949 Minister, Tel Aviv
1951 Ambassador, Istanbul

Governorships: Sudan 1955–56 (Governor-General)

Honours: OBE 1924; CBE 1932; CMG 1945; KCMG 1949;
GBE 1953

Clubs: Brooks's

Recreations: golf, gardening

Retired: 1956

Publications: —

Supplementary: —

Obit. 10 March, 16b; 16, 12e; 2 April, 14b

HELY-HUTCHINSON, Walter (Francis)

s/o. (2nd) Earl of Donoughmore and Thomasine, d/o
      Walter Steele, Moynalty, Co. Monaghan

b. 22 August 1849   **d.** 23 September 1913

m. May, d/o Major-General William Clive Justice, CMG,
      1881

ch. 4s 1d

Education: Harrow School
             Trinity College, Cambridge
             Called to the Bar, Inner Temple

Career: 1874 Private Secretary, Sir Hercules Robinson
                mission to Fiji
        1875 Private Secretary, Governor of New South
                Wales
        1877 Colonial Secretary, Barbados
        1883 Chief Secretary, Malta
        1884 Lieutenant-Governor

Governorships: Windward Island 1889–1893
                   Natal 1893–1901
                   Cape Colony 1901–1910

Honours: CMG 1883; KCMG 1888; GCMG 1897; PC 1909

Clubs: Carlton; Travellers'; Beefsteak

Recreations: golf

Retired: 1910
     LL.D. Edinburgh, 1904

Publications: —

Supplementary: E. H. Brookes and C. Webb, *A History of Natal*, 1965; T. R. Davenport, *South Africa: A Modern History*, 1978; C. J. F. Muller, *Five Hundred Years: A History of South Africa*, 1969; B. Sachs, *South Africa: An Imperial Dilemma*, 1967; L. M. Thompson, *The Unification of South Africa*, 1960; E. A. Walker, *A History of Southern Africa*, 1959; E. A. Walker, ed., *Cambridge History of the British Empire*, VIII, 1963

Obit. 24 Sept.; 7 Nov.

HODGSON, Frederic (Mitchell)

s/o. The Reverend O. A. Hodgson, Wareham
b. 22 November 1851   **d.** 6 July 1925
m. Mary Alice, d/o William A. G. Young, CMG,
       Governor of the Gold Coast
ch. 1d

Education: —

Career: 1869 entered Home Civil Service, Imperial Post
                  Office
             1882 Postmaster-General, British Guiana
             1888 Colonial Secretary, Gold Coast
             1889 Acting Governor
             1892 raised Gold Coast Reserve Volunteers
             1901 raised Barbados Volunteer Force

Governorships: Gold Coast 1898–1900
                    Barbados 1900–04
                    British Guiana 1904–11

Honours: CMG 1891; KCMG 1899

Clubs: Conservative; Ranelagh; West Indian

Recreations: —

Retired: 1911
   Member, West African Lands Committee, 1912

Publications: —

Supplementary: C. H. Armitage and A. F. Montanaro,
   The Ashanti Campaign of 1900, 1901; W. Walton Claridge,
   A History of the Gold Coast and Ashanti, 1915; David
   Kimble, *A Political History of Ghana*, 1963; Margery
   Perham and Mary Bull, *Diaries of Lord Lugard*, 1963

   Obit. 7 Aug. 14b; 14 Sept. 15d

HODSON, Arnold (Wienholt)

s/o. (1st) Algernon Hodson, Llanwern Park,
Monmouthshire, Wales

b. 1881, Devon   **d.** 26 May 1944
m. Elizabeth, d/o Major Malcolm V. Hay, 1928
ch. 2d

Education: Felsted School
privately, in Italy

Career: 1900 travelling in Queensland, Australia
1902 service in Transvaal with Australian
Commonwealth Horse
1904 Sub-Inspector, Bechuanaland Border
Police
1910 Assistant Commissioner,
Bechuanaland
1912 District Commissioner, Somaliland
1914 Consul, Southern Abyssinia
1917 war service, Europe and Abyssinia
1923 Consul, South-West Abyssinia

Governorships: Falkand Islands 1926–31
Sierra Leone 1931–34
Gold Coast 1934–41

Honours: CMG 1922; KCMG 1932

Clubs: Travellers'; St James's; Shikar; Royal Yacht, Cowes

Recreations: big game shooting, fishing, yachting, golf,
rifle shooting. Vice-President, National Rifle Association

Retired: 1941

Publications: *Seven Years in Southern Abyssinia*, 1927,
autobiog.; *Trekking the Great Thirst*, 1912; *Where Lion
Reign*, 1929; *A Practical Galla Gramma*, 1922; *The Downfall
of Zachariah Fee* (play); (Pantomime at Government
House, Accra)

Supplementary: F. M. Bourret, *Ghana: the Road to
Independence*, 1960; Sir Alan Burns, *Colonial Civil Servant*,
1949

Obit. 29 May 6e

HOLLIS, (Alfred) Claud

s/o. (2nd) George Hollis, Inner Temple, and Worthing
b. 12 May 1874   **d.** 22 November 1961
m. Enid Mabel, d/o Valentine Longman, Highgate, 1910
ch. 1s 2d

Education: privately, in Switzerland and Germany

Career: 1897 Cadet, Kenya
1900 Collector
1902 Secretary to the Administration
1905 Political Officer, Nandi expedition
1907 Secretary for Native Affairs
1913 Colonial Secretary, Sierra Leone
1913 Acting Governor
1916 Secretary to the Administration, German
East Africa
1919 Chief Secretary, Tanganyika

Governorships: Zanzibar 1924–30 (Resident)
Trinidad and Tobago 1930–36

Honours: CMG 1911; CBE 1919; KCMG 1927;
GCMG 1934

Clubs: Athenaeum; East India and Sports

Recreations: —

Retired: 1936
Chairman, Civil Defence Joint Committee, North West
Essex, 1938; Director, Trinidad Petroleum Development
Co, 1944; Chairman, Imperial Communications Advisory
Board, 1945

Publications: *The Masai: their Language and Folklore*, 1905;
The Nandi: their Language and Folklore, 1909; *A Brief History
of Trinidad under the Spanish Crown*, 1941

Supplementary: Sir Geoffrey Archer, *Personal and
Historical Memoirs*, 1964; A. V. Clayton and D. Savage,
Government and Labour in Kenya, 1974; G. H. Mungeam,

British Rule in Kenya, 1966; M. P. K. Sorrenson, *Origins of British Settlement in Kenya*, 1968; Robert L. Tignor, *The Colonial Transformation of Kenya*, 1976

Obit. 23 Nov. 19a; 27, 12b; 29, 17b   OCRP

HONE, Evelyn (Dennison)

s/o. (2nd) Arthur Hone, MBE, Salisbury, Rhodesia, and
Olive Scanlon

b. 13 December 1911   **d.** 18 September 1979

m. Helen Mellor, 1946

ch. 1s 2d

Education: Wellington College
Rhodes University, Grahamstown
New College, Oxford (Rhodes Scholar)
Law, Class II, 1934
Called to the Bar, Lincoln's Inn

Career: 1935 Cadet, Tanganyika
1944 Secretary to the Government, Seychelles
1946 Assistant Secretary, Palestine
1948 Colonial Secretary, British Honduras
1953 Chief Secretary, Aden
1957 Chief Secretary, Northern Rhodesia

Governorships: Northern Rhodesia 1959–64

Honours: OBE 1946; CMG 1953; CVO 1954;
KCMG 1959; GCMG 1965. Hon. LL.D., Rhodes, 1964

Clubs: —

Recreations: —

Retired: 1964
Adviser to the West Africa Committee, 1967; Member,
Southern Gas Board, 1968; Board of Governors, Overseas
Service College, 1969; Central Council, Royal Overseas
League, 1969; President, Zambia Society, 1969; Beit
Trustee, 1970; Vice Chairman, Commonwealth Institute,
1971

Publications: —

Supplementary: Harry Franklin, *Unholy Wedlock*, 1963;
David C. Mulford, *Zambia: the Politics of Independence*,
1967; Robin Short, *African Sunset*, 1973

Obit. 23 Nov. 1979

HONEY, (de Symons) Montagu (George)

s/o. J. W. Honey, Civil Commissioner and Resident Magistrate, Cape Service

b. 1 November 1872, Cape Province   **d.** 18 January 1945

m. Violet Marguerite, d/o Charles Jones, Stellenbosch

ch. 2s

Education: the Public School, Caernarvon, Wales

Career:
- 1891 British South Africa Company Police, Mashonaland
- 1893 British Central Africa Administration
- 1896 railway construction, Beira-Mashonaland
- 1899 South African war
- 1901 Transvaal Civil Service, Customs Department
- 1902 Native Affairs Department
- 1904 Secretary to the Government for Swaziland Affairs
- 1907 Secretary to the Government, Swaziland
- 1910 Deputy Resident Commissioner

Governorships: Swaziland 1917–28 (Resident Commissioner)
Seychelles 1928–33

Honours: CMG 1919; Kt. 1932

Clubs: —

Recreations: —

Retired: 1933

Publications: —

Supplementary: —

Obit. 19 Jan 8e

HOWE, Robert (George)

s/o. H. Howe
b. 19 September 1893, Derby   **d.** —
m. Loveday Mary Hext, 1919
ch. 15

Education: Derby School
St Catharine's College, Cambridge

Career:
1920	entered Diplomatic Service
1922	Belgrade
1924	Rio de Janeiro
1926	Bucharest
1930	Foreign Office
1934	Counsellor, Pekin
1940	Minister, Riga
1942	Minister, Addis Ababa
1945	Assistant Under-Secretary, Foreign Office

Governorships: Sudan 1947–55 (Governor-General)

Honours: CMG 1937; KCMG 1947; GBE 1949

Clubs: —

Recreations: riding

Retired: 1955

Publications: —

Supplementary: K. D. D. Henderson, *The Making of the Modern Sudan*, 1953; Sir James Robertson, *Transition in Africa*, 1974

HUDDLESTON, Hubert (Jervoise), Major-General

s/o. Thomas Jervoise Huddleston, Suffolk
b. 1880   **d.** 2 October 1950
m. Constance Eila, d/o F. H. M. Corbet, 1928
ch. 1d

Education: Felsted School

Career: 1899 South African war
       1910 Sudan campaign
       1914 war service, France
       1924 General Officer Commanding, Sudan
             Brigade
       1930 Commander, 14th Infantry Brigade
       1933 Major-General
       1934 Commander, Eastern Command, India
       1935 Commander, Western Command, India

Governorships: Sudan 1940–47 (Governor-General)

Honours: MC 1915; DSO 1917; CMG 1918; CB 1925;
KCMG 1940; GBE 1946; GCMG 1947.
Colonel of the Dorsetshire Regiment, 1933

Clubs: Army and Navy

Recreations: —

Retired: 1938
Lieutenant-Governor and Secretary, Royal Hospital,
Chelsea, 1938

Publications: —

Supplementary: Hugh Boustead, *The Wind of Morning*,
1971; J. S. R. Duncan, *The Sudan*, 1952; K. D. D.
Henderson, *The Making of the Modern Sudan*, 1953; H. C.
Jackson, *Behind the Modern Sudan*, 1955; Sir Harold
Macmichael, *Sudan Republic*, 1954; Sir James Robertson,
Transition in Africa, 1974

Obit. 3 Oct. 8e; 5, 8d; 7, 8b; 17, 8f; 18, 6g

                                    DNB Supp. VI

JACKSON, Frederick (John)

s/o. John Jackson, Oran Hall, Yorkshire, and Jane Outhwaite

b. 17 February 1860, Yorkshire **d.** 3 February 1929

m. Aline Louise, d/o William Wallace Cooper, Dublin, barrister

ch. —

Education: Shrewsbury School
Jesus College, Cambridge

Career: 1883 shooting expedition, Kashmir
1884 residing in Lamu
1886 shooting expedition, Kilimanjaro
1888 Imperial British East Africa Company
1889 Commanded Uganda expedition
1894 First–class Administrative Assistant, Uganda
1895 Vice-Consul
1896 Deputy Commissioner
1897 Acting Governor
1900 Chief Political Officer, Nandi expedition
1902 Deputy Commissioner, Kenya
1907 Lieutenant-Governor

Governorships: Uganda 1911–17

Honours: CB 1898; CMG 1902; KCMG 1913

Clubs: —

Recreations: ornithology ('fine collection of 12,000 specimens'), big game shooting

Retired: 1917

Publications: *Early Days in East Africa*, 1930, autobiog.; *Big-Game Shooting in East Africa*, 1897; *Notes on the Game-Birds of Kenya and Uganda*, 1926

Supplementary: H. H. Bell, *Glimpses of a Governor's Life*, 1946; James Barber, *The Imperial Frontier*, 1967; Robert G. Gregory, *India and East Africa*, 1971; M. F. Hill, *Permanent Way*, I, 1950; Elspeth Huxley, *White Man's Country*, 1935; Kenneth Ingham, *The Making of Modern Uganda*, 1958;

D. A. Low and Cranford Pratt, *Buganda and British Overrule*, 1960; G. H. Mungeam, *British Rule in Kenya*, 1966; Roland Oliver, *Sir Harry Johnston*, 1957; Margery Perham and Mary Bull, *The Diaries of Lord Lugard*, 1959; W. McGregor Ross, *Kenya From Within*, 1927; M. P. K. Sorrenson, *Origins of European Settlement in Kenya*, 1968; H. B. Thomas, *Uganda*, 1935

Obit. 4 Feb. 12c, 17d; 8, 8g; 16, 17a   DNB Supp. IV

JACKSON, Wilfrid (Edward Francis)

s/o. Sir Henry Moore Jackson, GCMG, Governor of Fiji and of Trinidad

b. 1883   **d.** 28 March 1971

m. Isabel Morgan, d/o Humphrey Morgan, Co. Donegal, and widow of Captain H. D'Estamps Vallency

ch. —

Education: Stonyhurst College
Lincoln College, Oxford (Scholar) Classics, Class II, 1905

Career: 1905 Personal Secretary to Governor of Trinidad
1906 Private Secretary to Governor of Bahamas
1907 Assistant Collector, Uganda
1912 District Commissioner
1916 Colonial Secretary, Bermuda
1921 Colonial Secretary, Barbados
1922 Acting Governor
1926 Colonial Secretary, Trinidad
1929 Colonial Secretary, Gold Coast

Governorships: Mauritius 1930–37
British Guiana 1937–41
Tanganyika 1941–45

Honours: CMG 1919; KCMG 1931; GCMG 1943

Clubs: —

Recreations: —

Retired: —

Publications: —

Supplementary: —

Obit. 31 March, 16f.

JARDINE, Douglas (James)

s/o. (1st) James Jardine, MD, Richmond, Surrey
b. 1888   **d.** 11 December 1946
m. Jessie Mary, d/o Lachlan A. Macpherson, Inverness,
      1923
ch. 2d

Education: Westminster School
                Trinity College, Cambridge   Classics, Class
                II, 1910

Career: 1910 Assistant Secretary, Cyprus
          1911 Private Secretary to High Commissioner
          1916 Secretary to the Administration, Somaliland
          1920 Headquarters, Somaliland Expeditionary
               Force
          1921 Senior Assistant Secretary, Nigeria
          1927 Deputy Chief Secretary, Tanganyika
          1929 Chief Secretary; Acting Governor

Governorships: North Borneo 1933–37
                   Sierra Leone 1937–41
                   Leeward Islands 1941–44

Honours: OBE 1918; CMG 1932; KCMG 1938

Clubs: United University; Surrey County Cricket

Recreations: —

Retired: 1944

Publications: *The Mad Mullah of Somaliland*, 1923,
autobiog.; *Handbook of Cyprus*, 1913; *Handbook of
Tanganyika Territory*, 1930

Supplementary: Darrell Bates, *A Gust of Plumes*, 1972;
Walter Morris-Hale, *British Administration in Tanganyika*,
1969; Margery Perham, *East African Journey*, 1976; Sir
Stewart Symes, *Tour of Duty*, 1946

Obit. 12 Dec. 7e; 16, 7b

JOHNSTON, Harry (Hamilton)

s/o. John Brookes Johnston, Secretary to Royal Exchange
Assurance Co, and Esther L. Hamilton, d/o Robert
Bloomfield, jewel merchant, India

b. 12 June 1858, London **d.** 31 July 1927

m. Hon. Winifred Irby, OBE, d/o Lord Boston

ch. —

Education: Stockwell Grammar School
King's College, London Modern Languages
(no degree)
Royal Academy of Arts, studied painting in
France and Spain

Career: 1879 explored North Africa
1882 explored Portuguese West Africa and River
Congo
1884 led Royal Society expedition to Kilimanjaro
1885 Vice-Consul, Cameroons
1887 Consul, Niger Coast Protectorate
1888 Consul, Mozambique
1889 expedition to Lakes Nyasa and Tanganyika
1897 Consul-General, Tunis

Governorships: Nyasaland 1891–97 (Commissioner)
Uganda 1899–1901 (Commissioner)

Honours: CB 1890; KCB 1896; GCMG 1901; Gold
Medallist of several learned societies; Hon. D.Sc.,
Cambridge 1902; Gold Medal, Royal Geographical
Society, 1904

Clubs: —

Recreations: painting, music, biology

Retired: 1901
President, Royal African Society, 1902; contested
Rochester by-election (Liberal) 1903; Adviser to President
of Liberia, 1904; visited America and West Indies to
research African origins of the black population, 1908.

Publications: *The Story of My Life*, 1923, autobiog.; *River*

Congo, 1884; *Kilimanjaro*, 1885; *History of A Slave*, 1889; *Life of Livingstone*, 1891; *British Central Africa*, 1897; *The Uganda Protectorate*, 1902; *A History of the Colonization of Africa by Alien Races*, 1899–1913; *The Nile Quest*, 1903; *Liberia*, 1906; *The Negro in the New World*, 1910; *Comparative Study of the Bantu and Semi-Bantu Languages*, 1919–22

Supplementary: Roland Oliver, *Sir Harry Johnson and the Scramble for Africa*, 1957, biog.; Alex Johnston, *The Life and Letters of Sir Harry Johnston*, 1929, biog.; James Cassada, *A Bio-Bibliography of Sir Harry Johnston*, 1977, biog.; Robert G. Gregory, *India and East Africa*, 1971; A. J. Hanna, *The Beginnings of Nyasaland*, 1956; Vincent Harlow and E. M. Chilver, *History of East Africa*, II, 1965; Kenneth Ingham, *The Making of Modern Uganda*, 1958; H. Moyse-Bartlett, *The King's African Rifles*, 1956; Margery Perham, *Lugard*, I, 1956; M. P. K. Sorrenson, *Origins of European Settlement in Kenya*, 1968; A. J. Wills, *An Introduction to the History of Central Africa*, 1973

Obit. 1 Aug. 10d, 12c; 3, 13c; 5, 13b; 31, 9c

DNB Supp. IV

JONES, Glyn (Smallwood)

s/o. G. I. Jones, Chester
b. 9 January 1908   **d.** —
m. Nancy, d/o J. H. Featherstone, Cape Town, 1942
ch. 1s 1d

Education: King's School, Chester
St Catherine's College, Oxford   English,
Class III, 1930

Career: 1931 Cadet, Northern Rhodesia
1951 Commissioner, Native Development
1955 Provincial Commissioner
1958 Secretary for Native Affairs
1959 Minister of Native Affairs
1960 Chief Secretary, Nyasaland

Governorships: Nyasaland 1961–66 (Governor-
General from 1964)

Honours: MBE 1944; CMG 1957; KCMG 1960; GCMG
1964

Clubs: Athenaeum; Royal Commonwealth Society

Recreations: shooting, fishing, golf, tennis

Retired: 1966
Chairman, London Advisory Board, Commercial Bank
of Malawi, 1972

Publications: —

Supplementary: Robin Short, *African Sunset*, 1973; Sir Roy
Welensky, *4000 Days*, 1964

KENNEDY, John (Noble), Major-General

s/o. (1st) The Reverend James Russell Kennedy and Sarah
Maud Noble

b. 31 August 1893   **d.** 15 June 1970

m. 1st Isabella Rosamund Georginana, d/o Colonel Lord
John Joicey-Cecil, 1926
2nd Catherine, d/o Major John Gurney Fordham, 1942

ch. 3s 2d

Education: Stranraer School, Scotland
Royal Military Academy, Woolwich
Imperial Defence College, 1938

Career: 1911 entered Royal Navy
1915 transferred to Royal Artillery
1916 war service; attached to Australian Corps
1920 Turkey
1922 Egypt
1938 Deputy Director, Military Operations, War
Office
1940 Northern Ireland
1941 War Office
1943 Assistant Chief of Imperial General Staff

Governorships: Southern Rhodesia 1946–53

Honours: CB 1942; KBE 1945; KCVO 1947; KCMG 1952;
GCMG 1953
Royal Company of Archers (Queen's Bodyguard,
Scotland)

Clubs: Travellers'; Pratts'

Recreations: salmon and trout fishing, ornithology

Retired: 1946
Colonel Commandant, Royal Artillery, 1945; Chairman,
National Convention of Southern Rhodesia, 1960

Publications: *The Business of War*, 1957

Supplementary: L. H. Gann and M. Gelfand, *Huggins
of Rhodesia*, 1964

Obit. 17 June, 12h; 19, 12h.

KING-HARMAN, Charles (Anthony)

s/o. (5th) Hon. L. H. King-Harman

b. 26 April 1851   **d.** 17 April 1939

m. Constance, d/o General Sir Robert Biddulph, GCB, High Commissioner of Cyprus, 1888

ch. 2s 1d

Education: Cheltenham College
Trinity College, Cambridge, 1872;   LL.D., Edinburgh.

Career: 1874   Private Secretary to Governor of Bahamas
1879   Private Secretary to High Commissioner, Cyprus
1880   Assistant Commissioner
1881   Assistant Chief Secretary
1883   Auditor-General, Barbados
1893   Colonial Secretary, Mauritius
1894   Acting Governor
1897   Administrator, St Lucia

Governorships: Sierra Leone 1900–04
Cyprus 1904–11 (High Commissioner)

Honours: CMG 1893; KCMG 1900

Clubs: National

Recreations: —

Retired: 1911
JP Bedfordshire

Publications: —

Supplementary: Christopher Fyfe, *A History of Sierra Leone*, 1962; John Hargreaves, *A Life of Sir Samuel Lewis*, 1958

Obit. 19 Apr. 16c; 22, 15c

KITCHENER, (Horatio) Herbert

s/o. Lieutenant-Colonel H. H. Kitchener, Leicester, and
Frances, d/o The Reverend J. Chevallier, Aspall Hall,
Suffolk

b. 24 June 1850,   **d.** 5 June, 1916
Co. Kerry, Ireland

m. —

ch. —

Education: Royal Military Academy, Woolwich

Career: 1871 commissioned into Royal Engineers
1874 Palestine Survey
1878 Cyprus Survey
1884 Intelligence Department, Cairo
1886 Governor of Suakim
1890 Sirdar of the Egyptian Army
1899 Governor-General of the Sudan
1900 Field Marshal, South Africa
1902 Commander-in-Chief, India
1909 Commander-in-Chief,
    Mediterranean
1911 Agent and Consul-General, Eqypt
1914 Secretary of State for War

Governorships: Sudan 1899 (Governor-General)

Honours: GCB 1898; GCMG 1902; GCIE 1908; GCSI
1909; KP 1911; PC 1914; KG 1915; OM
elevated to peerage as Baron Kitchener of Khartoum,
1898; as Viscount Kitchener of the Vaal and Aspall, 1902;
and as Earl Kitchener of Khartoum and Broome, 1914

Clubs: Athenaeum; United Service

Recreations: —

Retired: died in office, 1916

Publications: —

Supplementary: Sir George Arthur, *Life of Lord Kitchener*,
1920, biog.; A. Hodges, *Lord Kitchener*, 1936, biog.; Philip
Magnus, *Kitchener: Portrait of an Imperialist*, 1959, biog.;

Winston Churchill, *The River War*, 1899; David Dilks, *Curzon in India*, II, 1969; K. D. D. Henderson, *Sudan Republic*, 1965; Sir Harold Macmichael, *The Sudan*, 1954; Leonard Mosley, *Curzon: the End of an Epoch*, 1960; Mekki Shibeika, *The Independent Sudan*, 1959; Sir Ronald Storrs, *Orientations*, 1937; Sir Ronald Wingate, *Wingate of the Sudan*, 1955

Obit. June 9, 11; June, passim   DNB Supp. III

KITTERMASTER, Harold (Baxter)

s/o. (4th) The Reverend Frederick Wilson Kittermaster, Coventry

b. 14 May 1879   **d.** 14 January 1939

m. Winifred Elsie, d/o R. A. Rotherham, Coventry

ch. —

Education: Shrewsbury School
Christ Church, Oxford   Classics,
Class III, 1902

Career: 1902 Transvaal Education Department
1908 Cadet, Kenya
1915 District Commissioner
1916 in charge, Northern Frontier District
1921 Secretary to the Administration,
Somaliland

Governorships: Somaliland 1926–31
British Honduras 1932–34
Nyasaland 1934–39

Honours: OBE 1918; CMG 1926; KBE 1928;
KCMG 1936

Clubs: Oxford and Cambridge

Recreations: shooting, golf, motoring

Retired: died in office, 1939

Publications: —

Supplementary: Sir Geoffrey Archer, *Personal and
Historical Memoirs*, 1964; H. Moyse-Bartlett, *The King's
African Rifles*, 1956; Robert I. Rotberg, *The Rise of
Nationalism in Central Africa*, 1965; Sir Stewart Symes,
Tour of Duty, 1946

Obit. 16 Jan. 14e; 17, 11g; 1 Feb. 16c

LAGDEN, Godfrey (Yeatman)

s/o.   The Reverend Richard Dowse Lagden,
          Cambridgeshire and Dorset

b.   1 September 1851   **d.**   26 June 1934

m.   Frances Rebekah, d/o The Right Reverend Henry
         Brougham Bonsfield, Bishop of Pretoria, 1887

ch.   2s 2d

Education: Sherborne School

Career: 1869   entered Home Civil Service, Post Office
              1878   Private Secretary to the Administrator,
                     Transvaal
              1881   Secretary to Transvaal Commission on
                     Compensation
              1882   Special war correspondent, Egyptian
                     campaign
              1883   Assistant Colonial Secretary, Sierra Leone;
                     Finance Commissioner, Gold Coast
              1884   Secretary to the Government and
                     Accountant, Basutoland
              1885   Assistant Commissioner
              1893   Resident Commissioner
              1899   South African war
              1901   Commissioner for Native Affairs, Transvaal
              1902   Chairman, South Africa Native Affairs
                     Commission

Governorships: Basutoland 1893–1901 (Resident
                     Commissioner)

Honours: CMG 1894; KCMG 1897; KBE 1927

Clubs: MCC; Authors'

Recreations: 'all games and sports; has had considerable
experience big game hunting; walked from Cape Coast
Castle through Ashantee; shooting and collecting
specimens'

Retired: 1907
Director, South African Gold Trust and other companies;
Vice-President, Royal African Society; Vice-President,

Royal Empire Society; Vice-President, British and
Foreign Bible Society

Publications: *The Basutos*, 1909; *The Native Races of the
British Empire*, 1924

Supplementary: *Dictionary of South African Biography*, I,
1968

Obit. 27 June 11a; 30, 15a   OCRP

LAWRANCE, Arthur (Salisbury), Major

s/o. —
b. 1880   **d.** 12 January 1965
m. —
ch. —

Education: privately educated

Career: 1900 commissioned into Imperial Yeomanry, South African war
1905 seconded to King's African Rifles, Somaliland
1911 Assistant Resident, Northern Nigeria
1913 Commandant, Somaliland Camel Corps
1914 District Commissioner, Somaliland
1921 Acting Governor
1926 Secretary to the Government

Governorships: Somaliland 1932–39 (Commissioner to 1935)

Honours: DSO 1920; CMG 1931; KBE 1934; KCMG 1937

Clubs: Victoria (Jersey)

Recreations: —

Retired: 1939
British Red Cross Representative, Lisbon, 1941; Intelligence Officer, Home Guard, 1943

Publications: —

Supplementary: Sir Geoffrey Archer, *Personal and Historical Memoirs*, 1964

Obit. 14 Jan. 14b

LLEWELYN, Robert (Baxter)

s/o. John Llewelyn

b. 1845   **d.** 19 February 1919

m. Theodora Louisa, d/o Charles Harvey, Campbeltown, Argyllshire

ch. 2d

Education: —

Career: 1868 entered Colonial Office
1869 Registrar to Colonial Secretary, Jamaica
1873 Private Secretary to the Governor
1878 Commissioner, Turks and Caicos Islands
1885 Administrator, Tobago
1888 Administrator, St Vincent
1889 Administrator, St Lucia

Governorships: The Gambia 1891–1900 (Administrator)
Windward Islands 1900–06

Honours: CMG 1889; KCMG 1898

Clubs: Junior Carlton

Recreations: —

Retired: —

Publications: —

Supplementary: —

LOCH, Henry (Brougham)

s/o. James Loch, M.P., Drylaw, Midlothian, and Anne Orr, Kincardineshire

b. 23 May 1827 **d.** 20 June 1900

m. Elizabeth, d/o Hon. Edward Villiers, niece of Earl of Clarendon, 1862.

ch. 1s 2d

Education: —

Career: 1840 served in the Royal Navy
1844 commissioned, 3rd Bengal Cavalry
1845 ADC to Commander-in-Chief, India, Sutlej Campaign
1846 Adjutant, Skinner's Horse
1854 Crimean War
1860 Private Secretary, Earl of Elgin in China
1861 Private Secretary, Sir George Grey, Secretary of State
1882 Commissioner of H.M. Woods and Forests

Governorships: 1863–1882 Isle of Man
1884–1889 Victoria
1889–1895 Cape Colony (High Commissioner)

Honours: CB 1860; KCB 1880; GCMG 1887; GCB 1892; PC elevated to the peerage as Baron Loch of Drylaw, 1895

Clubs: Athenaeum; Marlborough; Travellers'

Recreations: —

Retired: Hon. D.C.L. Oxford; Hon. Col., Cheshire Regt., 1884

Publications: —

Supplementary: C. F. J. Muller, *Five Hundred Years: A History of South Africa*, 1969

Obit. 21 June DNB XXII.

LOYD, Francis (Alfred)

s/o.   Major A. W. K. Loyd, Royal Sussex Regiment
b.   5 September 1916   **d.** —
m.   Katharine Layzell, 1946
ch.   2d

Education: Eton College
Trinity College, Oxford   Classics, Class III,
1938
Harkness (Commonwealth Fund) Fellow, 1953

Career: 1939 Cadet, Kenya
1940 war service, East Africa
1942 Private Secretary to Governor of Kenya
1945 Consul, Ethiopia
1947 District Commissioner, Kenya
1956 Provincial Commissioner
1962 Permanent Secretary

Governorships: Swaziland 1964–68 (Commissioner)

Honours: MBE 1951; OBE 1954; CMG 1961; KCMG 1965

Clubs: Vincent's

Recreations: golf

Retired: 1968
Warden, Dominions Students Hall Trust, University of
London

Publications: —

Supplementary: A. V. Clayton and D. Savage,
Government and Labour in Kenya, 1974; M. P. K.
Sorrenson, *Land Reform in the Kikuyu Country*, 1967;
Richard P. Stevens, *Lesotho, Botswana and Swaziland*,
1967.

LUGARD, Frederick (Dealty)

s/o. The Reverend Frederick Grueber Lugard, Chaplain to the East India Company, Madras, and Mary Jane Howard, Church Missionary Society, India

b. 22 January 1858   **d.** 11 April 1945

m. Flora Louise, DBE, d/o Major-General Shaw, CB, 1902

ch. —

Education: Rossall School
Royal Military College, Sandhurst (passed in sixth)

Career: 1878 commissioned into 9th Foot, posted to India
1879 Afghan war
1885 Sudan campaign
1886 Burma campaign
1888 expedition to Nyasaland
1889 expedition to Uganda for British East Africa Co.; Administrator
1894 expedition to Borgu for Royal Niger Company
1896 expedition to Kalahari for British West Charterland Company
1897 Commissioner and Commandant, West African Frontier Force, Nigeria

Governorships: Northern Nigeria 1900–06 (High Commissioner; resigned)
Hong Kong 1907–12
Nigeria 1912–19 (Governor-General from 1914; resigned)

Honours: DSO 1887; CB 1895; KCMG 1901; GCMG 1911; PC 1920
elevated to peerage as Baron Lugard of Abinger, 1928; Gold Medallist, Royal Geographical Society 1902, Royal Commonwealth Institute, 1926 and Royal African Society, 1923; Silver Medallist, Royal Scottish Geographical Society, 1892; Hon. DCL, Oxford, 1912, Durham 1913; Hon. LL.D., Hong Kong 1916, Cambridge 1928, Glasgow 1929.

Clubs: Athenaeum

Recreations: —

Retired: 1919 (resigned)
British Member, Permanent Mandates Commission,
1922; Director, Barclay's Bank DCO; Chairman,
International African Institute

Publications: *Our East African Empire*, 1893; *Political
Memoranda*, 1906 and 1919; *The Dual Mandate in British
Tropical Africa*, 1922

Supplementary: Margery Perham, *Lugard*, I, 1966; II,
1960, biog.; J. E. Flint in P. Duignan and L. H. Gann, eds.,
The African Proconsul, 1978; E. Moberly Bell, *Flora
Shaw*, 1947; Sonia Graham, *Government and Mission
Education in Northern Nigeria*, 1966; M. F. Hill, *Permanent
Way*, I, 1950; A. H. M. Kirk-Greene, *Lugard and the
Amalgamation of Nigeria*, 1968; M. M. Mahood, *Joyce
Cary's Africa*, 1964; D. J. M. Muffett, *Concerning Brave
Captains*, 1964; I. F. Nicolson, *The Administration of
Nigeria*, 1969; C. W. J. Orr, *The Making of Northern
Nigeria*, 1911

Obit. 12 Apr. 7d, 5c; 17, 6b; 25, 7b; 26, 7d; 19 May, 3c;
30, 7e   DNB Supp VI   OCRP

McCALLUM, Henry (Edward), Colonel

s/o. (1st) Major H. A. M'Callum, Royal Marines, and
Eleanor, d/o Major Brutton, Royal Marines

b. 28 October 1852, Somerset **d.** 24 November 1919

m. Maud, d/o Lieutenant-Colonel Creighton, Royal
Marines, 1897

ch. 1s 3d

Education: privately
Royal Military Academy, Woolwich Passed
out in first place, 1871
Pollock Medallist, Fowke Medallist

Career: 1871 commissioned into Royal Engineers
1875 Private Secretary to Governor of Straits
Settlements
1877 Superintendent, Admiralty Works, Hong
Kong
1879 Superintendent, Admiralty Works,
Singapore
1880 Deputy Colonial Engineer, Penang
1884 Colonial Engineer and Surveyor-General,
Malaya

Governorships: Lagos 1897–98
Newfoundland 1899–1901
Natal 1901–07
Ceylon 1907–13

Honours: CMG 1887; KCMG 1898; GCMG 1904;
ADC to the King, 1900

Clubs: Junior United Service

Recreations: shooting, fishing, cricket, golf

Retired: 1913

Publications: —

Supplementary: H. A. J. Hulugalle, *British Governors of
Ceylon*, 1963; I. F. Nicolson, *The Administration of Nigeria*,
1968; Margery Perham, *Lugard*, I, 1956; Margery Perham
and Mary Bull, *The Diaries of Lord Lugard*, 1963

Obit. 27 Nov. 18a; 29, 15c

MACDONALD, Claude (Maxwell)

s/o. Major-General J. D. Macdonald
b. 12 June 1852 **d.** 10 September 1915
m. Ethel, d/o Major W. Cairns Armstrong, 1892
ch. 2d

Education: Uppingham School
Royal Military College, Sandhurst

Career: 1872 commissioned into 74th Highlanders
1882 Egyptian campaign; Military Attaché, British
Agency, Cairo
1888 Acting Consul-General, Zanzibar
1889 Special Commissioner, Niger Territories
1891 Commissioner, Oil Rivers Protectorate
1896 Minister Plenipotentiary, Peking
1900 Ambassador, Tokyo

Governorships: Oil Rivers Protectorate 1891–96
(Commissioner)

Honours: KCMG 1892; KCB 1898; GCMG 1900; GCVO
1906; PC 1906

Clubs: Brooks's; Junior United Service; Travellers'; Royal
Automobile; Ranelagh

Recreations: —

Retired: 1912

Publications: —

Supplementary: J. C. Anene, *Southern Nigeria in Transition*,
1966; Sir Alan Burns, *History of Nigeria*, 1969; A. N. Cook,
British Enterprise in Nigeria, 1942; J. E. Flint, *Sir George
Goldie and the Making of Nigeria*, 1960; O. Ikime, in *Odu*,
April 1970; Sir William Geary, *Nigeria Under British Rule*,
1927; A. F. Mockler-Ferryman, *Up the Niger*, 1892;
Margery Perham and Mary Bull, *The Diaries of Lord
Lugard*, 1963; Ellen Thorp, *Ladder of Bones*, 1957

Obit. 11 Sept. DNB Supp. III

MACGREGOR, James (Comyn)

s/o. (1st) Ronald Macgregor, Writer to the Signet, Fort
William, Scotland

b. 1861   **d.** January 1935

m. Emma, d/o The Reverend D. F. Ellenberger, Paris
Evangelical Missionary Society, Basutoland, 1889

ch. 1s 3d

Education: Felsted School
privately, in Germany

Career: 1880 commissioned into King's Royal Rifles
1884 Sub-Inspector, Basutoland Mounted Police
1893 Assistant Commissioner, Basutoland
1912 Secretary to the Government
1913 Acting Governor
1916 Deputy Resident Commissioner

Governorships: Bechuanaland 1917–23 (Resident
Commissioner)

Honours: CMG 1920; Kt. 1923

Clubs: Caledonian; Civil Service, Cape Town

Recreations: golf

Retired: 1923

Publications: *Basuto Traditions*, 1905; *A History of the
Basuto*, 1909

Supplementary: —

Obit. 14 Jan. 19b

MACGREGOR, William

s/o.   (1st) John Macgregor, crofter, Aberdeenshire, and
         Agnes, d/o William Smith, farmer

b.   20 October 1847,   **d.** 3 July 1919
         Towie, Aberdeen

m.   1st Mary, d/o Peter Thomson, 1868
         2nd Mary Jane, d/o Captain Robert Cocks, Merchant
         Navy, 1883

ch.   1s 3d

Education: Aberdeen Grammar School
             Aberdeen University   Medicine, MD 1874
                Watson Medallist
             Glasgow University   FFPS

Career: 1872 Resident Physician, Royal Infirmary,
                    Glasgow
             1873 Assistant Medical Officer, Seychelles
             1874 Resident Surgeon, Mauritius
             1875 Chief Medical Officer, Fiji
             1877 Receiver-General
             1885 Deputy Administrator
             1888 Administrator, New Guinea
             1895 Lieutenant-Governor

Governorships: Nigeria 1899–1904 (Governor of Lagos)
                  Newfoundland 1904–09
                  Queensland 1909–14

Honours: CB 1897; KCMG 1889; GCMG 1907; PC 1914
            Founder's Medal, Royal Geographical Society; Mary
            Kingsley Medal, 1910; Hon. LL.D., Edinburgh,
            Aberdeen, Queensland; Hon. DSc., Cambridge; Albert
            Medal and Clarke Medal for saving life at sea, 1884;
            Chancellor, University of Queensland, 1910

Clubs: Athenaeum

Recreations: Fellow, Royal Anthropological Society of
            Italy; Fellow, Royal Geographical Societies, Scotland and
            Berlin

Retired: 1914, to Berwickshire

Publications: *British New Guinea: Country and People*, 1897

Supplementary: R. B. Joyce, *Sir William MacGregor*, 1971, biog.; I. F. Nicolson, *The Administration of Nigeria*, 1969; Margery Perham, *Lugard*, II, 1960; Ellen Thorp, *Ladder of Bones*, 1957; R. W. Reid, In Memoriam, *Aberdeen University Review*, 1919

Obit. 4 July 16e   DNB Supp. III

MACKENZIE, William Forbes

s/o. (1st) A. J. Mackenzie, MD, Salisbury, Southern
          Rhodesia
b.   5 June 1907   **d.** —
m.   Marion Elizabeth, d/o F. H. Glenton, Johannesburg,
          1934
ch.   —

Education: Plumtree School, Southern Rhodesia
                Merchiston Castle School, Edinburgh
                Caius College, Cambridge

Career: 1927 Clerk, Native Affairs Department, Southern
                   Rhodesia
             1936 Assistant District Officer, Bechuanaland
             1949 Deputy Resident Commissioner, Swaziland
             1950 Deputy Resident Commissioner,
                   Bechuanaland

Governorships: Bechuanaland 1953–55 (Resident
                    Commissioner)

Honours: OBE 1946; CBE 1951; CMG 1955

Clubs: Country, Johannesburg; Bulawayo; Salisbury

Recreations: fishing, shooting, golf

Retired: 1956

Publications: —

Supplementary: —

MACKENZIE-KENNEDY, (Henry Charles) Donald (Cleveland)

s/o. (1st) Major-General E. C. W. Mackenzie-Kennedy, KBE, CB

b. 1889   **d.** 2 August 1965

m. Mildred, d/o The Reverend J. G. Munday, 1919

ch. 3s 1d

Education: Marlborough College

Clare College, Cambridge   History, Class III, 1911

Career: 1912 Cadet, Northern Rhodesia
1918 Native Commissioner
1926 Assistant Magistrate
1927 Principal Assistant Chief Secretary
1930 Chief Secretary
1931 Acting Governor
1935 Chief Secretary, Tanganyika
1939 Chief Political Officer, East African Forces

Governorships: Nyasaland 1939–42
Mauritius 1942–49

Honours: CMG 1932; KCMG 1939

Clubs: —

Recreations: —

Retired: 1949

Publications: —

Supplementary: Walter Morris-Hale, *British Administration in Tanganyika*, 1969; Robert I. Rotberg, *The Rise of Nationalism in Central Africa*, 1965

MACMICHAEL, Harold (Alfred)

s/o.   The Reverend C. MacMichael, Rector of Wisbech, and
       Hon. Sophia, d/o Lord Scarsdale

b.   15 October 1882   **d.**   19 September 1969

m.   Nesta, d/o Canon J. Otter Stephens, 1919

ch.   2d

Education: Bedford School   Public Schools Fencing
              Champion, 1901
              Magdalene College, Cambridge (Scholar)
              Classics, Class I, 1904

Career: 1905 entered Sudan Political Service
          1926 Civil Secretary
          1934 Governor of Tanganyika
          1938 High Commissioner, Palestine
          1945 Special British Representative, Malaya
          1946 Constitutional Commissioner, Malta

Governorships: Tanganyika 1934–38
                 Palestine 1938–44 (High Commissioner)

Honours: DSO 1917; CMG 1927; KCMG 1932; GCMG
    1941; Burton Memorial Medal, Royal Asiatic Society,
    1928; Hon. Fellow, Magdalene College, Cambridge

Clubs: Athenaeum

Recreations: reading

Retired: 1947

Publications: *Tribes of Northern and Central Kordofan*, 1912;
    A History of the Arabs in the Sudan, 1922; *The Anglo-
    Egyptian Sudan*, 1934; *The Sudan*, 1954

Supplementary: Sir Geoffrey Archer, *Personal and
    Historical Memoirs*, 1964; N. and H. Bentwick, *Mandate
    Memories*, 1965; Ralph A. Austen, *Northwest Tanzania
    Under German and British Rule*, 1968; B. T. G. Chidzero,
    Tanganyika and International Trusteeship, 1961; K. D. D.
    Henderson, *The Making of the Modern Sudan*, 1953; Collie
    Knox, *It Might Have Been You*, 1938; Walter Morris-Hale,
    British Administration in Tanganyika, 1969

Obit. 22 Sept. 10f; 17 Oct. 14c   OCRP

MACPHERSON, John (Stuart)

s/o. James P. Macpherson, JP
b. 25 August 1898 **d.** 5 November 1971
m. Joan, d/o W. E. Fry, MD
ch. 1s

Education: Watson's College, Edinburgh
Edinburgh University

Career: 1918 war service, France
1921 Cadet, Malaya
1928 District Officer
1933 Colonial Office
1937 Principal Assistant Secretary, Nigeria
1939 Chief Secretary, Palestine
1943 Head of British Colonies Supply Mission, Washington DC
1945 Comptroller of Development and Welfare, West Indies
1948 Governor of Nigeria
1956 Permanent Secretary, Colonial Office

Governorships: Nigeria 1948–55 (Governor-General from 1954)

Honours: CMG 1941; KCMG 1945; GCMG 1951

Clubs: —

Recreations: —

Retired: 1959
Chairman, Trusteeship Council Visiting Mission, Pacific, 1956; Chairman, Cable and Wireless Ltd, 1962; Deputy Chairman, Basildon Development Corporation

Publications: —

Supplementary: Obafemi Awolowo, *Awo*, 1960; Sir Ahmadu Bello, *My Life* 1962; J. S. Coleman, *Nigeria: Background to Nationalism*, 1958; Michael Crowder, *The Story of Nigeria*, 1973; Kalu Ezera, *Constitutional Developments in Nigeria*, 1964; Sir Hugh Foot, *A Start in Freedom*, 1964; Elspeth Huxley, *Four Guineas*, 1954; Sir

Bryan Sharwood Smith, *But Always As Friends*, 1969; John Smith, *Colonial Cadet in Nigeria*, 1968

Obit. 6 Nov. 1e; 11, 18g; 3 Dec. 16b   OCRP/t

MAFFEY, John (Loader) (Lord Rugby)

s/o.   Thomas Maffey

b.   1 July 1877   **d.**   20 April 1969

m.   Dorothy, OBE, d/o Charles L. Huggins, JP, Buxted

ch.   2s 2d

Education: Rugby School
Christ Church, Oxford

Career: 1899   entered Indian Civil Service
1905   transferred to Indian Political Service
1909   Political Agent, Khyber
1914   Deputy Commissioner, North West Frontier
Province
1915   Deputy Secretary, Government of India
1916   Private Secretary to the Viceroy
1921   Chief Commissioner, North West Frontier
Province
1926   Governor-General of the Sudan
1933   Permanent Secretary, Colonial Office

Governorships: Sudan 1926–33 (Governor-General)

Honours: CIE 1916; CSI 1920; KCVO 1921; KCMG 1931;
KCB 1934; GCMG 1935
elevated to the peerage as Baron Rugby, 1947
Hon. Student, Christ Church

Clubs: —

Recreations: —

Retired: 1937 (resigned ICS 1924)
Director, Imperial Airways, 1937; Director, Rio Tinto
Co, 1937; British Representative to Eire, 1939; Governor
of Rugby School (resigned)

Publications: —

Supplementary: Reginald Davies, *The Camel's Back*, 1957;
Sir Harold Macmichael, *The Sudan*, 1954; Sir James
Robertson, *Transition in Africa*, 1974; Viscount Swinton,
I Remember, 1947

Obit. 21 Apr., 10f; 25; 12e; 29, 12h

MANNING, William (Henry), Brigadier-General

s/o. (2nd) Henry Manning
b. 19 July 1863   **d.** 1 January 1932
m. Olga May, d/o H. Sefton-Jones
ch. 3d

Education: Royal Military College, Sandhurst

Career: 1886 commissioned into South Wales Borderers
1888 transferred to Indian Army
1891 North West Frontier operations
1893 Matabele war
1897 Deputy Commissioner, British Central
        Africa Protectorate
1900 Commanded Central Africa Regiment
1901 Inspector-General, King's African Rifles
1902 Commanded Somaliland Field Force
1907 Acting Governor, Somaliland

Governorships: Somaliland 1910
                    Nyasaland 1910–13
                    Jamaica 1913–18
                    Ceylon 1918–25

Honours: CB 1903; KCMG 1904; KBE 1918; GCMG 1921

Clubs: Naval and Military; Ranelagh

Recreations: golf

Retired: 1925 (retired Indian Army, 1910)

Publications: —

Supplementary: Sir Geoffrey Archer, *Personal and Historical Memoirs*, 1964; H. A. Hulugalle, *British Governors of Ceylon*, 1963; Douglas Jardine, *The Mad Mullah of Somaliland*, 1963; H. Moyse-Bartlett, *The King's African Rifles*, 1956; Robert I. Rotberg, *The Rise of Nationalism in Central Africa*, 1965; H. F. P. Battersby, *Richard Corfield of Somaliland*, 1914

Obit. 4 Jan. 12c; 6, 13e

MARWICK, Allan Graham

s/o. —
b. 1877   **d.** —
m. —
ch. —

Education: —

Career: 1895   Natal Civil Service
               1899   South African war
               1903   Sub-Native Commissioner, Swaziland
               1907   Assistant Commissioner
               1933   Deputy Resident Commissioner

Governorships: Swaziland 1935–37

Honours: OBE 1925

Clubs: —

Recreations: —

Retired: 1937

Publications: —

Supplementary: —

MARWICK, Brian (Allan)

s/o. James Walter Marwick and Elizabeth Jane Flett
b. 18 June 1908 **d.** —
m. Riva Lee, d/o Major H. C. Cooper
ch. 2d

Education: University of Cape Town
Corpus Christi College, Cambridge

Career: 1925 Cadet, Swaziland
1937 District Officer, Northern Nigeria
1941 District Commissioner, Swaziland
1949 Assistant Secretary, Basutoland
1952 Deputy Resident Commissioner
1955 Administrative Secretary for High
Commission Territories
1956 Assistant Chief Secretary

Governorships: Swaziland, 1956–64 (as Resident
Commissioner; Commissioner from
1963)

Honours: OBE 1946; CBE 1954; CMG 1958; KBE 1963

Clubs: Royal Commonwealth Society

Recreations: polo, tennis, golf

Retired: 1964
Permanent Secretary, Bahamas, 1965–71

Publications: *The Swazi*, 1940

Supplementary: Richard P. Stevens, *Lesotho, Botswana and
Swaziland*, 1967

MAXWELL, James (Crawford)

s/o. James Maxwell, Dundee, Scotland
b. 1869   **d.** 16 November 1932
m. Muriel, d/o T. J. Davies, Gloucestershire, 1909
ch. —

Education: Dundee High School
Edinburgh University   MA 1889; MD 1896
Called to Bar, Gray's Inn

Career: 1897 Assistant Colonial Surgeon, Sierra Leone
1900 District Commissioner
1914 Provincial Commissioner, Southern Nigeria
1918 Special Commissioner, Abeokuta
                  Disturbances
1920 Colonial Secretary, Sierra Leone
1921 Acting Governor
1922 Colonial Secretary, Gold Coast

Governorships: Northern Rhodesia 1927–32

Honours: CMG 1911; KBE 1925; KCMG 1930

Clubs: Athenaeum

Recreations: —

Retired: 1932

Publications: —

Supplementary: A. E. Afigbo, *The Warrant Chiefs*, 1972;
Sir Alan Burns, *Colonial Civil Servant*, 1949; L. H. Gann, *A
History of Northern Rhodesia*, 1964; Margery Perham,
Lugard, II, 1960; Margery Perham, *African Apprenticeship*,
1974

Obit. 18 Nov. 16d; 25, 17d; 29, 17b

MAXWELL, William (Edward)

s/o. Sir Peter Benson Maxwell
b. 1846   **d.** 10 December 1897
m. Lilias, d/o The Rev. J. Aberigh-Mackay, DD, 1870
ch. —

Education: Repton School
Called to the Bar, Inner Temple, 1881

Career: 1865 Cadet, Malaya
1878 Assistant Resident
1892 Colonial Secretary
1893 Acting Governor

Governorships: Gold Coast 1895–97

Honours: CMG 1893; KCMG 1896

Clubs: Conservative; Wellington

Recreations: 1897 (died in office)

Retired: —

Publications: —

Supplementary: W. Walton Claridge, *A History of the Gold Coast and Ashanti*, 1915; David Kimble, *A Political History of Ghana*, 1963

MAYBIN, John (Alexander)

s/o. William Maybin, Ayr, Scotland
b. 5 August 1889   **d.** 9 April 1941
m. —
ch. —

Education: Edinburgh University

Career:
- 1914 Cadet, Ceylon
- 1916 Police Magistrate
- 1924 Assistant Colonial Secretary
- 1932 Deputy Registrar, Co-operative Societies
- 1934 Chief Secretary, Nigeria
- 1935 Acting Governor

Governorships: Northern Rhodesia 1938–41

Honours: CMG 1935; KCMG 1939

Clubs: East India and Sports

Recreations: golf, fishing, philately

Retired: died in office, 1941

Publications: —

Supplementary: L. H. Gann, *A History of Northern Rhodesia*, 1964; Robert I. Rotberg, *The Rise of Nationalism in Central Africa*, 1965; Robert I. Rotberg, *Black Heart*, 1917

Obit. 10 April 4f; 12, 6d; 14, 3e

MEREWETHER, Edward (Marsh)

s/o. (2nd) Major-General Sir W. L. Merewether, KCSI, CB
b.   9 September 1858   **d.**   28 December 1938
m.   Honoria Clementina, d/o Thomas Braddell, CMG,
          Attorney-General, Malaya, 1883
ch.   —

Education: Harrow School
               Wren's Tutors

Career: 1880 Cadet, Malaya
             1886 District Officer
             1891 Superintendent of Census
             1893 Inspector of Prisons
             1897 Assistant Colonial Secretary
             1901 Resident, Selangor
             1902 Lieutenant-Governor, Malta

Governorships: Sierra Leone 1911–15
                    Leeward Islands 1916–21

Honours: CMG 1902; CVO 1903; KCVO 1907; KCMG 1916

Clubs: St Stephen's

Recreations: shooting, fishing, motoring, golf

Retired: 1921

Publications: —

Supplementary: —

   Obit. 29 Dec. 10b

METHUEN, Paul Sanford, Field–Marshal Lord

s/o. (1st) Lord Frederick Methuen and Anna Horatia, d/o The Reverend John Sanford, Somerset

b. 1 September 1845   **d.** 30 October 1932

m. 1st Evelyn, d/o Sir Frederick Hervey-Bathurst, Bt, 1878
2nd Mary Ethel, CBE, d/o William Sanford, Colonial Service, Nynehead Court, Somersetshire, 1884

ch. 3s 1d

Education: Eton College

Career: 1862 joined Royal Wiltshire Yeomanry
1864 commissioned into Scots Guards
1873 Ashanti Campaign
1877 Assistant Military Secretary, Commander in Chief, Ireland
1878 Military Attaché, Berlin
1882 Egyptian Expeditionary Force
1884 Commanded Methuen's Horse, Bechuanaland Expeditionary Force
1888 General Staff, South Africa
1892 Commanded Home District
1897 Tirah Campaign
1899 Divisonal Commander, Anglo-Boer War
1903 Commander-in-Chief, Eastern Command
1908 G.O.C. South Africa
1911 promoted Field-Marshal

Governorships: Natal 1909–1910
Malta 1915–1919

Honours: CB 1882; CMG 1886; KCVO 1897; KCB 1900; GCB 1902; GCVO 1910; GCMG 1919;
succeeded father as Baron Methuen of Corsham, 1891

Clubs: Guards'; Travellers'

Recreations: —

Retired: 1919
Colonel, Scots Guards, 1904; Hon. LL.D. Malta 1919;

Governor and Constable of the Tower, 1920; voluntary work with British Legion, Church Lads' Brigade, Boy Scouts, V.A.D.

Publications: —

Supplementary: E. H. Brookes and C. Webb, *A History of Natal*, 1965; C. J. F. Muller, *Five Hundred Years: A History of South Africa*, 1969; E. A. Walker, *A History of Southern Africa*, 1959

Obit. 31 Oct.; 2 Nov.   DNB Supp. V

MIDDLETON, John

s/o.   Dr James Middleton, MD, Midlothian, Scotland
b.   1870   3d.   5 November 1954
m.   Mabel, d/o Lieutenant-Colonel G. Wilbraham Northey,
         DL, JP, Ashley Manor, and widow of R. K.
         Granville, 1920
ch.   —

Education: Sedbergh School
                 Edinburgh University

Career: 1901   Assistant District Commissioner, Southern
                     Nigeria
              1904   Senior Assistant Secretary
              1906   District Commissioner
              1907   Senior Assistant Colonial Secretary
              1908   Assistant Colonial Secretary, Mauritius
              1913   Colonial Secretary
              1914   Acting Governor

Governorships: Falkland Islands 1920–27
                     The Gambia 1927–28
                     Newfoundland 1928–32

Honours: CMG 1916; KBE 1924; KCMG 1931

Clubs: —

Recreations: —

Retired: 1932

Publications: —

Supplementary: —

Obit. 6 Nov. 8g; 10, 8d

MILNER, Alfred, Viscount

s/o. Charles Milner, M.D. and Mary Ierne, d/o Major-
General John Ready, Governor of Prince Edward's
Island and of the Isle of Man

b. 23 March 1854 **d.** 13 May 1925

m. Violet Georgina, d/o Admiral Frederick Augustus
Maxse and widow of Lord Edward Cecil, 1921

ch. —

Education: privately in Germany
King's College, London
Balliol College, Oxford (Scholar) Classics,
Class I
Hertford Scholar 1874; Craven Scholar 1877;
Elden Scholar 1878; Derby Scholar 1878;
President of the Union Inner Temple, 1881

Career: 1876 Fellow of New College, Oxford
1883 Assistant Editor, *Pall Mall Gazette*
1885 contested Harrow Division
1887 Private Secretary, Chancellor of Exchequer
1889 Under-Secretary of Finance, Egypt
1892 Chairman, Board of Inland Revenue
1916 Minister without Portfolio, War Cabinet
1918 Secretary of State for War
1919 Secretary of State for the Colonies

Governorships: Cape Colony 1897–1901
Transvaal and Orange River 1902–1905
South Africa 1897–1905 (High
Commissioner)

Honours: CB 1894; KCB 1895; GCMG 1897; GCB 1901;
KG 1921; PC
elevated to peerage as Baron Milner of St James's, London
and Cape Town, 1901; Viscountcy 1902

Clubs: Athenaeum; Brooks's; New University

Recreations: —

Retired: 1921
Trustee, Rhodes Trust; Hon. D.C.L. Oxford 1896; Hon.
LL.D. Cambridge; Chancellor, Oxford University, 1925

Publications: *England in Egypt*, 1892; *The Nation and the Empire*, 1913; *Questions of the Hour*, 1923

Supplementary: E. Crankshaw, *The Forsaken Idea*, 1952, (biog.); A. M. Gollin, *Proconsul in Politics*, 1964 (biog.); V. Halperin, *Lord Milner and the Empire*, 1952 (biog.); Cecil Headlam, *The Milner Papers, 1897–1905*, I, 1931; II, 1933 (biog.); John Marlowe, Milner, *Apostle of Empire*, 1976 (biog.); Evelyn Wrench, *Alfred, Lord Milner: The Man of No Illusions*, 1958 (biog.)

L. S. Amery, *My Political Life*, II, 1953; T. R. Davenport, *South Africa: A Modern History*, 1978; L. M. Thompson, *The Unification of South Africa*, 1960; E. A. Walker, ed., *Cambridge History of the British Empire*, VIII, 1963; M. Wilson and L. M. Thompson, *Oxford History of South Africa*, II, 1971

Obit. May 14; 16; 17   DNB Supp. IV

MITCHELL, Lieutenant-Colonel, Charles (Bullen Hugh)

s/o. (1st) Colonel Hugh Mitchell and Constance, d/o Major
    R. Bullen, Scots Greys

b. —   **d.**   7 December 1899

m. —

ch. —

Education: Royal Naval School, New Cross
                       Royal Naval College, Portsmouth

Career: 1852 commissioned into Royal Marines
             1868 Colonial Secretary, British Honduras
             1870 Acting Governor
             1877 Colonial Secretary, Natal

Governorships: Fiji 1887–1888
                         Leeward Islands 1888 (never assumed
                            office)
                         Natal 1889–1893
                         Straits Settlements 1893–1899

Honours: CMG 1880; KCMG 1883; GCMG 1895

Clubs: United Service

Recreations: from Royal Marines, 1878

Retired: died in office

Publications: —

Supplementary: E. H. Brookes and C. Webb, *A History of
Natal*, 1965; E. A. Walker, *A History of Southern Africa*,
1959

   Obit. 6 Dec.; 8

MITCHELL, Philip (Euen)

s/o. (5th) Captain Hugh Mitchell, Royal Engineers
b.   1 May 1890   **d.**   11 October 1964
m.   Margery, d/o John D'Urban Tyrwhitt Drake
ch. —

Education: St Paul's School
              Trinity College, Oxford   Classics, Class II
              1911

Career: 1912 Assistant Resident, Nyasaland
         1915 Lieutenant, King's African Rifles
         1918 ADC and Private Secretary to Governor of
               Nyasaland
         1919 Assistant Political Officer, Tanganyika
         1926 Assistant Secretary for Native Affairs
         1928 Provincial Commissioner
         1934 Chief Secretary, Tanganyika
         1935 Governor, Uganda
         1941 Political Adviser to General Sir Archibald
               Wavell
         1942 British Plenipotentiary in Ethiopia and Chief
               Political Officer to GOC East Africa, in
               rank of Major-General

Governorships: Uganda 1935–40
                  Fiji 1942–44
                  Kenya 1944–52

Honours: MC 1917; CMG 1933; KCMG 1937; GCMG 1947
US Legion of Honor

Clubs: Savile; Little Ship

Recreations: golf, shooting, fishing

Retired: 1952
settled on a farm in Kenya

Publications: *African Afterthoughts*, 1954, autobiog.; chapter
in C. Grove Haines, *Africa Today*, 1955

Supplementary: Fay Carter in Kenneth King and Ahmed
Salim, *Kenya Historical Biographies*, 1971, biog.; Lord

Altrincham, *Kenya's Opportunity*, 1955; David Apter, *The Political Kingdom in Uganda*, 1961; Sir Michael Blundell, *So Rough A Wind*, 1964; Lord Chandos, *An Unexpected View from the Summit*, 1962; A. V. Clayton and D. Savage, *Government and Labour in Kenya*, 1974; Richard A. Frost, *Race Against Time*, 1978; Vincent Harlow and E. M. Chilver, *History of East Africa*, II, 1965; K. D. D. Henderson, *The Making of the Modern Sudan*, 1953; Kenneth Ingham, *The Making of Modern Uganda*, 1958; D. A. Low and Alison Smith, *History of East Africa*, III, 1976; Margery Perham, *East African Journey*, 1976; M. P. K. Sorrenson, *Land Reform in the Kikuyu Country*, 1967

Obit. 13 Oct. 14e; 19, 17a; 23, 18d   OCRP

MOLONEY, (Cornelius) Alfred, Captain

s/o. —

b. 1848   **d.** 13 August 1913

m. 1st Constance, d/o W. Clifford Knight, 1881
2nd Frances, d/o H. Owen Lewis, JP, DL

ch. —

Education: Royal Military College, Sandhurst

Career: 1867 commissioned into army
1871 ADC to Governor of Bahamas
1873 Ashanti campaign
1874 Private Secretary to Governor of Gold Coast
1875 Acting Inspector-General, Gold Coast
Constabulary
1877 Assistant Colonial Secretary
1879 Colonial Secretary
1880 Acting Governor of Lagos

Governorships: The Gambia 1884–85 (Administrator)
Lagos 1886–90 (Administrator till 1887)
British Honduras 1891–97
Windward Islands 1897–1900
Trinidad and Tobago 1900–04

Honours: CMG 1882; KCMG 1890

Clubs: Naval and Military

Recreations: 1904

Retired: —

Publications: *Forestry of West Africa*, 1887

Supplementary: Michael Crowder, *The Story of Nigeria*, 1973; John Hargreaves, *Prelude to the Partition of West Africa*, 1963; Samuel Johnson, *The History of the Yorubas*, 1921; Ellen Thorp, *Ladder of Bones*, 1956

MOOR, Ralph (Denham Rayment)

s/o.   W. H. Moor, MD, Hertfordshire, and Sarah Pears
b.   31 July 1860, Buntingford   **d.**   13 September 1909
m.   Adrienne Burns, widow of J. Burns, 1898
ch.   —

Education: privately

Career: 1880 learner in the tea trade
   1882 Cadet, Royal Irish Constabulary
   1892 Deputy Commissioner, Oil Rivers
      Protectorate
   1893 Acting Governor

Governorships: Niger Coast 1896–1900 (Commissioner)
      Southern Nigeria 1900–03 (High
      Commissioner)

Honours: CMG 1895; KCMG 1897

Clubs: St James's

Recreations: —

Retired: 1903 (from Constabulary, 1891)
   Adviser, British Cotton Growing Association;
   Consultant to Sir Alfred Jones on West African affairs

Publications: —

Supplementary: A. E. Afigbo, *The Warrant Chiefs*, 1972;
   J. C. Anene, *Southern Nigeria in Transition*, 1966; Sir Alan
   Burns, *History of Nigeria*, 1969; A. Norton Cook, *British
   Enterprise in Nigeria*, 1942; E. D. Morel, *Nigeria: its People
   and its Problems*, 1911; I. F. Nicolson, *The Administration of
   Nigeria*, 1969

   Obit. 15 Sept. 11c; 17, 5f; 18, 11a; 28 Oct. 11d
                              DNB Supp. II

MOORE, Henry (Monck–Mason)

s/o. (y) The Reverend E. W. Moore and Laetitia Monck-Mason

b. 1887   **d.** 26 March 1964

m. Daphne, d/o W. J. Benson, CBE, Consular Service

ch. 2d

Education: King's College School, Cambridge
Jesus College, Cambridge

Career: 1910 Cadet, Ceylon
1914 Assistant Colonial Secretary
1916 Salonika campaign
1919 Assistant Colonial Secretary, Ceylon
1920 Private Secretary to the Governor
1922 Colonial Secretary, Bermuda
1924 Principal Assistant Secretary, Nigeria
1927 Deputy Chief Secretary
1929 Colonial Secretary, Kenya
1930 Acting Governor
1934 Governor, Sierra Leone
1937 Assistant Under-Secretary, Colonial Office

Governorships: Sierra Leone 1934–37
Kenya 1940–44
Ceylon 1944–49 (Governor-General 1948–49)

Honours: CMG 1930; KCMG 1935; GCMG 1943
Hon LL.D., Ceylon

Clubs: Athenaeum; Oxford and Cambridge; Civil Service (Cape Town)

Recreations: —

Retired: 1949 to Cape Town

Publications: —

Supplementary: Lord Altrincham, *Kenya's Opportunity*, 1955; George Bennett, *Kenya*, 1963; A. V. Clayton, *Government and Labour in Kenya*, 1974; H. A. J. Hulugalle, *British Governors of Ceylon*, 1963; Sir Philip Mitchell, *African Afterthoughts*, 1954
Obit. 28 March 10d; 10 Apr. 17d

MOORING, (Arthur) George (Rixson)

s/o. Arthur Mooring, Biddenham, Bedford
b. 23 November 1908   **d.** 13 January 1969
m. Patricia, d/o Algernon Hare Duke, County Down,
       Ireland
ch. 1s 1d

Education: Bedford Modern School
       Queen's College, Cambridge   Modern
          Languages, Class II/2, 1930

Career: 1931 Cadet, Nigeria
       1939 war service, Royal West African Frontier
             Force
       1951 Financial Secretary, Western Nigeria
       1954 Deputy-Governor

Governorships: Zanzibar 1960–63 (Resident)

Honours: CMG 1955; Kt 1958; KCMG 1961

Clubs: Royal Commonwealth; East India and Sports;
   Hawks'

Recreations: golf, sailing

Retired: 1964
   Member, Constituency Delimination Commission, St
   Vincent, 1967; Chairman, Gilbert and Ellice Islands Socio-
   Economy Survey, 1967

Publications: —

Supplementary: —

   Obit. 15 Jan. 10f; 24, 14h

MORGAN, David Loftus

s/o.   George Morgan, CIE, West Bengal
b.   21 November 1904   d.   —
m.   Phyllis Russell, 1929
ch.   1d

Education: Harrow School
Trinity College, Cambridge   History, II/2,
1922

Career: 1926 Cadet, Kenya
1947 Provincial Commissioner

Governorships: Swaziland 1951–56 (Resident
Commissioner)

Honours: MBE 1943; CMG 1952

Clubs: Caledonian; Nairobi

Recreations: golf

Retired: 1956, to Swaziland
Member, Swaziland Public Service Commission;
Member, Swaziland Railway Board, 1963; Director of
several companies

Publications: —

Supplementary: —

NATHAN, Matthew, Lieutenant-Colonel

s/o. (2nd) Jonah Nathan, manufacturer, Paddington, and
      Miriam, d/o Lewis Jacobs

b.   3 January 1862   **d.**   18 April 1939

m.   —

ch. —

Education: Royal Military Academy, Woolwich

Career: 1880 commissioned into Royal Engineers
           1884 Nile expedition
           1895 Secretary, Colonial Defence Committee
           1899 Acting Governor, Sierra Leone
           1900 [various Colonial Governorships]
           1909 Permanent Secretary, General Post Office,
                   London
           1911 Chairman, Board of Inland Revenue
           1914 Under-Secretary for Ireland
           1916 Permanent Secretary, Ministry of Pensions
           1920 Governor of Queensland
           1926 Chairman, Colonial Secretary's Advisory
                   Committee on Rubber
           1927 Member, Ceylon Constitutional
                   Commission
           1928 Chairman, Civil Service Sub-Commission
                   on Irrigation Research

Governorships: Gold Coast 1900–03
                      Hong Kong 1903–07
                      Natal 1907–09
                      Queensland 1920–25

Honours: CMG 1899; KCMG 1902; GCMG 1908; PC
(Ireland) 1914. Hon. LL.D. Queensland, 1925

Clubs: Athenaeum

Recreations: Fellow, Society of Antiquaries; Fellow, Royal
Geographical Society; Fellow, Royal Historical Society

Retired: 1930 to Somerset
President, Somerset Archaeological and Natural History

Society, 1930; Chancellor, University of Queensland, 1922; Alderman, Somerset County Council, 1927; Sheriff of Somerset, 1934; Deputy Lieutenant, Somerset; JP

Publications: —

Supplementary: Anthony P. Haydon, *Sir Matthew Nathan: British Colonial Governor and Civil Servant*, 1976, biog; W. Walton Claridge, *A History of the Gold Coast and Ashanti*, 1915; H. Curtis, *Regimes and Governors in Natal*, 1930; David Kimble, *A Political History of Ghana*, 1963; Leonard M. Thompson, *The Unification of South Africa*, 1960; *Dictionary of South African Biography*, II, 1972

Obit. 19 Apr. 16d; 22, 15c; 25, 16c; 26, 18b; 8 June, 21b

DNB Supp. V   OCRP

NEWTON, Francis (James)

s/o. F. R. Newton, Santa Cruz, West Indies
b. 13 September 1857,   **d.** 9 May 1948
West Indies
m. Henrietta, d/o D. Cloete, Cape of Good Hope, 1889
ch. —

Education: Rugby School
University College, Oxford
Called to the Bar, Inner Temple

Career: 1881 Private Secretary to Governor of Cape
Colony
1883 Private Secretary to Prime Minister
1884 Private Secretary to Governor
1886 Secretary to Royal Commission on Mauritius
1889 Colonial Secretary, Bechuanaland
1894 Special Commissioner, Matabeleland
1895 Resident Commissioner, Bechuanaland
1898 Colonial Secretary, British Honduras
1901 Colonial Secretary, Barbados
1903 Treasurer, Southern Rhodesia

Governorships: Bechuanaland 1895–97 (Resident
Commissioner)

Honours: CMG 1892; CVO 1911; KCMG 1919

Clubs: Carlton

Recreations: —

Retired: 1919, to Rhodesia
Colonial Secretary, Southern Rhodesian Ministry, 1923;
High Commissioner for Southern Rhodesia, London,
1924; Chairman, Rhodesian Committee of Barclay's Bank
DCO, 1930

Publications: —

Supplementary: A. Sillery, *The Bechuanaland Protectorate*,
1952

Obit. 10 May 6d

NORMAN-WALKER, Hugh (Selby)

s/o. Colonel J. N. Norman-Walker, CIE
b. 17 December 1916   **d.** —
m. Janet Baldock, 1948
ch. —

Education: Sherborne School
Corpus Christi College, Cambridge   History
II/1

Career: 1938 entered Indian Civil Service
1949 transferred to Colonial Service, Nyasaland
1953 Cabinet Office, Federation of Rhodesia and
Nyasaland
1954 Development Secretary, Nyasaland
1961 Secretary to Treasury
1965 Commissioner, Bechuanaland
1967 Governor, Seychelles
1969 Colonial Secretary, Hong Kong

Governorships: Bechuanaland 1965–66 (Commissioner)
Seychelles 1967–69
Isle of Man 1974 (did not assume office)

Honours: OBE 1961; CMG 1964; KCMG 1966

Clubs: East India and Sports; Island Sailing, Cowes

Recreations: sailing, shooting, bridge

Retired: 1974

Publications: —

Supplementary: —

NORTHEY, Edward, Major-General

s/o. The Reverend Edward W. M. Northey, and Florence,
       d/o Sir John Honywood, Bt.

b. 28 May 1868   **d.** 25 December 1953

m. Evangeline Cloete, d/o Daniel Cloete, Cape Town,
       1897

ch. 2s 2d

Education: Eton College
            Royal Military Academy, Sandhurst

Career: 1891 North West Frontier operations
          1899 South African war
          1914 commanded Brigade, France and Belgium
          1916 commanded Nyasaland/Rhodesia Field Force

Governorships: Kenya 1919–22

Honours: CB 1917; KCMG 1918; GCMG 1922
          Extra ADC to the King, 1915
          Promoted Major-General for distinguished service in the
          field, 1918

Clubs: —

Recreations: Fellow, Royal Geographical Society; Fellow,
          Zoological Society

Retired: 1926
          GOC 43rd Division (Wessex) Territorial Army, 1924

Publications: —

Supplementary: Lord Altrincham, *Kenya's Opportunity*,
          1955; George Bennett, *Kenya*, 1963; A. V. Clayton and
          D. Savage, *Government and Labour in Kenya*, 1974;
          Marjorie Ruth Dilley, *British Policy in Kenya Colony*, 1937;
          Robert G. Gregory, *India and East Africa*, 1971; Vincent
          Harlow and E. M. Chilver, *History of East Africa*, II, 1965;
          M. F. Hill, *Permanent Way*, I, 1950; Elspeth Huxley, *White
          Man's Country*, 1935; H. Moyse-Bartlett, *The King's
          African Rifles*, 1956; Norman Leys, *Kenya*, 1925;
          W. McGregor Ross, *Kenya From Within*, 1927; Robert L.
          Tignor, *The Colonial Transformation of Kenya*, 1976

Obit. 29 Dec. 9b

PALMER, (Herbert) Richmond

s/o. —

b. 20 April 1877   **d.** 22 May 1958

m. Margaret, d/o Reginald Abel Smith, Hertfordshire,
     1924

ch. 2d

Education: Oundle School
            Trinity Hall, Cambridge (Scholar)
            Called to the Bar, Middle Temple, 1904

Career: 1904 Assistant Resident, Northern Nigeria
         1911 Commissioner, Native Revenue
         1912 Revenue mission to the Sudan
         1917 Resident, Northern Nigeria
         1918 Education mission to the Sudan
         1925 Lieutenant-Governor, Northern Nigeria

Governorships: The Gambia 1930–33
                 Cyprus 1933–39

Honours: CMG 1922; CBE 1924; KCMG 1933

Clubs: Travellers'; Winckley, Preston

Recreations: —

Retired: 1939
Barrister at Law, Northern Circuit

Publications: *Sudanese Memoirs*, 1926–28; *The Bornu Sahara and Sudan*, 1936

Supplementary: A. E. Afigbo in *Journal of Historical Society of Nigeria*, 3, 1965; A. E. Afigbo, *The Warrant Chiefs*, 1972; Michael Crowder, *Revolt in Bussa*, 1973; C. Foley and W. I. Scobie, *The Struggle for Cyprus*, 1975; Harry A. Gailey, *A History of the Gambia*, 1964; Robert Heussler, *The British in Northern Nigeria*, 1968; Margery Perham, *Lugard*, II, 1960; Sir Bryan Sharwood Smith, *But Always As Friends*, 1969

Obit. 26 May 8d; 3 June 14b

PALMER, William Waldegrave
(Viscount Wolmer; Lord Selborne)

s/o. Earl and Lady Laura Waldegrave, d/o 8th Earl
     Waldegrave

b.   17 October 1859   **d.**   26 February 1942

m.   Lady Beatrix Maud Cecil, d/o Marquis of Salisbury,
     KG, 1883

ch.   3s 1d

Education: Winchester College
         University College, Oxford   Modern
             History, Class I

Career: 1882 Assistant Private Secretary, Chancellor of
             Exchequer
       1885 M.P. East Hants
       1886 Alderman, Hampshire County
             Council
       1892 M.P., West Edinburgh
       1895 Under-Secretary of State for the
             Colonies
       1896 Chairman, Pacific Cable Committee
       1900 First Lord of the Admiralty
       1915 President, Board of Agriculture and
             Fisheries

Governorships: Orange River 1905–1907
             Transvaal 1905–1910
             South Africa 1905–1910 (High
                 Commissioner)

Honours: PC 1900; GCMG 1905; KG 1909
     succeeded as Viscount Wolmer, 1883; and as Earl of
     Selborne, 1895

Clubs: Brooks's

Recreations: —

Retired: resigned 1916.
     JP; LL.D. Cambridge 1910; D.C.L. Oxford, 1911; Elder
     Brother of Trinity House, 1904; Chairman, Agriculture

Policy Sub-Committee of the Reconstruction
Committee, 1917; Director, Lloyds Bank; Chairman,
Parliamentary Joint Committee on Montagu-Chelmsford
Reforms Report, 1919; Lord High Steward of Winchester,
1920; Warden of Winchester College, 1920

Publications: —

Supplementary: T. R. Davenport, *South Africa: A Modern
History*, 1978; R. Hyam, *The Failure of South African
Expansion*, 1972; C. F. S. Muller, *Five Hundred Years: A
History of South Africa*, 1969; B. Sachs, *South Africa: An
Imperial Dilemma*, 1967; L. M. Thompson, *The Unification
of South Africa*, 1960; F. Troup, *South Africa: An Historical
Introduction*, 1972; E. A. Walker, *A History of Southern
Africa*, 1959; E. A. Walker, ed., *Cambridge History of the
British Empire*, VIII, 1963

Obit. 27 Feb.; 3 March   DNB Supp. VII

PANZERA, Francis William, Lieutenant-Colonel

s/o. J. G. I. A. Panzera, civil engineer

b.   1851   **d.**   14 June 1917

m.   —

ch.   1s 2d

Education: —

Career: 1870   served with Artillery Militia
1888   Engineer, Submarine Miners, Harwich
1893   Engineer, Public Works Department, Bechuanaland
1894   Government Engineer, Rhodesia Railways
1896   Magistrate, Bechuanaland
1898   Special Commissioner, Ngamiland
1901   Assistant Commissioner, Bechuanaland
1907   Resident Commissioner
1917   Commandant, Alien Detention Camp, Isle of Man

Governorships: Bechuanaland 1907–16

Honours: CMG 1911

Clubs: British Empire; Junior Army and Navy; Royal Harwich Yacht

Recreations: Fellow, Royal Society of Arts

Retired: died in office 1917

Publications: *Questions and Answers in Gunnery*, n.d.; *The Officering of the Artillery Militia*, n.d.

Supplementary: A. Sillery, *The Bechuanaland Protectorate*, 1952

Obit. 15 June 3c

PAUL, John (Warburton)

s/o. (2nd) Walter George Paul and Phoebe Bull, Weymouth, Dorset

b. 29 March 1916 **d.** —

m. Kathleen Audrey, d/o A. D. Weeden, MD, Weymouth, 1946

ch. 3d

Education: Weymouth College
Selwyn College, Cambridge Law, Class III
Called to the Bar, Inner Temple, 1947

Career: 1936 Secretary, Maddermarket Theatre, Norwich
1937 commissioned into Royal Tank Regiment
1940 prisoner of war
1945 Private Secretary to Governor of Sierra Leone
1947 Cadet
1952 District Commissioner
1956 Permanent Secretary
1959 Provincial Commissioner
1960 Secretary to the Cabinet

Governorships: The Gambia 1962–66 (Governor-General from 1965)
British Honduras 1966–72
Bahamas 1972–73
Isle of Man 1974–

Honours: MC 1940; OBE 1959; KCMG 1962; GCMG 1965

Clubs: Athenaeum; Royal Commonwealth Society; Royal Dorset Yacht, Weymouth

Recreations: painting, sea-fishing, sailing, shooting

Retired: —

Publications: —

Supplementary: *West Africa*, 22 Aug. 1964

PEARCE, Francis Barrow, Major

s/o. —
b.   16 September 1866, London **d.**   11 June 1926
m. —
ch. —

Education: Cheltenham College
                Royal Military College, Sandhurst

Career: 1886 commissioned into West Yorkshire
                    Regiment
              1895 Ashanti campaign
              1897 seconded as Assistant Deputy
                    Commissioner, Nyasaland
              1899 commanded Anglo–Portuguese force
              1900 South African war
              1901 Deputy Commissioner, Nyasaland
              1903 Acting Commissioner
              1907 Deputy Governor
              1910 Acting Governor

Governorships: Zanzibar 1914–22 (Resident)

Honours: CMG 1904

Clubs: —

Recreations: —

Retired: 1921

Publications: *Zanzibar: the Island-Metropolis of Eastern Africa*, 1920; *Rambles in Lion-Land*, 1898

Supplementary: Robert G. Gregory, *India and East Africa*, 1971; A. J. Wills, *An Introduction to the History of Central Africa*, 1973

Obit. 16 June 11b

PIKE, Theodore (Ouseley)

s/o. (3rd) Canon W. Pike, Co. Tipperary, Ireland
b. 1904   **d.** —
m. Violet, d/o Sir William Robinson, DL, JP
ch. 2s 1d

Education: The Abbey, Tipperary
Trinity College, Dublin
University College, Oxford

Career: 1928 Cadet, Tanganyika
1940 District Officer
1950 Provincial Commissioner

Governorships: Somaliland 1954–59

Honours: CMG 1953; KCMG 1956
Hon. LL.D., Dublin

Clubs: —

Recreations: —

Retired: 1959

Publications: —

Supplementary: —

PILLING, (Henry) Guy

s/o. —
b.   1886, East Dereham   **d.**   13 June 1953
m.   Gladys Neville, d/o J. H. Ganwick, Fiji, 1912
ch.   1s 1d

Education: King's School, Ely
                      Keble College, Oxford   Modern History,
                           Class II, 1907

Career: 1907 Cadet, Fiji
                 1914 District Commissioner
                 1921 Assistant Colonial Secretary
                 1926 Secretary, Western Pacific High Commission
                 1929 Colonial Secretary, British Honduras
                 1930 Acting Governor
                 1933 Deputy Colonial Secretary, Kenya

Governorships: St Helena 1938–41
                            Zanzibar 1941–46 (Resident)

Honours: CMG 1932; KCMG 1941

Clubs: —

Recreations: —

Retired: 1946, to Kenya
        Speaker, East African Central Legislative Assembly 1949

Publications: —

Supplementary: —

   Obit. 15 June 8e

PLEASS, Clement (John)

s/o. J. W. A. Pleass, Tiverton, Devon
b.   19 November 1901   **d.** —
m.   Sybil, d/o Alwyn Child, Gerrard's Cross,
          Buckinghamshire, 1927
ch.   1s

Education: Royal Masonic School
               Selwyn College, Cambridge   History, Class II/1,
               1923

Career: 1924 Cadet, Nigeria
            1952 Lieutenant-Governor, Eastern Nigeria

Governorships: Eastern Nigeria 1954–56

Honours: CMG 1950; KBE 1953; KCMG 1955;
             KCVO 1956

Clubs: Royal Commonwealth Society

Recreations: golf

Retired: 1956
             Member, Colonial Development Corporation, 1957

Publications: —

Supplementary: Sir James Robertson, *Transition in Africa*,
                   1974

PORTAL, Gerald (Herbert)

s/o. (2nd) Melville Portal, Hampshire, and Lady Charlotte
     Mary Elliott, d/o Earl of Minto
b.   13 March 1858, Laverstoke   **d.**   25 January 1894
m.   Lady Alice Josephine Bertie, d/o Earl of Abingdon,
     1890
ch. —

Education: Eton College   First XI, cricket

Career: 1879 entered Diplomatic Service
       1880 posted to Rome
       1882 posted to Cairo
       1887 mission to Abyssinia
       1888 Chargé d'affaires, Cairo
       1889 Consul-General, Zanzibar
       1891 Consul-General for German East Africa
       1892 commanded expedition to Uganda

Governorships: Uganda 1893–94 (Commissioner)

Honours: CB 1888; KCMG 1892

Clubs: —

Recreations: —

Retired: died in office, 1894

Publications: *The British Mission to Uganda*, 1894,
autobiog.; *My Mission to Abyssinia*, 1888, autobiog.

Supplementary: J. W. Gregory, *The Foundation of British
East Africa*, 1901; M. F. Hill, *Permanent Way*, I, 1950;
Kenneth Ingham, *The Making of Modern Uganda*, 1958;
Margery Perham, *Lugard*, I, 1956; H. B. Thomas, *Uganda*,
1935

Obit. 19 Feb. 8c   DNB XVI   OCRP

POTTER, Henry (Steven)

s/o. Charles Edward Potter, MD
b.   7 March 1904   **d.**   14 November 1976
m.   Ruth Newton, 1929
ch.   1s 1d

Education: Shrewsbury School
                 Queen's College, Cambridge   Law, Class III,
                 1926

Career: 1926 Cadet, Kenya
              1944 Deputy Financial Secretary
              1945 Financial Secretary, Uganda
              1948 Chief Secretary
              1952 Chief Secretary, Kenya

Governorships: Zanzibar 1954–59 (Resident)

Honours: CMG 1948; KCMG 1956

Clubs: Nairobi

Recreations: gardening

Retired: 1960

Publications: —

Supplementary: —

Obit. 20 Nov. 14th

PROBYN, Leslie

s/o. (3rd) Edmund Probyn, DL, JP, High Sheriff of
      Gloucestershire

b. 1862   **d.** 17 December 1938

m. Emily, OBE, d/o G. Davies, 1885

ch. 2s

Education: Charterhouse School
                privately, in France and Germany
                Called to the Bar, Middle Temple, 1884

Career: 1883 commissioned into Gloucestershire
                     Regiment (militia)
          1892 contested (Liberal) Uxbridge, Middlesex
          1893 Attorney-General, British Honduras
          1896 Attorney-General, Grenada
          1901 Secretary to the Government, Southern
                     Nigeria

Governorships: Sierra Leone 1904–10
                    Barbados 1911–18
                    Jamaica 1918–24

Honours: CMG 1903; KCMG 1909

Clubs: —

Recreations: —

Retired: 1924
    Vice-President of the Cremation Society; JP, Kent

Publications: *The Jurisdiction and Practice of the Mayor's
Court*, n.d., various legal treatises

Supplementary: Sir Harry Luke, *Cities and Men*, I, 1953

    Obit. 19 Dec. 14c; 21, 17e

RANKINE, John (Dalzell)

s/o. Sir Richard Rankine, KCMG, British Resident of
Zanzibar

b. 8 June 1907 **d.** —

m. Janet Grace, d/o Major R. L. Austin, Bristol, 1939

ch. 1d

Education: Christ's College, New Zealand
Exeter College, Oxford History, Class II,
1930

Career: 1931 Cadet, Uganda
1939 Assistant Secretary, East African Governors'
Conference
1942 Assistant Colonial Secretary, Fiji
1945 Colonial Secretary, Barbados
1946 Acting Governor
1947 Chief Secretary, Kenya

Governorships: Zanzibar 1952–54 (Resident)
Western Nigeria 1954–60

Honours: CMG 1947; KCMG 1954; KCVO 1956

Clubs: Athenaeum; MCC; Queen's

Recreations: tennis, squash, golf

Retired: 1960
Consultant, Turner and Newall Ltd

Publications: —

Supplementary: Sir James Robertson, *Transition in Africa*,
1974

RANKINE, Richard (Sims Donkin)

s/o. John Rankine

b. North Shields,   **d.**   24 June 1961
      Northumberland

m. Hilda Akerman, d/o Joseph Stelle Dalzell, New
      Zealand

ch. 1s 1d

Education: privately

Career: 1894 Cadet, Fiji
           1897 Private Secretary to three successive
                  Governors
           1909 Assistant Colonial Secretary
           1919 special mission to India, on immigration
           1920 Chief Secretary, Nyasaland
           1921 Acting Governor
           1927 Chief Secretary, Uganda

Governorships: Zanzibar 1930–37 (Resident)

Honours: CMG 1919; KCMG 1932

Clubs: —

Recreations: tennis, golf, cricket

Retired: 1937

Publications: —

Supplementary: Robert G. Gregory, *India and East Africa*,
1971

Obit. 26 June 14a

REECE, Gerald

s/o.   Edward Mackintosh Reece
b.   10 January 1897   **d.** —
m.   Alys, d/o H. E. H. Tracy, MD, 1936
ch.   2s 2d

Education: Rugby School

Career: 1915 commissioned into Sherwood Foresters
1921 Solicitor, Supreme Court, London
1925 Cadet, Kenya
1934 Consul for Southern Abyssinia
1939 in charge of Northern Frontier District,
Kenya

Governorships: Somaliland 1948–53

Honours: OBE 1937; CBE 1943; KCMG 1950

Clubs: —

Recreations: —

Retired: 1953
Scottish Chairman, Howard League for Penal Reform,
1961; Hon. Sheriff, East Lothian, 1962; Chairman,
Loaningdale Approved School, 1968; Deputy Lieutenant,
East Lothian, 1971

Publications: —

Supplementary: —

REEVE, Henry Fenwick

s/o. —
b.   7 April 1854, Kent   **d.**   18 January 1920
m. —
ch. —

Education: St Peter's College
                      Melbourne University

Career: 1868 entered Victoria Civil Service, Survey
                          Department
                   1874 Cadet, New South Wales Survey
                   1880 Surveyor, Fiji
                   1887 Colonial Engineer, St Lucia
                   1891 Director of Survey, Windward Islands
                   1894 Colonial Engineer, The Gambia
                   1895 Chief Commissioner, Anglo-French
                          Boundary Commissions
                   1901 Director of Public Works, Lagos
                   1902 Acting Governor
                   1903 Deputy Governor

Governorships: Lagos 1903–04

Honours: CMG 1900

Clubs: Royal Societies; St Stephen's

Recreations: shooting, fishing, yachting
Fellow, Royal Geographical Society; Fellow, Society of
Antiquaries

Retired: 1904

Publications: *The Gambia*, 1912; *The Black Republic*, n.d.

Supplementary: —

RENISON, Patrick (Muir)

s/o. (2nd) William J. H. Renison
b. 24 March 1911   **d.** 11 November 1965
m. Eleanor Hope Gibb, 1936
ch. 1d

Education: Uppingham School
Corpus Christi College, Cambridge
Anthropology, Class I

Career: 1932 entered Colonial Service, seconded to
Colonial Office
1935 Cadet, Ceylon
1936 Private Secretary to the Governor
1940 Assistant Chief Secretary
1944 Colonial Office
1948 Colonial Secretary, Trinidad and Tobago

Governorships: British Honduras 1952–55
British Guiana 1955–59
Kenya 1959–62

Honours: CMG 1950; KCMG 1955; GCMG 1962
Hon. Fellow, Corpus Christi College, Cambridge, 1959

Clubs: —

Recreations: —

Retired: 1963
Adviser to Lord Hailsham on Sport and Recreation, 1963;
Joint Vice-Chairman, British Red Cross, 1964; Member,
Governing Body Queen Elizabeth House, Oxford; JP,
Sussex, 1965

Publications: —

Supplementary: George Bennett, *Kenya*, 1963; George
Bennett and Carl Rosberg, *The Kenyatta Election*, 1963; Sir
Michael Blundell, *So Rough A Wind*, 1964; Sir Ralph Furse,
Aucuparius, 1962

Obit. 12 Nov. 14f; 20, 10f; 3 Dec. 14c   OCRP

RENNIE, Gilbert (McCall)

s/o. (2nd) John Rennie
b. 1895   **d.** —
m. Jean Huggins, 1929
ch. 2s 1d

Education: Stirling High School
               Glasgow University

Career: 1915 war service
         1920 Cadet, Ceylon
         1923 Police Magistrate
         1934 Secretary to the Governor
         1937 Financial Secretary, Gold Coast
         1939 Chief Secretary, Kenya
         1942 Acting Governor

Governorships: Northern Rhodesia 1948–54

Honours: MC; CMG 1941; Kt. 1946; KCMG 1949;
     GBE 1954
   Hon. LL.D., Glasgow

Clubs: Royal Commonwealth Society

Recreations: gardening, fishing, golf

Retired: 1961
   High Commissioner in London for Federation of
   Rhodesia and Nyasaland, 1954; Chairman, UK
   Committee, Freedom from Hunger Campaign, 1965;
   Joint Treasurer, Royal Society of Arts, 1965

Publications: —

Supplementary: Harry Franklin, *Unholy Wedlock*, 1963; A. J.
   Hanna, *The Story of the Rhodesias and Nyasaland*, 1960;
   Robert I. Rotberg, *The Rise of Nationalism in Central Africa*,
   1965; Robert I. Rotberg, *Black Heart*, 1977; Sir Roy
   Welensky, *4000 Days*, 1964; Robin Short, *African Sunset*,
   1973

REY, Charles (Fernand)

s/o. —
b.   7 August 1877, London   **d.**   30 March 1968
m.   Georgina, d/o J. Hume Webster
ch. —

Education: privately
Royal Military Academy, Woolwich
Royal School of Mines

Career: 1899 exploring and prospecting in West Africa
1900 Assistant Principal, Board of Trade
1902 Secretary, China Tariff Commission
1903 Secretary, Imperial Institute Trustees
1904 Secretary, All Red Route Committee
1909 General Manager, Labour Exchange and
Unemployment Insurance
1917 Director of Employment, Board of Trade
1919 mission to Abyssinia
1920 Unemployment Grants Committee
1929 Assistant Resident Commissioner,
Bechuanaland

Governorships: Bechuanaland 1930–37 (Resident
Commissioner)

Honours: CMG 1932; Kt. 1938

Clubs: Civil Service, Cape Town

Recreations: Fellow, Royal Geographical Society

Retired: 1937
Member, Portuguese Academy of History, 1945; Hon.
Life President, South African Association of Arts, 1952

Publications: *Unconquered Abyssinia*, 1923; *In the Country of the Blue Nile*, 1927; *The Romance of the Portuguese in Abyssinia*, 1929; *The Real Abyssinia*, 1935; *The Union of South Africa and Some of its Problems*, 1948

Supplementary: —

RICHARDS, Arthur (Frederick) (Lord Milverton)

s/o. (2nd) William Richards
b. 21 February 1885   **d.** 27 October 1978
m. Noelle Benda Whithead, 1927
ch. 2s 1d

Education: Clifton College
Christ Church, Oxford

Career: 1908 Cadet, Malayan Civil Service
1923 Acting Secretary to High Commissioner
1926 Under-Secretary
1929 Acting General Adviser, Government of
Johore

Governorships: North Borneo 1930–33
The Gambia 1933–36
Fiji 1936–38
Jamaica 1938–43
Nigeria 1943–47

Honours: CMG 1933; KCMG 1935; GCMG 1942
elevated to peerage as Baron Milverton of Lagos and
Clifton, 1947

Clubs: Athenaeum; United University; Number 10

Recreations: golf, sailing

Retired: 1947
part-time Director, Colonial Development Corporation,
1948; Chairman of Council, London School of Hygiene
and Tropical Medicine, 1948; Chairman, Empire Day
Movement, 1948; Vice-President, Royal Empire Society;
President, Association of British Malaya, 1948; Board of
Governors, Clifton College; Chairman, British Leprosy
Relief Association, 1948; Director, West Indies Sugar Co,
1950; Director, Bank of West Africa, 1950; Director, Perak
Rubber and Tin Co, 1956; Chairman, Royal African
Society 1963

Publications: —

Supplementary: Obafemi Awolowo, *Awo*, 19; Darrell
Bates, *A Gust of Plumes*, 1972; Ian Brook, *The One-Eyed
Man Is King*, 1966; Sir Alan Burns, *Colonial Civil Servant*,
1949; James S. Coleman, *Nigeria: Background to
Nationalism*, 1958; Sir Hugh Foot, *A Start in Freedom*, 1964;
Sir Ralph Furse, *Aucuparius*, 1962; Sir Alexander
Grantham, *Via Ports*, 1965; Molly Huggins, *Too Much To
Tell*, 1967; Sir Bryan Sharwood Smith, *But Always As
Friends*, 1969; Viscount Swinton, *I Remember*, 1947;
Stanhope White, *Dan Bana*, 1966; *West Africa*, 2 Oct. 1948

OCRP/t

RICHARDS, Edmund (Charles)

s/o. Edmund Richards, civil servant, and Amelia Symes
b.   6 October 1889   **d.**   28 June 1955
m.   Jean, d/o George Barron Beattie, Aberdeenshire, 1926
ch.   1d

Education: —

Career: 1909 Department of Agriculture, Kenya
1912 Secretariat, Nyasaland
1914 war service, King's African Rifles
1917 Political Officer, German East Africa
1922 District Commissioner, Tanganyika
1927 Assistant Secretary for Native Affairs
1931 Provincial Commissioner
1934 Deputy Chief Secretary

Governorships: Basutoland 1935–42 (Resident
Commissioner)
Nyasaland 1942–48

Honours: CMG 1937; Kt. 1941; KCMG 1944

Clubs: Athenaeum; East India and Sports

Recreations: golf, shooting, fishing

Retired: 1948 to East Griqualand, South Africa

Publications: —

Supplementary: Sir Philip Mitchell, *African Afterthoughts*,
1954; Margery Perham, *East African Journey*, 1976

Obit. 4 July 11d

ROBERTSON, James (Wilson)

s/o. (1st) James Robertson, Broughty Ferry, Angus, and
Mrs Robertson, Colinton, Midlothian

b. 27 October 1899 **d.** —

m. Nancy, d/o H. S. Walker, Huddersfield, Yorkshire,
1926

ch. 1s 1d

Education: Merchiston Castle School, Edinburgh
Balliol College, Oxford   Classics, Class II;
rugger blue

Career: 1918 commissioned into Black Watch
1922 Assistant District Commissioner, Sudan
Political Service
1937 Sub-Governor
1939 Deputy Governor
1940 Assistant Civil Secretary
1942 Deputy Civil Secretary
1945 Civil Secretary

Governorships: Nigeria 1955–60 (as Governor-General,
two months)

Honours: MBE 1931; KBE 1948; KCMG 1953;
GCVO 1956; GCMG 1957; KT 1965
Hon. Fellow, Balliol College, Oxford, 1953; Hon. LL.D.,
Leeds, 1961; Wellcome Medal, Royal African Society,
1961; Fellow of the Royal Society of Arts, 1961

Clubs: Athenaeum

Retired: 1960 (from Sudan Political Service, 1953)
Chairman, British Guiana Constitutional Commission,
1953; Chairman, Kenya Coastal Strip Commission, 1961;
Director, Uganda Co. Ltd. 1954 and 1961; Chairman,
Commonwealth Institute, 1961; Governor, Queen Mary
College, London University, 1961; Central Council Royal
Overseas League, 1962; Director, Barclay's Bank, DCO,
1961; President, Britain-Nigeria Association, 1961;
Councillor for Aid to African Students, 1961; President,
Overseas Service Pensioners' Association, 1961; Member,

Council, Royal Commonwealth Society for the Blind;
Deputy Chairman, National Committee for Commonwealth Immigrants, 1961

Publications: *Transition in Africa*, 1974, autobiog.

Supplementary: K. G. Bradley, *Once A District Officer*,
1966; Sir Hugh Foot, *A Start in Freedom*, 1964; K. D. D.
Henderson, *The Making of the Modern Sudan*, 1953; *West
Africa*, 23 April 1955; 3 Sept. 1960

OCRP/t

ROBINSON, Hercules (George Robert) (Lord Rosmead)

s/o.   (2nd) Admiral Hercules Robinson of Rosmead,
Westmeath, Ireland, and Frances Widman-Wood
b.   19 December 1824   **d.**   28 October 1897
m.   Nea, d/o Viscount Valentia, 1846
ch.   1s 1d

Education: Royal Military Academy, Sandhurst

Career: 1843 commissioned into 87th Royal Irish Fusiliers
1846 served with Poor Law Commissioners,
Ireland
1852 Chief Commissioner, Fairs and Markets,
Ireland
1854 President of Montserrat
1855 Lieutenant-Governor, St Christopher
1863 on special duty, Straits Settlements
1874 on special duty as Commissioner in Fiji
1886 on special duty as Commissioner in Mauritius

Governorships: Hong Kong 1859–1865
Ceylon 1865–1872
New South Wales 1872–1878
New Zealand 1879–1880
Cape Colony 1881–1889
Cape Colony 1895–1897

Honours: KB 1859; KCMG 1869; GCMG 1875; PC 1889;
Baronetcy 1891; elevated to peerage as Baron Rosmead,
1898

Clubs: Carlton; Arthur's

Recreations: —

Retired: 1889 (from army, 1846)
Director, London and Westminster Bank, 1890

Publications: —

Supplementary: Sir Henry Parkes, *Fifty Years in the Making
of Australian History*, 1892 (biog.); T. R. Davenport, *South*

Africa: A Modern History, 1978; H. A. J. Hulugalle, *British Governors of Ceylon*, 1963; C. J. F. Muller, *Five Hundred Years: A History of South Africa*, 1969; D. Schreuder, *Gladstone and Kruger*, 1969; F. Troup, *South Africa: An Historical Introduction*, 1972; M. Wilson and L. M. Thompson, *Oxford History of South Africa*, II, 1971

Obit. 29 Oct.; 2 Nov.   DNB XXII

RODGER, John (Pickersgill)

s/o.   (3rd) Robert Rodger, Hadlow Castle, Kent
b.   12 February 1851   **d.**   19 September 1910
m.   Maria, d/o George Tyser, Hollanden Park, Kent, 1872
ch.   1d

Education: Eton College
Christ Church, Oxford
Called to the Bar, Inner Temple, 1877

Career: 1882 Chief Magistrate, Malaya
1888 Resident

Governorships: Gold Coast 1904–10

Honours: CMG 1899; KCMG 1904

Clubs: St James'; MCC; Prince's

Recreations: —

Retired: died in office, 1910

Publications: —

Supplementary: David Kimble, *A Political History of Ghana*, 1963; Ronald E. Wraith, *Guggisberg*, 1967

Obit. 20 Sept. 11e; 23, 9a; 3 Oct. 13d   OCRP

RODWELL, Cecil (Hunter)*

s/o. William Hunter-Rodwell, Woodlands, Holbrook, and
Constance d/o Sir S. Ruggles-Brise, KCB, Spain
Hall, Essex

b. 29 December 1874   **d.** 23 February 1953
m. Ethel Clarissa, d/o Herbert Ralland, 1908
ch. 3s 2d

Education: Eton College (Scholar)
King's College, Cambridge (Scholar)
Classics, II/1, 1896
Editor, *The Granta*

Career: 1899 South African war, on Milner's staff
1900 on staff of High Commissioner, South Africa
1903 Imperial Secretary, High Commission for
South Africa

Governorships: Fiji 1918–24
British Guiana 1925–28
Southern Rhodesia 1928–34

Honours: CMG 1909; KCMG 1919; GCMG 1934

Clubs: Marlborough-Windham; MCC

Recreations: shooting, fishing, golf, tennis, chess

Retired: 1934
Controller of Diamonds, Ministry of Supply, 1942; JP,
Suffolk

Publications: —

Supplementary: Margery Perham, *African Apprenticeship*,
1974

Obit. 24 Feb., 10e; 26, 10b

---

*Sometimes given as Hunter-Rodwell. *Who's Who* indexes the name under
R but observes the hyphen.

ROWE, Samuel, Surgeon–Major

s/o. —
b. —   **d.** 1888
m. —
ch. —

Education: —

Career: 1862 Army Surgeon, posted to Lagos
              1873 Ashanti war
              1875 Lieutenant-Governor, West Africa
                    Settlements

Governorships: The Gambia 1875–77 (Administrator)
                     Sierra Leone 1877–81 (West African
                         Settlements)
                     Gold Coast 1881–84
                     Sierra Leone 1885–88

Honours: CMG 1874; KCMG 1880

Clubs: —

Recreations: —

Retired: died in office, 1888

Publications: —

Supplementary: W. Walton Claridge, *A History of the Gold Coast and Ashanti*, 1915; Christopher Fyfe, *A History of Sierra Leone*, 1962; John Hargreaves, *A Life of Sir Samuel Lewis*, 1958; David Kimble, *A Political History of Ghana*, 1963

SADLER, James (Hayes)★

s/o. Sir J. Hayes Sadler

b. 1851   **d.** 21 April 1922

m. Rita Annie, d/o Colonel Weymiss Smith, Indian Army

ch. 15

Education: —

Career: 1870   commissioned into 61st Regiment, Indian Army

         1870   served with 40th Regiment and 33rd Bengal Infantry

         1877   transferred to Political Department, Government of India

         1892   Consul, Muscat

Governorships: Somali Protectorate 1898–1901 (Consul-General)

                 Uganda 1902–05 (Commissioner)

                 Kenya 1905–09 (Commissioner till 1906)

                 Windward Islands 1909–14

Honours: CB 1902; KCMG 1907

Clubs: —

Recreations: —

Retired: 1914

Publications: —

Supplementary: George Bennett, *Kenya*, 1963; A. V. Clayton and D. Savage, *Government and Labour in Kenya*, 1974; Majorie Ruth Dilley, *British Policy in Kenya Colony*, 1937; Vincent Harlow and E. M. Chilver, *History of East Africa*, II, 1965; M. F. Hill, *Permanent Way*, I, 1950; C. W. Hobley, *Kenya: from Chartered Company to Crown*

★This is in the form used in most books of reference in the Colonial Office records. Kenneth Ingham, however, prefers the hyphenated form and so indexes the Governor under the letter H.

Colony, 1929; Elspeth Huxley, *White Man's Country*, 1935; D. A. Low and C. Pratt, *Buganda and British Overrule*, 1960; Douglas Jardine, *The Mad Mullah of Somaliland*, 1923; R. Meinertzhagen, *Kenya Diary*, 1957; G. H. Mungeam, *British Rule in Kenya*, 1966; W. McGregor Ross, *Kenya From Within*, 1927; M. P. K. Sorrenson, *Origins of European Settlement in Kenya*, 1968

Obit. 27 April 18d

SHARPE, Alfred

s/o. (3rd) Edmund Sharpe, Lancashire, and Elizabeth
Fletcher

b. 19 May 1853, Lancaster **d.** 10 December 1935

m. Rosamond, d/o Reverend E. Bolling, Lancashire, 1881

ch. 2s

Education: Haileybury College

Career: 1876 Solicitor, Supreme Court, Westminster
1885 Stipendiary Magistrate, Fiji
1891 Vice-Consul, Nyasaland
1894 Acting Commissioner
1896 Deputy Commissioner

Governorships: Nyasaland 1897–1910 (Commissioner till
1907)

Honours: CB 1897; KCMG 1903

Clubs: St Stephen's

Recreations: —

Retired: 1910

Publications: *The Backbone of Africa*, 1921

Supplementary: A. J. Hanna, *The Beginnings of Nyasaland*,
1956; A. J. Hanna, *The Story of the Rhodesias and Nyasaland*,
1960; H. M. Hole, *The Making of Rhodesia*, 1926; H. H.
Johnston, *The Story of My Life*, 1923; H. Moyse-Bartlett,
The King's African Rifles, 1956; Roland Oliver, *Sir Harry
Johnston*, 1957; Margery Perham and Mary Bull, *The
Diaries of Lord Lugard*, 1959; Robert I. Rotberg, *The Rise of
Nationalism in Central Africa*, 1965

Obit. 11 Dec. 21a; 13, 16c; 14, 15d   OCRP

SHARWOOD SMITH, Bryan (Evers)★

s/o. Edward Sharwood-Smith
b. 5 January 1899   **d.** —
m. 1st, 1926
       2nd Winifred Joan, d/o Thomas Mitchell, 1939
ch. 1d; 2s 1d

Education: Aldenham School (Scholar)

Career: 1917 war service, Royal Flying Corps; India
            1920 Cadet, Southern Nigeria
            1927 District Officer, Northern Nigeria
            1938 Senior District Officer
            1940 war service
            1942 Resident
            1952 Lieutenant-Governor

Governorships: Northern Nigeria 1954–57

Honours: CMG 1950; KBE 1953; KCMG 1955;
    KCVO 1956

Clubs: Royal Air Force

Recreations: —

Retired: 1957

Publications: *Recollections of British Administration in the
    Cameroons and Northern Nigeria: 'But Always As Friends'*,
    1969, autobiog.

Supplementary: Sir Ahmadu Bello, *My Life*, 1962; Robert
    Heussler, *The British in Northern Nigeria*, 1968; Elspeth
    Huxley, *Four Guineas*, 1954; Sir James Robertson,
    Transition in Africa, 1974; John Smith, *Colonial Cadet in
    Nigeria*, 1968

OCRP/t

★Found under Smith in *Colonial Office List* before 1948. *Who's Who* shows a
hyphen in the father's name only.

SHIPPARD, Sydney (Godolphin Alexander)

s/o. (1st) Captain William Henry Shippard, and grandson of Rear-Admiral Shippard, Perthshire

b.   29 May 1837, Brussels   **d.**   29 March 1902

m.   1st Maria Susanna, d/o Sir Andries Stockenström, Bt., Cape Colony, 1864
2nd Rosalind, d/o W. A. Sandford, Nynehead Court, Somerset, 1894

ch.   —

Education: King's College School, London
Oriel (Exhibitioner) and Hertford (Scholar) Colleges, Oxford   Law, 1863
Called to the Bar, Inner Temple, 1867
DCL, Oxford, 1878

Career: 1868   practised as advocate, Supreme Court, Cape Colony
1873   Attorney-General, Griqualand West
1877   resigned
1880   Puisne Judge, Supreme Court, Cape Colony
1885   British Commissioner, Anglo-German Commission, Angra Pequena

Governorships: Bechuanaland 1885–95 (Resident Commissioner)

Honours: CMG 1886; KCMG 1887

Clubs: Union; Garrick; Royal Societies

Recreations: painting, music
Fellow, Royal Geographical Society

Retired: 1895
Legal Adviser, Consolidated Goldfields of South Africa Co.; Director, British South Africa Co.

Publications: —

Supplementary: M. H. Hole, *The Making of Rhodesia*, 1926; M. H. Hole, *The Passing of the Black Kings*, 1932; A. Sillery, *The Bechuanaland Protectorate*, 1952; A. J. Wills, *An Introduction to the History of Central Africa*, 1973; *Dictionary of South African Biography*, II, 1972

Obit. 31 March 4e   DNB Supp. II

SHUCKBURGH, John (Evelyn)

s/o. (1st) Evelyn Shirley Shuckburgh, Litt.D., assistant
master, Eton College

b. 18 March 1877   **d.** 8 February 1953

m. Lilian Violet, d/o Arthur George Peskett, Fellow of
Magdalene College, Cambridge, 1906

ch. 3s 2d

Education: Eton College
King's College, Cambridge   Classics, Class I,
1899

Career: 1900 entered Home Civil Service, India Office
1902 Private Secretary to Permanent Under-
Secretary of State
1917 Secretary, Political Department
1921 Assistant Under-Secretary, Colonial Office
1931 Deputy Under-Secretary

Governorships: Nigeria 1939 (did not assume office)

Honours: CB 1918; KCMG 1922

Clubs: Athenaeum; MCC

Recreations: —

Retired: 1942
Narrator, Historical Section, Cabinet Office, 1942

Publications: *An Ideal Voyage and other Essays*, 1942,
autobiog.; ed., *The India Office List*, 1901; *History of the
Colonial Empire in the Second World War* (unpublished)

Supplementary: —

Obit. 10 Feb. 8d; 17, 11c   DNB Supp. VII

SILLERY, Anthony

s/o. Lieutenant-Colonel C. C. A. Sillery, Indian Army, and
Edith, Scarborough, Yorkshire

b. 19 April 1903   **d.** 7 March 1976

m. Valentine Kennerly, d/o A. H. Goddard, 1941

ch. 2d

Education: Perse School, Cambridge
St John's College, Oxford   French, Class I
Heath Harrison Prizewinner; D.Phil.,
Oxford, 1962

Career: 1925 Cadet, Tanganyika
1942 Occupied Territories Administrator,
Madagascar
1943 British Military Administration, Cyrenaica
1944 Deputy Provincial Commissioner,
Tanganyika
1945 Civil Affairs Branch, GHQ, Middle East

Governorships: Bechuanaland 1947–50 (Resident
Commissioner)

Honours: CVO 1947

Clubs: Ski Club of Great Britain

Recreations: winter sports, fishing, 'African studies',
France. Fellow, Royal Historical Society; Fellow, Royal
Society of Arts

Retired: 1951
Secretary, Taylorian Institute, 1951

Publications: *The Bechuanaland Protectorate*, 1952; *Sechele*,
1954; *Africa: A Social Geography*, 1961; *Founding A
Protectorate*, 1965; *Bechuanaland: A Short Political History*,
1974

Supplementary: Charles Douglas-Home, *The Last
Proconsul: Evelyn Baring*, 1978

Obit. 8 March, 14h   OCRP

SINCLAIR, John Houston

s/o. (2nd) W. H. Sinclair, Isle of Wight

b. 1871   **d.** 17 August 1961

m. Muriel Eveleen, MBE, d/o Colonel Cockburn, Black
      Watch, 1902

ch. 1d

Education: —

Career: 1893 appointed to Colonial Audit Branch, Uganda
            Railway
       1899 Vice-Consul, Zanzibar
       1906 Consul
       1914 Chief Secretary

Governorships: Zanzibar 1922–24 (Resident)

Honours: CMG 1915; CBE 1919

Clubs: Caledonian

Recreations: golf, polo

Retired: 1924, to Tangiers

Publications: *The Laws of Zanzibar*, 1836–1911

Supplementary: —

    Obit. 19 Aug. 10b; 28, 10d

SLATER, (Alexander) Ransford

s/o. The Reverend C. S. Slater, Plymouth
b. 28 November 1874   **d.** 23 April 1940
m. Dora Waterfield, d/o H. T. S. Ward, Director of
     Irrigation, Ceylon, 1906
ch. 2s 3d

Education: King Edward's School, Birmingham
          Emmanuel College, Cambridge (Scholar)
          Mathematics, 31st Wrangler, 1897

Career: 1898 Cadet, Ceylon Civil Service
         1900 Assistant Post-Master General
         1904 Clerk to Legislative Council
         1906 District Judge
         1910 Deputy Controller of Customs
         1912 Principal Assistant Colonial Secretary
         1914 Colonial Secretary, Gold Coast
         1915 Acting Governor

Governorships: Sierra Leone 1922–27
             Gold Coast 1927–32 (resigned)
             Jamaica 1932–34 (resigned)

Honours: CMG 1916; CBE 1918; KCMG 1924;
      GCMG 1933

Clubs: Royal Societies

Recreations: golf

Retired: 1934 (resigned)

Publications: —

Supplementary: David Kimble, *A Political History of the
     Gold Coast*, 1963; Sir Harry Luke, *Cities and Men*, III, 1956;
     Ronald E. Wraith, *Guggisberg*, 1967

     Obit. 25 Apr. 8e; 27, 9b

SLOLEY, Herbert (Cecil)

s/o. (3rd) Robert Hugh Sloley, North Devon and Calcutta

b. 4 February 1855, Calcutta   **d.** 22 September 1937

m. Charlotte, d/o John Dick, Falkirk, Scotland, and Cape Colony, 1886

ch. 2d

Education: Greenwich Proprietary School

Career: 1873 Clerk, London and Westminster Bank
1875 Cape Mounted Rifles
1880 Captain, Native Contingent, Basuto war
1883 Sub-Inspector, Cape Police
1884 Sub-Inspector, Basutoland Mounted Police
1886 Inspector
1889 Assistant Commissioner, Basutoland
1895 Acting Governor
1898 Secretary to the Government

Governorships: Basutoland 1900–16 (Resident Commissioner)

Honours: CMG 1905; KCMG 1911

Clubs: Civil Service, Cape Town

Recreations: —

Retired: 1916
Special Commissioner into Ngwato Succession, Bechuanaland, 1922

Publications: Introduction to J. C. Macgregor, *Basuto Traditions*, 1905

Supplementary: —

SMITH, George

s/o. Hugh Smith, Ayrshire, Scotland

b. 8 March 1858 **d.** 14 June 1938

m. Lucie M'Duff, CBE, d/o W. W. Cargill, Kensington, 1893

ch. 3d

Education: privately

Career: 1878 Home Civil Service, War Office
1879 entered Colonial Service, Cyprus
1881 Chief Clerk
1883 Assistant Chief Secretary
1891 District Commissioner
1895 Registrar-General
1904 Acting Director of Agriculture
1905 Acting Chief Collector of Customs
1910 Colonial Secretary, Mauritius
1911 Acting Governor

Governorships: Nyasaland 1913–23

Honours: CMG 1911; KCMG 1914

Clubs: —

Recreations: —

Retired: 1923

Publications: —

Supplementary: Robert I. Rotberg, *The Rise of Nationalism in Central Africa*, 1965; G. Shepperson and T. Price, *Independent African*, 1958

Obit. 15 June 16b; 17, 19b

SOAMES, (Arthur) Christopher (John)

s/o. —

b.   12 October 1920   **d.** —

m.   Mary, d/o Rt. Hon. Sir Winston Churchill, Prime
Minister, 1947

ch.   3s, 2d

Education: Eton College
Royal Military College, Sandhurst

Career: 1939   commissioned into Coldstream Guards,
war service
1946   Assistant Military Attaché, Paris
1950   MP (Conservative) for Bedford
1952   Parliamentary Private Secretary to the Prime
Minister
1958   Secretary of State for War
1960   Minister of Agriculture, Fisheries and Food
1968   Ambassador to France
1973   Vice-President, EEC Commission

Governorships: Southern Rhodesia: 1979–80

Honours: CBE 1955; PC 1958; GCVO 1972; GCMG 1972;
created Baron Soames of Fletching, 1978

Clubs: White's; Portland

Recreations: —

Retired: 1977
Director, N. M. Rothschild, 1977; National Westminster
Bank, 1978

Publications: —

Supplementary: Mary Soames, *Clementine Churchill*, 1979

SOUTHORN, (Wilfrid) Thomas

s/o. Josiah Southorn, Leamington Spa, Warwickshire
b. 4 August 1879   **d.** 15 March 1957
m. Bella, OBE, d/o Sidney Woolf, QC, and widow of
        R. H. Lock, Sc.D.
ch. —

Education: Warwick School
               Corpus Christi College, Oxford   Classics,
               Class III, 1902

Career: 1903 Cadet, Ceylon
             1907 District Judge
             1914 Private Secretary to the Governor
             1920 Principal Assistant Colonial Secretary
             1923 Principal Collector of Customs
             1926 Colonial Secretary, Hong Kong
             1927 Acting Governor
             1942 Colonial Service Liaison Officer

Governorships: The Gambia 1936–42

Honours: CMG 1927; KBE 1933; KCMG 1938;
        Hon. LL. D., Hong Kong 1936

Clubs: Athenaeum

Recreations: —

Retired: 1946

Publications: —

Supplementary: —

   Obit. 18 March 10d; 23, 11b

STACK, Lee (Oliver Fitzmaurice), Major-General

s/o. —

b.   15 May 1868   **d.**   20 November 1924

m.   Flora C. Moodie, 1902

ch.   1d

Education: Clifton College
Royal Military College, Sandhurst

Career: 1888 commissioned into Border Regiment
1899 seconded to Egyptian army
1904 transferred to Sudan Government
1908 Director of Military Intelligence, Cairo
1913 Civil Secretary, Sudan

Governorships: Sudan 1917–24 (Governor-General)

Honours: CMG 1914; KBE 1918; GBE 1923

Clubs: United Service; Travellers'

Recreations: —

Retired: died in office, 1924

Publications: —

Supplementary: Sir Geoffrey Archer, *Personal and Historical Memoirs*, 1964; K. D. D. Henderson, *Sudan Republic*, 1955; H. C. Jackson, *Behind the Modern Sudan*, 1955; Sir Harold Macmichael, *The Sudan*, 1954; Sir James Robertson, *Transition in Africa*, 1974; Sir Ronald Wingate, *Wingate of the Sudan*, 1965

Obit. 21 Nov., 11a; Nov. passim   DNB Supp. IV

STANLEY, Herbert (James)

s/o. Sigismund Sonnenthal (later Stanley), merchant,
  Manchester, and Anna Rose Meyer

b. 25 July 1872   **d.** 5 June 1955

m. Reneira, DBE, d/o Henry Cloete, CMG, South Africa,
  1918

ch. 2s 2d

Education: Eton College
  Balliol College, Oxford   Classics, Class III,
    1893

Career: 1897 Private Secretary to British Minister,
      Dresden
  1906 Private Secretary to First Lord of the
      Admiralty
  1908 Private Secretary to Lord President of the
      Council
  1910 Private Secretary to Governor-General of
      South Africa
  1913 Secretary to the Governor-General
  1915 Resident Commissioner, Northern and
      Southern Rhodesia
  1918 Imperial Secretary, South Africa

Governorships: Northern Rhodesia 1924–27
  Ceylon 1927–31
  South Africa 1931–35 (High
    Commissioner)
  Southern Rhodesia 1935–42

Honours: CMG 1913; KCMG 1924; GCMG 1930

Clubs: Brooks's; Athenaeum; Beefsteak; St James's Bath

Recreations: —

Retired: 1942, to South Africa
  Director, De Beers Mining Co; Director, Anglo-
American Co; Chief Scout, South Africa; President,
Toc H, Southern Africa

Publications: —

Supplementary: L. H. Gann, *A History of Northern Rhodesia*, 1964; H. A. J. Hulugalle, *British Governors of Ceylon*, 1963; Margery Perham, *African Apprenticeship*, 1974; Robert I. Rotberg, *The Rise of Nationalism in Central Africa*, 1965

Obit. 6 June 8g   DNB Supp. VII   OCRP

STAPLEDON, Robert (de Stapledon)

s/o. Ernest A. Stapledon, and Vivien, née Garvice

b. 6 February 1909 **d.** —

m. Marjorie Radford, 1933

ch. —

Education: Marlborough College
Trinity College, Cambridge Geography,
Class II/2, 1930

Career: 1931 Cadet, Nigeria
1940 Secretary, West African Governors'
Conference
1942 Secretary, Resident Minister, West Africa
1945 Financial Secretary, Western Pacific High
Commission
1948 Economic Secretary, East Africa High
Commission
1954 Chief Secretary, Tanganyika

Governorships: Eastern Nigeria 1956–60
Bahamas 1960–64

Honours: OBE 1944; CBE 1953; CMG 1955; KCMG 1956

Clubs: East India and Sports

Recreations: —

Retired: 1964

Publications: —

Supplementary: —

STEVENSON, Hubert (Craddock), Major

s/o. —

b. 1888   **d.** 13 June 1971

m. —

ch. —

Education: Harrow School

Career: 1915 war service, France
1920 Cadet, Southern Nigeria
1926 Assistant Secretary
1934 Resident
1936 Chief Commissioner, Ashanti, Gold Coast

Governorships: Sierra Leone 1941–48

Honours: MC; OBE 1934; CMG 1938; Kt. 1941; KCMG 1942

Clubs: —

Recreations: shooting, fishing

Retired: —

Publications: —

Supplementary: Sir Alan Burns, *Colonial Civil Servant*, 1949

Obit. 14 June 14b

STEWART, Donald (William), Captain

s/o. Sir Donald Stewart

b. 1860   **d.** 1 October 1905

m. —

ch. —

Education: Clifton College
Royal Military College, Sandhurst

Career: 1879 commissioned into Gordon Highlanders
1880 Afghan war
1881 Transvaal war
1882 ADC to Commander-in-Chief, India
1884 Sudan campaign
1896 Political Officer, Ashanti expedition;
      Resident, Kumasi
1897 Political Officer, Northern Territories, Gold
      Coast
1902 Chief Commissioner, Ashanti

Governorships: Kenya 1904–05 (Commissioner)

Honours: CMG 1897; KCMG 1902

Clubs: —

Recreations: —

Retired: died in office, 1905

Publications: —

Supplementary: George Bennett, *Kenya*, 1963; A. V.
Clayton and D. Savage, *Government and Labour in Kenya*,
1974; Robert E. Gregory, *India and East Africa*, 1971; M. F.
Hill, *Permanent Way*, I, 1950; C. W. Hobley, *Kenya: from
Chartered Company to Crown Colony*, 1929; Elspeth
Huxley, *White Man's Country*, 1935; R. Meinertzhagen,
Kenya Diary, 1957; G. H. Mungeam, *British Rule in Kenya*,
1966; W. McGregor Ross, *Kenya From Within*, 1927;
M. P. K. Sorrenson, *Origins of European Settlement in
Kenya*, 1968

Obit. 2 Oct. 6b

STORRS, Ronald

s/o. The Very Reverend John Storrs, Vicar, Eaton Square, and Dean of Rochester, and Hon. Lucy Anna Maria Cust

b. 19 November 1881, **d.** 1 November 1955
Bury St Edmunds

m. Louisa Lucy, d/o Rear-Admiral Hon. Algernon Littleton, and widow of Lieutenant-Colonel H. Clowes, 1923

ch. —

Education: Charterhouse School (Scholar)
Pembroke College, Cambridge (Scholar)
Classics, Class I, 1903

Career: 1904 entered Egyptian Civil Service
1909 Oriental Secretary, British Agency, Cairo
1917 Military Governor, Jerusalem
1920 Civil Governor, Jerusalem and Judaea

Governorships: Cyprus 1926–32
Northern Rhodesia 1932–34

Honours: CMG 1916; CBE 1919; Kt. 1924; KCMG 1929
Hon. LL.D., Aberdeen and Trinity College, Dublin;
Fellow of the Royal Society of Literature

Clubs: Travellers'; Beefsteak

Recreations: music, chess, Eastern travel

Retired: 1934 (invalided)
Member, London County Council, 1937; Deputy Lieutenant, Essex; Trustee, Royal Philharmonic Society; Governor, Shakespeare Memorial Theatre; Chairman, Lesser Eastern Churches Committee, Church of England Council on Foreign Relations; lecturing and various arts activities

Publications: *Orientations*, 1937, autobiog.; *Handbook of Cyprus*, 1930; *A Quarterly Record of the War*, 1940; *Drawing the RAF*, 1942; *Dunlop in War and Peace*, 1946; Contr. *T. E. Lawrence by his Friends*, 1937

Supplementary: Sir Geoffrey Archer, *Personal and Historical Memoirs*, 1964; Harry Franklin, *The Flag-Wagger*, 1974; Albert M. Hyamson, *Palestine Under the Mandate*, 1950; Sir George Hill, *A History of Cyprus*, IV, 1952; T. E. Lawrence, *Seven Pillars of Wisdom*, 1935; Sir Harry Luke, *Cities and Men*, II, 1953

Obit. 2 Nov. 11a; 5, 8b; 9, 11d   DNB Supp. VII

STURROCK, John (Christian Ramsay)

s/o. (2nd) John Sturrock, CIE, ICS, Madras

b. 1875   **d.** 13 February 1937

m. Blanche Walker, 1917

ch. 1s

Education: Charterhouse School
Balliol College, Oxford   Classics, Class III,
1898

Career: 1905 tutor to the Kabaka of Buganda
1914 District Commissioner, Uganda
1921 Provincial Commissioner
1923 Assistant Chief Secretary
1924 Acting Governor

Governorships: Basutoland 1926–35 (Resident
Commissioner)

Honours: CMG 1927; Kt. 1934

Clubs: —

Recreations: —

Retired: 1935

Publications: —

Supplementary: Sir Geoffrey Archer, *Personal and
Historical Memoirs*, 1964; H. Hesketh Bell, *Glimpses of a
Governor's Life*, 1946; D. A. Low and Cranford Pratt,
Buganda and British Overrule, 1960; Margery Perham,
African Apprenticeship, 1974; J. R. P. Postlethwaite, *I Look
Back*, 1974

Obit. 15 Feb. 14b; 18, 17e

SUMMERS, Gerald (Henry), Lieutenant–Colonel

s/o. The Reverend Walter Summers, Sussex

b. 12 October 1885   **d.** 29 November 1925

m. Margaret Troath, d/o Lieutenant-Colonel T. R. Swinburne, Pontop Hall, Durham

ch. 1s 1d

Education: Bradfield College
Royal Military College, Sandhurst

Career: 1904 commissioned into Indian Cavalry
1905 seconded to Burma Infantry
1912 Somaliland Indian Contingent, King's African Rifles
1914 Intelligence Officer, Somaliland
1916 Deputy Commissioner

Governorships: Somaliland 1922–25

Honours: CMG 1920; KCMG 1925

Clubs: Cavalry

Recreations: Fellow, Royal Geographical Society

Retired: died in office, 1925

Publications: —

Supplementary: H. Moyse-Bartlett, *The King's African Rifles*, 1956

Obit. 1 Dec. 16e; 4, 17c

SWAYNE, Eric (John Eagles), Brigadier-General

s/o. The Reverend G. C. Swayne
b. 14 May 1863   **d.** 9 September 1929
m. Yda Peach, d/o Sir T. Holdich and widow of Major Edmund Peach, Indian Army, 1908
ch. —

Education: —

Career: 1883 commissioned into Indian Staff Corps
          1886 Burma War
          1890 special duty, Somaliland reconnaissance
          1892 Intelligence Department, India
          1898 Uganda mutiny and Jubaland campaign
          1901 Commander, Somaliland Field Force

Governorships: Somaliland 1902–06 (Commissioner)
                      British Honduras 1906–13

Honours: CB 1904; KCMG 1910; CBE 1921

Clubs: —

Recreations: —

Retired: 1913
re-enlisted 1914; Assistant Inspector Recruiting, Northern Command Labour Commandant, 3rd Corps, 1917

Publications: *Seventeen Trips Through Somaliland*

Supplementary: Sir Geoffrey Archer, *Personal and Historical Memoirs*, 1964; H. F. P. Battersby, *Richard Corfield of Somaliland*, 1914; R. E. Drake-Brockman, *British Somaliland*, 1912; Douglas Jardine, *The Mad Mullah of Somaliland*, 1923; I. M. Lewis, *The Modern History of Somaliland*, 1965; H. Moyse-Bartlett, *The King's African Rifles*, 1956

Obit. 10 Sept. 16d; 14, 13b; 9 Nov. 15d   OCRP

SYMES, (George) Stewart

s/o. Lieutenant-Colonel W. A. Symes, 71st Highland Light Infantry, and Hon. Emily Shore

b. 29 July 1882   **d.** 5 December 1962

m. Viola, d/o J. Felix Brown, 1913

ch. 1s 1d

Education: Malvern College
Royal Military College, Sandhurst

Career:
- 1900 commissioned into Hampshire Regiment
- 1902 South African war
- 1903 Aden campaign
- 1905 Assistant Director of Intelligence, Egyptian Army
- 1906 seconded to Sudan Government
- 1907 ADC to Governor-General of Sudan
- 1909 Assistant Director of Intelligence, Sudan
- 1913 Private Secretary to Governor-General
- 1920 District Governor, Palestine
- 1925 Chief Secretary; Acting Governor

Governorships: Aden 1928–31 (Resident)
Tanganyika 1931–33
Sudan 1934–40 (Governor-General)

Honours: DSO 1904; CMG 1917; KBE 1928; KCMG 1932; GBE 1939

Clubs: —

Recreations: —

Retired: 1940

Publications: *Tour of Duty*, 1946, autobiog.

Supplementary: Ralph A. Austen, *Northwest Tanzania Under German and British Rule*, 1968; Hugh Boustead, *The Wind of Morning*, 1971; N. and H. Bentwick, *Mandate Memories*, 1965; Vincent Harlow and E. M. Chilver, *History of East Africa*, II, 1965; K. D. D. Henderson, *Sudan*

Republic, 1965; K. D. D. Henderson, *Making of the Modern Sudan*, 1953; Walter Morris-Hale, *British Administration in Tanganyika*, 1969; Sir James Robertson, *Transition in Africa*, 1974; Viscount Swindon, *I Remember*, 1947

Obit. 7 Dec. 15c; 10, 14c; 20, 11f

TAIT, (William Eric) Campbell, Admiral

s/o. Deputy Surgeon-General William Tait, MB, RN, Hampshire

b. 1886   **d.** 7 July 1946

m. Katie Cynthia, d/o Captain H. H. Grenfell, RN

ch. 2d

Education: —

Career: 1914 war service
1919 with Royal Yacht *Victoria and Albert*
1921 Commander, Flagship, China Station
1928 Captain, Mediterranean Station
1929 West Indies Station
1932 Deputy Director, Naval Intelligence, Admiralty
1938 Rear-Admiral
1942 Commander-in-Chief, Atlantic Station
1945 Admiral

Governorships: Southern Rhodesia 1945–46

Honours: MVO 1917; CB 1940; KCB 1943; ADC to the King, 1938

Clubs: United Service

Recreations: —

Retired: 1945 (from Royal Navy; died in office, 1946)

Publications: —

Supplementary: —

Obit. 18 July   DNB Supp. VI

THOMAS, (Thomas) Shenton (Whitelegge)

s/o. The Reverend T. W. Thomas, Cambridgeshire

b. 1879 **d.** 15 January 1962

m. Lucy, d/o Colonel J. A. L. Montgomery, CSI, CBE, County Donegal, Ireland

ch. 1d

Education: St John's School, Leatherhead
Queens' College, Cambridge (Scholar)

Career: 1909 Assistant District Commissioner, Kenya
1919 Assistant Chief Secretary, Uganda
1921 Principal Assistant Secretary, Nigeria
1924 Deputy Chief Secretary
1927 Colonial Secretary, Gold Coast

Governorships: Nyasaland 1929–32
Gold Coast 1932–34
Malaya 1934–42

Honours: OBE 1919; CMG 1929; KCMG 1931; GCMG 1937. Hon. Fellow, Queens' College, Cambridge, 1936

Clubs: MCC

Recreations: cricket, tennis, golf

Retired: 1946 (interned by Japanese, 1942–45)
Vice-President, British Empire Leprosy Relief Association; Vice-President, Fauna Preservation Society; Chairman, Overseas League, 1946–49

Publications: —

Supplementary: J. G. Farrell, *The Singapore Grip*, 1978; R. H. Bruce Lockhart, *Return to Malaya*, 1936; Molly Huggins, *Too Much To Tell*, 1967

Obit. 17 Jan. 14c; 8 Feb. 14d; 14 June 14d

THOMSON, Graeme

s/o. John Thomson, Bowdon
b. 9 August 1875   **d.** September 1933
m. —
ch. —

Education: Winchester College
New College, Oxford   Classics, Class III,
     1898
Called to the Bar, Middle Temple, 1902

Career: 1900 entered Home Civil Service, Admiralty
1914 Director of Transports
1917 Director of Shipping
1919 Colonial Secretary, Ceylon
1920 Acting Governor

Governorships: British Guiana 1923–25
Nigeria 1926–31
Ceylon 1931–33

Honours: CB 1917; KCB 1919; GCMG 1928

Clubs: Oxford and Cambridge; Windham

Recreations: shooting, fishing

Retired: died in office, 1933

Publications: —

Supplementary: A. E. Afigbo, *The Warrant Chiefs*, 1972;
Michael Crowder, *The Story of Nigeria*, 1973; H. A. J.
Hulugalle, *British Governors of Ceylon*, 1963; I. F.
Nicolson, *The Administration of Nigeria*, 1969

Obit. 30 Sept. 10b, 12b; 3 Oct. 7c; 4, 17a; 6, 15e; 17, 15b; 13
Nov, 19e

THORBURN, James (Jamieson)

s/o. William Thorburn, Edinburgh
b. 1864   **d.** 14 September 1929
m. Ruth, widow of R. Bertram Parsey, 1924
ch. —

Education: Edinburgh Collegiate School

Career: 1886 Cadet, Ceylon
        1900 Principal Assistant Colonial Secretary
        1905 Provincial Commissioner, Southern Nigeria
        1906 Lieutenant-Governor, Southern Nigeria
        1907 Acting Governor

Governorships: Gold Coast 1910–12

Honours: CMG 1907

Clubs: Royal and Ancient, St Andrews

Recreations: golf

Retired: 1912

Publications: —

Supplementary: David Kimble, *A Political History of Ghana*, 1963

Obit. 17 Sept. 17f

TURNBULL, Richard (Gordon)

s/o.   Richard Turnbull, Chartered Accountant, Glasgow
b.   7 July 1909   **d.**   —
m.   Beatrice, d/o John Wilson, Glasgow, 1939
ch.   —

Education: University College School, London
University College, London   B.Sc.,
Chemistry
Magdalene College, Cambridge

Career: 1931 Cadet, Kenya
1948 Provincial Commissioner in charge
Northern Frontier District
1954 Minister for Internal Security and Defence
1955 Chief Secretary
1957 Acting Governor

Governorships: Tanganyika 1958–62 (Governor-General
from 1961)
Aden 1965–67

Honours: CMG 1953; KCMG 1958; GCMG 1962
Hon. Fellow, Magdalene College, Cambridge 1970

Clubs: —

Recreations: fine wine

Retired: —

Publications: —

Supplementary: Darrell Bates, *A Gust of Plumes*, 1972;
Sir Michael Blundell, *So Rough A Wind*, 1964; Charles
Chenevix-Trench, *The Desert's Dusty Face*, 1969; Judith
Listowel, *The Making of Tanganyika*, 1965; D. A. Low and
Alison Smith, *History of East Africa*, III, 1976; Cranford
Pratt, *The Critical Phase in Tanzania*, 1976; M. K. P.
Sorrenson, *Land Reforms in the Kikuyu Country*, 1967; J.
Clagett Taylor, *The Political Development of Tanganyika*,
1963

OCRP/t

TWINING, Edward (Francis)

s/o. Reverend W. H. G. Twining, St Stephen's,
         Westminster
b.   1899   **d.**   21 July 1967
m.   Helen Mary (MRCS), d/o A. E. Du Boisson
ch. 2s

Education: Lancing College
                 Royal Military College, Sandhurst

Career: 1918 commissioned into Worcestershire
                    Regiment
              1923 seconded to King's African Rifles, Uganda
              1929 joined Colonial Service, Uganda, as Cadet
              1939 Director of Labour, Mauritius
              1944 Administrator, St Lucia

Governorships: North Borneo 1946–49
                     Tanganyika 1949–58

Honours: MBE 1923; CMG 1943; KCMG 1949; GCMG
      1953
      elevated to peerage as Baron Twining of Tanganyika and
      Godalming, 1958; Hon. Colonel, 6th Brigade, King's
      African Rifles

Clubs: Athenaeum; United Service

Recreations: crown jewels

Retired: 1958 (from army, 1929)
      Chairman, Ross Institute of Tropical Hygiene; Director,
      Business Archives Council; Director, National and
      Grindlay's Bank; Chairman, Victoria League

Publications: *A History of the Crown Jewels of Europe*, 1960

Supplementary: Darrell Bates, *A Gust of Plumes*, 1972,
      biog.; B. T. G. Chidzero, *Tanganyika and International
      Trusteeship*, 1961; John Gunther, *Inside Africa*, 1955; J. Gus
      Liebenow, *Colonial Rule and Political Development in
      Tanzania*, 1971; Judith Listowel, *The Making of
      Tanganyika*, 1965; D. A. Low and Alison Smith, *History of*

East Africa, III, 1976; Cranford Pratt, *The Critical Phase in Tanzania*, 1976; J. Clegett Taylor, *The Political Development of Tanganyika*, 1963

Obit. 24 July 10g; 2 Aug. 8h

USSHER, Herbert Taylor

s/o. —
b. —   **d.**   December 1880
m. —
ch. —

Education: —

Career: 1854 Commissariat, Crimean War
            1864 Private Secretary to Governor of Lagos
            1866 Collector of Customs, Gold Coast
            1867 Acting Governor

Governorships: Gold Coast 1867–72 (Administrator)
                     Tobago 1872–75
                     Labuan 1875–79
                     Gold Coast 1879–80

Honours: CMG 1872

Clubs: —

Recreations: —

Retired: —

Publications: —

Supplementary: W. Walton Claridge, *A History of the Gold Coast and Ashanti*, 1915; David Kimble, *A Political History of Ghana*, 1963

WADDINGTON, (Eubule) John

s/o. Thomas Waddington

b. 9 April 1890   **d.** 18 January 1957

m. Edith, d/o George Galloway

ch. 2s

Education: Dulwich College
Merton College, Oxford   Mathematics, Class II, 1913

Career: 1913   Cadet, Kenya
1923   Senior Assistant Secretary
1928   Provincial Commissioner
1932   Colonial Secretary, Bermuda
1935   Colonial Secretary, British Guiana

Governorships: Barbados 1938–41
Northern Rhodesia 1941–47

Honours: OBE 1919; CMG 1935; KCMG 1939; KCVO 1947; GBE 1948

Clubs: East India and Sports

Recreations: golf, tennis

Retired: 1947

Publications: —

Supplementary: Harry Franklin, *The Flag-Wagger*, 1974; L. H. Gann, *A History of Northern Rhodesia*, 1964; Molly Huggins, *Too Much To Tell*, 1967; R. I. Rotberg, *Black Heart*, 1977

Obit. 21 Jan. 10s; 26, 8b; 7 Feb. 13a

WALLACE, Lawrence (Aubrey)

s/o. John Henry Wallace

b. 2 February 1857 **d.** 26 January 1942

m. Marguerite-Marie, CBE, d/o Professor Henry Duboc, Le Havre, France, 1907

ch. 1s 1d

Education: —

Career: 1879 civil engineer on railway construction, South Africa
1894 travel and sport in Central Africa
1902 Chief Surveyor, North-Eastern Rhodesia
1907 Acting Administrator
1909 Acting Administrator, North-Western Rhodesia

Governorships: Northern Rhodesia, 1911–21 (Administrator)

Honours: CMG 1910; KBE 1918

Clubs: —

Recreations: —

Retired: 1921, to Calvados, France

Publications: —

Supplementary: L. H. Gann, *A History of Northern Rhodesia*, 1964

WILKINSON, Richard James

s/o. (1st) R. Wilkinson, British Consul, Salonika
b. 1867   **d.** 5 December 1941
m. Edith, d/o James Baird, Glasgow, 1912
ch. —

Education: Trinity College, Cambridge (Exhibitioner)

Career: 1889 Cadet, Malaya
             1896 Magistrate
             1902 District Officer
             1903 Inspector of Schools
             1911 Colonial Secretary;
                   Acting Governor

Governorships: Sierra Leone, 1916–22

Honours: CMG 1912

Clubs: —

Recreations: —

Retired: 1922

Publications: —

Supplementary: —

Obit. 11 Dec. 7e; 17, 7c

WILLIAM-POWLETT, Peveril (Barton Reibey Wallop), Vice-Admiral

s/o. (2nd) Major Barton William-Powlett
b. 5 March 1898   **d.** —
m. 1st   Helen Constance, d/o James Forbes Crombie, Aberdeen
     2nd   Barbara Patience, widow of Captain Newton William-Powlett, RN
ch. 3d

Education: Cordwalles School
     Osborne and Dartmouth Naval Colleges

Career: 1914 Midshipman
     1915 war service
     1944 Captain of Home Fleet
     1946 Commandant, Royal Naval College, Dartmouth
     1948 Naval Secretary to First Lord of the Admiralty
     1950 Flag Officer, Mediterranean Fleet
     1952 Commander in Chief, South Atlantic

Governorships: Southern Rhodesia 1954–59

Honours: DSO 1942; CBE 1945; CB 1949; KCB 1953; KCMG 1959

Clubs: United Service; Chelsea Arts

Recreations: rugby (played for England, 1922), golf, shooting, fishing

Retired: 1954
Chairman, Appledore Shipbuilders Ltd.; Sheriff of Devonshire, 1972

Publications: —

Supplementary: —

WILLIAMS, Ralph (Champneys)

s/o. The Reverend T. N. Williams, Anglesey, and Rector of
Aber, Wales, and Phoebe Howard

b. 9 March 1848   **d.** 22 June 1927

m. Jessica, d/o Samuel Dean, 1875

ch. 1s

Education: King's School, Chester
Rossall School

Career: 1865 articled to solicitors, Bangor, Wales
1870 emigrated to Australia
1873 exploring in South America
1876 travelling in Canada
1883 exploring in Central Africa
1884 Head of Civil Intelligence, Bechuanaland
expedition
1885 Special Correspondent *The Standard* and *Cape
Argus*
1887 British Agent, Transvaal
1890 Colonial Treasurer, Gibraltar
1897 Colonial Secretary, Barbados
1898 Acting Governor

Governorships: Bechuanaland 1901–06 (Resident
Commissioner)
Windward Islands 1907–09
Newfoundland 1909–13

Honours: CMG 1901; KCMG 1907

Clubs: St James's; MCC; Royal Thames Yacht

Recreations: 'ceaseless travelling to distant countries'

Retired: 1913
President of Second Line of Defence, East Africa 1914
(invalided 1915); Governor, Rossall School

Publications: *How I Became A Governor*, 1913, autobiog.;
The British Lion in Bechuanaland, 1885

Supplementary: —

Obit. 24 June 16d

WINDLEY, Edward (Henry)

s/o. E. C. Windley, Southern Rhodesia, and Vicomtesse de Toustain

b. 1909   **d.** 5 January 1972

m. Patience, d/o Lieutenant-General Sir B. Sergison-Brooke, 1939

ch. 1s 1d

Education: Repton
St Catharine's College, Cambridge
    Archaeology and Anthropology, Class II/2, 1930

Career: 1931 Cadet, Kenya
1949 Provincial Commissioner
1954 Chief Native Commissioner

Governorships: The Gambia 1958–62

Honours: CMG 1953; KCMG 1958; KCVO 1961

Clubs: —

Recreations: tennis, fishing, shooting, skiing, mountaineering

Retired: 1962
Director, Yullis Ltd; Chairman, Save the Children Fund, 1962; Chairman, Exchange Travel Agency Ltd, 1965

Publications: —

Supplementary: —

    Obit. 6 Jan 5d; 13, 14g

WINGATE, (Francis) Reginald

s/o. (7th) Andrew Wingate, textile merchant, Glasgow
b. 25 June 1861, Port Glasgow, **d.** 29 January 1953
Renfrewshire
m. Kitty, d/o Captain Sparkhall Rundle, RN, 1888
ch. 2s 1d

Education: St James' Collegiate School, Jersey
Royal Military Academy, Woolwich
Represented in athletics

Career: 1880 commissioned into Royal Artillery
1881 posted to India
1882 ADC to the Resident and Commander-in-
Chief, Aden
1883 transferred to the Egyptian Army
1884 ADC to the Commander-in-Chief, Egyptian
Army
1885 Nile expedition
1886 ADC to General Officer Commanding,
Eastern Command, England
Assistant Military Secretary to the Sirdar,
Cairo
1889 Director, Military Intelligence
1894 Governor of the Red Sea Littoral; Sirdar of the
Egyptian Army

Governorships: Sudan 1899–1916 (Governor-General)
Egypt 1917–1919 (High Commissioner)

Honours: DSO 1889; CB 1986; KCMG 1898; GCVO 1912;
GCB 1914; GBE 1918
elevated to the peerage as Baron Wingate of Dunbar and
Port Sudan

Clubs: Athenaeum

Recreations: study of languages, golf

Retired: 1919
Chairman, Tanganyika Concessions Ltd; Director, Union
Minière; Member, Governing Body Gordon College,
Khartoum; Chairman, Egyptian Army Dinner Club;

Trustee, Duchess of Fife Estate; Colonel Commandant, Royal Artillery; President, Dunbar Branch, British Legion; President, Dunbar Branch, Royal National Lifeboat Institution; Vice-President, Royal African Society

Publications: *Mahdism and the Egyptian Sudan*, 1891; transl. Joseph Ohrwalder, *Ten Years' Captivity in the Mahdi's Camp*, 1892; transl. Rudolf Slatin, *Fire and Sword in the Sudan*, 1896; *The Story of Gordon College*, n.d.

Supplementary: Sir Ronald Wingate, *Wingate of the Sudan*, 1955, biog.; Winston Churchill, *The River War*, 1899; K. D. D. Henderson, *Sudan Republic*, 1965; P. M. Holt, *A Modern History of the Sudan*, 1961; T. E. Lawrence, *Seven Pillars of Wisdom*, 1935; Mekki Shibeeka, *The Independent Sudan*, 1959; Sir Ronald Storrs, *Orientations*, 1937; Sir Stewart Symes, *Tour of Duty*, 1946; G. Warburg, *The Sudan Under Wingate*, 1971

DNB Supp. VII

WRAY, Martin Osterfield

s/o. C. N. O. Wray
b. 14 June 1912   **d.** —
m. Lilian Joyce, d/o R. W. Playfair, Nairobi, 1938
ch. 1s 2d

Education: St George's School, Harpenden, Hertfordshire
Wadham College, Oxford   History, Class II,
1934

Career: 1935 Cadet, Nigeria
1949 Administrative Secretary, Zanzibar
1952 Administrative Secretary, High Commission
Territories
1955 Resident Commissioner, Bechuanaland
1959 Chief Secretary, Northern Rhodesia

Governorships: Bechuanaland 1955–59 (Resident
Commissioner)

Honours: OBE 1954; CMG 1956

Clubs: Royal Commonwealth Society

Recreations: —

Retired: 1962

Publications: —

Supplementary: —

WRIGHT, Andrew (Barkworth)

s/o. The Reverend H. L. Wright

b. 30 November 1895   **d.** 24 March 1971

m. Rosemary Barret

ch. 1s 1d

Education: Haileybury College
Jesus College, Cambridge

Career: 1914 war service, France
1922 Cadet, Cyprus
1937 Colonial Secretary
1940 war service, Middle East
1943 Colonial Secretary, Trinidad

Governorships: The Gambia 1947–49
Cyprus 1949–54

Honours: CBE 1932; CMG 1941; KCMG 1948

Clubs: —

Recreations: —

Retired: 1954

Publications: —

Supplementary: —

WYN-HARRIS, Percy★

s/o. (1st) Percy Martin Harris, JP, and Catherine Mary Davis

b. 24 August 1903   **d.** 25 February 1979

m. Mary Macdonald, d/o Ranald Macdonald, CBE, New Zealand, 1932

ch. 1s

Education: Gresham's School
Caius College, Cambridge   Natural Sciences, Class II, 1925

Career: 1926 Cadet, Kenya
1941 District Commissioner
1944 Commissioner for Labour
1945 Provincial Commissioner
1947 Chief Native Commissioner

Governorships: The Gambia 1949–58

Honours: MBE 1941; CMG 1949; KCMG 1952

Clubs: Alpine; Savile; East India and Sports; Little Ship

Recreations: sail-cruising, mountaineering
Second ascent of Mount Kenya, with E. E. Shipton, 1929; member, Everest expeditions, 1933 and 1936

Retired: 1961
Member, Devlin Commission, Nyasaland, 1959; Administrator, Northern Cameroons (UN Plebiscite), 1960; toured Canada, Australia and New Zealand as special representative, Duke of Edinburgh's Award

Publications: —

Supplementary: A. V. Clayton and D. Savage, *Government and Labour in Kenya*, 1974; Harry A. Gailey, *A History of the Gambia*, 1964; Elspeth Huxley, *Four Guineas*, 1954; W. H. Murray, *The Story of Everest*, 1953; *West Africa*, 19 Nov. 1949

Obit. 17 Dec. 1979

★sometimes listed under Harris, P. Wyn.

YOUNG, Hubert (Winthrop), Major

s/o.   (2nd) Sir W. Mackworth Young, KCSI, Lieutenant-Governor of the Punjab, and Frances Mary, d/o Sir Robert Eyles Egerton, Lieutenant-Governor of the Punjab

b.   6 July 1885, Wrexham   **d.**   20 April 1950

m.   Margaret Rose Mary, d/o Colonel Frank Romilly Reynolds, Royal Engineers, 1924

ch.   3s

Education: Eton College (Scholar)
Royal Military Academy, Woolwich

Career: 1904 commissioned into Royal Garrison Artillery
1905 posted to Aden
1908 transferred to Indian Army
1915 Assistant Political Officer, Mesopotamia
1919 seconded to Foreign Office
1921 seconded to Colonial Office
1927 Colonial Secretary, Gibraltar
1929 Counsellor to High Commissioner, Iraq
1932 Minister Plenipotentiary, Iraq

Governorships: Nyasaland 1932–34
Northern Rhodesia 1934–38
Trinidad and Tobago 1938–42

Honours: DSO 1919; CMG 1923; Kt. 1932; KCMG 1934

Clubs: —

Recreations: —

Retired: 1945 (retired from army, 1927)
European Regional Officer, UNRRA, 1944; contested (Liberal) Harrow West 1945 and Edge Hill, 1947; Chairman, Royal Free Hospital Management Committee, Wiltshire, 1946; Consultant, Consultative Council, Southern Electricity Area

Publications: *The Independent Arab*, 1933; contr. *T. E. Lawrence by his Friends*, 1937

Supplementary: Sir Charles Dundas, *African Crossroads*,

1955; L. H. Gann, *A History of Northern Rhodesia*, 1964; Molly Huggins, *Too Much To Tell*, 1967; T. E. Lawrence, *Seven Pillars of Wisdom*, 1935; Robert I. Rotberg, *The Rise of Nationalism in Central Africa*, 1965; Robert I. Rotberg, *Black Heart*, 1977

Obit. 22 April 8f; 5 May, 7b   DNB Supp. VI

YOUNG, Mark (Aitchison)

s/o. (3rd) Sir W. Mackworth Young, KCSI, Lieutenant-Governor of the Punjab, and Frances Mary, d/o Sir Robert Eyles Egerton, Lieutenant-Governor of the Punjab

b. 30 June 1886   **d.** —
m. Josephine, d/o Walter C. Prince
ch. 2s 2d

Education: Eton College
King's College, Cambridge   Classics, Class I, 1908

Career: 1909 Cadet, Ceylon
1915 war service
1923 Principal Assistant Colonial Secretary
1928 Colonial Secretary, Sierra Leone
1929 Acting Governor
1930 Chief Secretary, Palestine

Governorships: Barbados 1933–38
Tanganyika 1938–41
Hong Kong 1941 (interned) and 1946–47

Honours: CMG 1931; KCMG 1934; GCMG 1946

Clubs: —

Recreations: —

Retired: 1947

Publications: —

Supplementary: G. B. Endacott, *A History of Hong Kong*, 1958; Sir Alexander Grantham, *Via Ports*, 1965; N. J. Miners, *The Government and Politics of Hong Kong*, 1975; Walter Morris-Hale, *British Administration in Tanganyika*, 1969

YOUNG, William Alexander George

s/o. —

b. —   **d.**   24 April 1885

m. —

ch.   1d

Education: —

Career: entered Royal Navy
                   1855 Secretary to Captain of the Fleet, Baltic
                   1859 Colonial Secretary, British Columbia
                   1866 Acting Governor
                   1869 Assistant Colonial Secretary, Jamaica
                   1873 Government Secretary, British Guiana
                   1877 Lieutenant-Governor

Governorships: Gold Coast 1884–85

Honours: CMG 1877

Clubs: —

Recreations: —

Retired: died in office, 1885

Publications: —

Supplementary: —

APPENDIX: A Chronology of the British Governors of Tropical Africa, c. 1875–1968.*

The Resident Commissioners of Basutoland 1884–1966

A Protectorate was proclaimed over Basutoland in 1868. Following a period of administrative attachment to Cape Colony after 1871, the post of Government Agent was replaced by that of Resident Commissioner in 1884 when Britain reassumed direct responsibility for the territory. In the colonial period Basutoland was known as one of the three High Commission Territories, from 1906 its Chief Administrator being responsible, along with those of Bechuanaland and Swaziland, to the British High Commissioner for South Africa, a post combined with the Governor-Generalship until 1931. The High Commissioner's post, which became coterminous with that of British Ambassador to South Africa in 1961, was abolished in 1964. Basutoland became independent in 1966 and changed its name to Lesotho.

The twelve Resident Commissioners were:

1	Sir Marshall Clarke	1884–1893
2	Sir Godfrey Lagden	1893–1901
3	Sir Herbert Sloley	1901–1916
4	R. T. Coryndon	1916–1917
5	Sir Edward Garraway	1917–1926
6	Sir John Sturrock	1926–1935
7	Sir Edward Richards	1935–1942
8	C. A. Arden-Clarke	1942–1946
9	A. D. Forsyth Thompson	1947–1952
10	E. P. Arrowsmith	1952–1956
11	A. G. T. Chaplin	1956–1961
12	Sir Alexander Giles	1962–1966

The Resident Commissioners of Bechuanaland 1885–1966

After the appointment of a Deputy Commissioner in 1884, a Protectorate was proclaimed over Bechuanaland in 1885 under an Administrator. The southern part was declared the Colony of British Bechuanaland and then annexed to Cape Colony. The northern part was recognized as the Bechuanaland Protectorate and in 1891 the post of Administrator was redesignated Resident Commissioner. During the colonial period Bechuanaland was recognized as one of the three High Commission Territories, from 1906 its chief administrator being responsible, along with those of Basutoland and Swaziland, to the British High Commissioner in South Africa, a post combined with the Governor Generalship until 1931. The High Commissioner's post, which became co-terminous with that of British Ambassador to South Africa in 1961, was abolished in 1964. Bechuanaland became independent in 1966 and changed its name to Botswana.

The eighteen Resident Commissioners were:

1	Sir Sidney Shippard	1885–1895
2	F. J. Newton	1895–1897
3	H. J. Goold-Adams	1897–1901
4	R. C. Williams	1901–1906
5	F. W. Panzera	1907–1916
6	E. C. F. Garraway	1916–1917
7	Sir James Macgregor	1917–1923
8	J. Ellenberger	1923–1927
9	R. M. Daniel	1928–1930
10	Sir Charles Rey	1930–1937
11	C. N. Arden-Clarke	1937–1942
12	A. D. Forsyth Thompson	1942–1947
13	A. Sillery	1947–1950
14	E. B. Beetham	1950–1953
15	W. F. Mackenzie	1953–1955
16	M. O. Wray	1955–1959
17	Sir Peter Fawcus	1959–1965
18	Sir Hugh Norman-Walker	1965–1966

The Governors of British Somaliland 1898–1960

In 1884 Great Britain established a Protectorate over that part of the Somali Coast opposite Aden, and the Government of India, which was responsible for Aden through the Bombay Presidency from 1839 to 1937, appointed an administrator from Aden. Up to 1898 he was variously styled President or Political Agent. When Somaliland was transferred from the Government of India to the Foreign Office in 1898, the post was redesignated Consul-General. On the assumption of control by the Colonial Office in 1905, the title was again changed, this time to Administrator. During World War I, and again between 1932 and 1935, the title was Commissioner, but otherwise it was that of Governor from 1919 onwards. Between 1941, after the Italian army of occupation had been ejected, and 1948 Somaliland was administered by a military governor, General A. R. Chater (1941–3) and Brigadier G. T. Fisher (1943–8). British Somaliland became independent in 1960 and joined the former Italian Somaliland to form the Republic of Somalia.

The thirteen British Governors or their equivalent for the period under Foreign (1898–1905) and Colonial (1905–41 and 1948–60) Office rule were:

1	Lieutenant-Colonel J. H. Sadler	1898–1901
2	Brigadier-General E. J. E. Swayne	1902–1906
3	H. E. S. Cordeaux	1906–1910
4	Brigadier-General W. Manning	1910–
5	H. A. Byatt	1911–1914
6	Sir Geoffrey Archer	1914–1922
7	Lieutenant-Colonel Sir Gerald Summers	1922–1925
8	Sir Harold Kittermaster	1926–1931
9	Major Sir Arthur Lawrance	1932–1939
10	V. G. Glenday	1939–1941
11	Sir Gerald Reece	1948–1953
12	Sir Theodore Pike	1954–1959
13	Sir Douglas Hall	1959–1960

The Governors of Cape Colony 1870–1910

The Cape Colony was taken from the Dutch in 1795 but returned in 1803. From 1806 it became a permanent British territory. Parliamentary government was introduced in 1872. Between 1847 and 1901 the Governor of Cape Colony was simultaneously High Commissioner for South Africa, in which latter capacity the Resident Commissioners of Basutoland, Bechuanaland and Swaziland were responsible to him. In 1910 Cape Colony became one of the four colonies which united to form the new Union of South Africa, thereafter administered by a Governor-General until South Africa withdrew from the Commonwealth in 1961.

The seven Governors of Cape Colony from 1870 were:

1	Sir Henry Barkly	1870–1877
2	Sir Bartle Frere	1877–1880
3	Sir Hercules Robinson	1881–1889
4	Sir Henry Loch	1889–1895
5	Sir Hercules Robinson	1895–1897
6	Sir Alfred Milner	1897–1901
7	Sir Walter Hely-Hutchinson	1901–1910

The Governors of The Gambia 1884–1965

In 1661 the Royal African Company nominated an administrator to James Fort on the River Gambia. Named variously Agent and Governor, the post continued until 1766, apart from the years 1695–99 and 1709–13 when the trading settlement was temporarily abandoned. In 1766 the area came under the jurisdiction of the French colony of the Senegambia. Soon after the resumption as an English settlement in 1816, this time on Banjul Island, The Gambia was annexed to the colony of Sierra Leone under a military Commander from 1821. From 1829 a Lieutenant-Governor was appointed until 1843, when The Gambia became a separate colony under its own Governor, but from 1866 to 1888 it was part of the West Africa

Settlements responsible to the Governor of Sierra Leone. During this period, and up to 1901, the post was designated as Administrator, but in 1901 it reverted to Governor. The Gambia became independent in 1965.

There were thirty-six Agents at James Fort between 1661 and 1766. These were followed, in 1829, by five Lieutenant-Governors and, from 1843, six Governors, until the incorporation of The Gambia in the West Africa Settlements in 1866. Then came eleven appointments as Administrator and, from 1901, fourteen Colonial Governors:

1	C. A. Moloney	1884–1885
2	J. S. Hay	1885–1887
3	G. T. Carter	1888–1890
4	Sir Robert B. Llewelyn	1891–1900
5	Sir George Denton	1900–1911
6	Lieutenant-Colonel Sir Henry Galway	1911–1914
7	Sir Edward Cameron	1914–1920
8	Captain Sir Cecil Armitage	1920–1927
9	Sir John Middleton	1927–1928
10	Sir Edward Denham	1928–1930
11	Sir Richard Palmer	1930–1933
12	Sir Arthur Richards	1933–1936
13	Sir Thomas Southorn	1936–1942
14	Sir Hilary Blood	1942–1947
15	Sir Andrew Wright	1947–1949
16	Sir Percy Wyn-Harris	1949–1958
17	Sir Edward Windley	1958–1962
18	Sir John Paul	1962–1965

The Governors of the Gold Coast 1879–1957

From 1632 to 1821 a number of merchant companies, among them the Company of Royal Adventurers (1663–72) and the Royal African Company (1672–1751), nominated a Chief Factor or Agent to administer their settlements along the Gold Coast. In 1821 the Crown assumed control of these settlements, their Governor being responsible to the Governor of Sierra Leone until 1850, when the Danish Gold Coast Settlements were brought under the former's jurisdiction. However, from 1866 to 1874 the Gold Coast again came under Sierra Leone, this time as part of the West Africa Settlements. Between 1874 and 1886 the Colony of Lagos was subordinate to the Gold Coast. The Gold Coast became independent in 1957 and changed its name to Ghana.

Twenty-three Chief Agents were nominated between 1751 and 1822. There were twenty-one Governors after 1822, followed by five Administrators from 1866 to 1874 and two more Governors before 1879. The seventeen Colonial Governors from 1879 were:

1	H. T. Ussher	1879–1880
2	Sir Samuel Rowe	1881–1884
3	W. A. G. Young	1884–1885
4	Sir William Griffith	1885–1895
5	Sir William Maxwell	1895–1897
6	Sir Frederic Hodgson	1898–1900
7	Sir Matthew Nathan	1900–1903
8	Sir John Rodger	1904–1910
9	J. J. Thorburn	1910–1912
10	Sir Hugh Clifford	1912–1919
11	Brigadier-General Sir Gordon Guggisberg	1919–1927
12	Sir Ransford Slater	1927–1932
13	Sir Shenton Thomas	1932–1934
14	Sir Arnold Hodson	1934–1941
15	Sir Alan Burns	1941–1947
16	Sir Gerald Creasy	1948–1949
17	Sir Charles Arden-Clarke	1949–1957

The Governors of Kenya 1896–1963

In 1887 the Sultan of Zanzibar ceded to the Imperial British East Africa Company the administration of his remnant mainland dominions after the establishment of German East Africa. From 1888 to 1906 the administration was in charge of a Commissioner, appointed by the I.B.E.A. up to 1895 and thereafter by the Foreign Office. In 1906 the Colonial Office assumed control and the post was redesignated Governor. The territory was known as the East Africa Protectorate until 1920, when it was renamed Kenya. Kenya became independent in 1963.

Four Commissioners were appointed by the I.B.E.A. Co. between 1888 and 1895. The four Commissioners appointed by the Foreign Office before 1906 and the twelve Colonial Governors were:

1	Sir Arthur Hardinge	1896–1900
2	Sir Charles Eliot	1900–1904
3	Sir Donald Stewart	1904–1905
4	Sir James Sadler	1905–1909
5	Colonel Sir Percy Girouard	1909–1912
6	Sir Henry Belfield	1912–1919
7	Major-General Sir Edward Northey	1919–1922
8	Sir Robert Coryndon	1922–1925
9	Lieutenant-Colonel Sir Edward Grigg	1925–1931
10	Brigadier-General Sir Joseph Byrne	1931–1936
11	Air Chief Marshal Sir Robert Brooke-Popham	1937–1939
12	Sir Henry Monck-Mason Moore	1940–1944
13	Sir Philip Mitchell	1944–1952
14	The Hon. Sir Evelyn Baring	1952–1959
15	Sir Patrick Renison	1959–1962
16	Malcolm Macdonald	1963

The Governors of Natal 1880–1910

The Colony of Natal was established in 1843. From then until 1880 it was administered by a Lieutenant-Governor. The first Governor was General Wolseley, appointed in 1880, and the first civilian, appointed in 1882, was Sir Henry Bulwer, who had already been Lieutenant-Governor since 1875. The colony was granted responsible government in 1893, and four years later Zululand, administered by a Resident Commissioner since 1879, was incorporated into it. In 1910 Natal became one of the four colonies which united to form the new Union of South Africa, thereafter administered by a Governor-General until South Africa withdrew from the Commonwealth in 1961.

The seven Governors of Natal from 1882 were:

1	Sir Henry Bulwer	1882–1885
2	Sir Arthur Havelock	1886–1889
3	Lieutenant-Colonel Sir Charles Mitchell	1889–1893
4	Sir Walter Hely-Hutchinson	1893–1901
5	Sir Henry McCallum	1901–1907
6	Sir Matthew Nathan	1907–1909
7	Lord Methuen	1909–1910

The Governors of Nigeria 1886–1960

Although there were Consuls assigned to the Bights of Biafra and of Benin from 1849 onwards, the first Colonial Office appointment was that of Administrator of Lagos Colony in 1862. The post was redesignated Governor in 1886, after the colony had been variously subordinated in Sierra Leone in 1866 as part of the West Africa Settlements, and to the Gold Coast in 1874. In 1885 the Bights of Biafra and Benin became the Oil Rivers Protectorate, under first a Consul and then, in 1891, a Commissioner. In 1893 this territory changed its name to the Niger Coast Protectorate, administered by a Commissioner until, in 1900, the Colonial Office assumed responsibility from the Foreign Office and the Royal Niger Company. It established the two colonies of Southern and Northern Nigeria, each under a High Commissioner, later Governor. In 1914 these were amalgamated under a single Governor of Nigeria, the post being personally recognized as Governor-General from 1914 to 1919 and again, institutionally as a consequence of the creation of the Federation of Nigeria, from 1954 to 1960.

There were four Consuls of the Bight of Biafra between 1849 and 1867, five Consuls of the Bight of Benin between 1852 and 1861, and four Consuls of the joint Bights from 1867 to 1885. There was one Consul for the Oil Rivers Protectorate from 1885 to 1891. There were six Administrators of Lagos from 1862 to 1886. The five Governors of Lagos from 1886 to 1906, the two Commissioners of the Niger Coast Protectorate from 1893 to 1900 and the eight Colonial Governors of Nigeria after 1912 were:

LAGOS

1	Sir Alfred Moloney	1886–1890
2	Sir Gilbert Carter	1890–1896
3	Sir Henry McCallum	1897–1898
4	Sir William Macgregor	1899–1904
5	Sir Walter Egerton	1904–1906

NIGER COAST PROTECTORATE

1	Sir Claude Macdonald	1891–1896
2	Sir Ralph Moor	1896–1900

NIGERIA

1	Sir Frederick Lugard	1912–1919
2	Sir Hugh Clifford	1919–1925
3	Sir Graeme Thomson	1926–1931
4	Sir Donald Cameron	1931–1935
5	Sir Bernard Bourdillon	1935–1942
5a	Sir John Shuckburgh	1939 (did not assume office)
6	Sir Arthur Richards	1943–1947
7	Sir John Macpherson	1948–1955
8	Sir James Robertson	1955–1960

The Governors of Eastern Nigeria 1954–1960

The Eastern Provinces, which had been part of Southern Nigeria until 1939, were advanced to a governorship in 1954 as the Eastern Region. It became independent as part of the Federation of Nigeria in 1960.

The two Governors were:

1 Sir John Pleass   1954–1956
2 Sir Robert Stapledon   1956–1960

The Governors of Northern Nigeria 1900–1914 and 1954–1960

Northern Nigeria was established as a Protectorate in 1900. In 1908 the title was changed from High Commissioner to Governor, but this was downgraded to that of Lieutenant-Governor in 1914 when the Northern and Southern Provinces were amalgamated under a single Governor of Nigeria. In 1933 the office was further reduced to that of Chief Commissioner. Under the constitutional provisions of 1951, the office of Lieutenant-Governor was re-established, and on the creation of the Federation of Nigeria in 1954 the post was designated as that of Governor of the Northern Region. It became independent as part of the Federation of Nigeria in 1960.

Excluding the periods of Lieutenant-Governorship and Chief Commissionership, the six Governors were:

1 Sir Frederick Lugard   1900–1906
2 Sir Percy Girouard   1907–1909
3 Sir Hesketh Bell   1909–1912
4 Sir Frederick Lugard   1912–1914
5 Sir Bryan Sharwood Smith   1954–1957
6 Sir Gawain Bell   1957–1961

The Governors of Southern Nigeria 1900–1914

Southern Nigeria was established as a Protectorate in 1900, under a High Commissioner. In 1906 the Colony of Lagos was incorporated and the office was redesignated Governor. On the amalgamation of the Northern and Southern Provinces in 1914 under a single Governor of Nigeria, the post was downgraded to that of Lieutenant-Governor, and further reduced to that of Chief Commissioner in 1935. In 1939 the Southern Provinces were divided into the Western and the Eastern Provinces, each under its own Chief Commissioner.

The three Governors were:

1	Sir Ralph Moor	1900–1903
2	Sir Walter Egerton	1903–1912
3	Sir Frederick Lugard	1912–1914

The Governors of Western Nigeria 1954–1960

The Western Provinces, which had been part of Southern Nigeria until 1939, were advanced to a governorship in 1954 as the Western Region of Nigeria. It became independent as part of the Federation of Nigeria in 1960.

The sole governor was:

1	Sir John Rankine	1954–1960

The Governors of Northern Rhodesia 1897–1964

Until 1911, the British South Africa Company administered this area of its Chartered territory in two parts, North-Eastern Rhodesia and North-Western Rhodesia, each under an Administrator. From 1911 these were merged into one territory, known as Northern Rhodesia, and brought under a single Administrator. In 1924 the Colonial Office assumed control from the B.S.A. Co. and the post was redesignated Governor. Between 1953 and 1963 Northern Rhodesia was, along with Nyasaland and Southern Rhodesia, part of the Federation of Rhodesia and Nyasaland. After the dissolution of this Central African Federation, Northern Rhodesia became independent in 1964 and changed its name to Zambia.

Two Administrators were nominated to North-Eastern Rhodesia by the British South African Company between 1895 and 1898. The B.S.A. Co. Administrators appointed between 1897 and 1924, and the nine subsequent Colonial Governors, were:

NORTH-EASTERN RHODESIA
1	R. E. Codrington	1898–1907
2	L. A. Wallace	1907–1909

NORTH-WESTERN RHODESIA
1	R. T. Coryndon	1900–1907
2	R. E. Codrington	1907–1908
3	L. A. Wallace	1909–1911

NORTHERN RHODESIA
1	Sir Lawrence Wallace	1911–1921
2	Sir Drummond Chaplin	1921–1923
3	R. A. J. Goode	1923–1924

COLONIAL GOVERNORS
1	Sir Herbert Stanley	1924–1927
2	Sir James Maxwell	1927–1932
3	Colonel Sir Ronald Storrs	1932–1934
4	Major Sir Hubert Young	1934–1938
5	Sir John Maybin	1938–1941
6	Sir John Waddington	1941–1947
7	Sir Gilbert Rennie	1948–1954
8	Sir Arthur Benson	1954–1959
9	Sir Evelyn Hone	1959–1964

The Governors of Nyasaland 1891–1964

A consul was appointed for the area round Lake Nyasa and another at Zomba in 1883. A Protectorate was proclaimed in

1889. This was extended in 1891, becoming in 1893 the British Central Africa Protectorate under a Commissioner. In 1907 the post was redesignated Governor and at the same time the name was changed to the Nyasaland Protectorate. From 1953 to 1963 Nyasaland was, along with Northern Rhodesia and Southern Rhodesia, part of the Federation of Rhodesia and Nyasaland. After the dissolution of the Central African Federation, Nyasaland became independent in 1964 and changed its name to Malawi.

The two Commissioners and twelve Colonial Governors were:

1	Sir Harry Johnston	1891–1897
2	Sir Alfred Sharpe	1897–1910
3	Brigadier-General Sir William Manning	1910–1913
4	Sir George Smith	1913–1923
5	Sir Charles Bowring	1923–1929
6	Sir Shenton Thomas	1929–1932
7	Major Sir Hubert Young	1932–1934
8	Sir Harold Kittermaster	1934–1939
9	Sir Donald Mackenzie-Kennedy	1939–1942
10	Sir Edmund Richards	1942–1948
11	Sir Geoffrey Colby	1948–1956
12	Sir Robert Armitage	1956–1961
13	Sir Glyn Jones	1961–1964

The Governors of Orange River Colony 1902–1910

On the conclusion of the Anglo–Boer War in 1902, the former Orange Free State was annexed and renamed the Orange River Colony. For the first five years it was administered by a Lieutenant-Governor, responsible to the High Commissioner for South Africa who was simultaneously Governor of Cape Colony. Responsible government was granted to the Orange River Colony in 1907 and the Lieutenant-Governorship was advanced to a Governorship. In 1910 the Orange River Colony became one of the four colonies which united to form the new Union of South Africa, thereafter administered by a Governor-General until South Africa withdrew from the Commonwealth in 1961.

The three Governors of the Orange River Colony were:

1	Viscount Milner	1902–1905
2	Lord Palmer	1905–1907
3	Sir Hamilton Goold-Adams	1907–1910

The Governors of Sierra Leone 1877–1961

In 1792 the Sierra Leone Company nominated a Governor for its Province of Freedom. In 1808 Sierra Leone became a crown colony. Between 1821 and 1850 the Governor of Sierra Leone also exercised jurisdiction over the Gold Coast, and similarly over the Gambia from 1821 to 1843. For the period 1827–1837 the Sierra Leone post was regarded as that of Lieutenant-Governor. From 1866 to 1888 the Governor of Sierra Leone was simultaneously Governor-in-Chief of the West Africa Settlements: these included the Gold Coast and Lagos up to 1874, and The Gambia until the Settlements were abolished in 1888 as an administrative unit. A protectorate was added to the Colony in 1896. Sierra Leone became independent in 1961.

There were five Sierra Leone Company nominations to the Governorship between 1792 and 1805 and nine Colonial Governors up to 1827. Then came ten Lieutenant-Governors. From 1837 to 1866 there were eight Colonial Governors, followed by eight Governors of the West Africa Settlements between 1860 and 1888. The nineteen Colonial Governors from 1877 to 1961 were:

1	Sir Samuel Rowe	1877–1881
2	Sir Arthur Havelock	1881–1884
3	Sir Samuel Rowe	1885–1888
4	Sir James Hay	1888–1891
5	Sir Francis Fleming	1892–1894

6	Colonel Sir Frederick Cardew	1894–1900
7	Sir Charles King-Harman	1900–1904
8	Sir Leslie Probyn	1904–1910
9	Sir Edward Merewether	1911–1915
10	R. J. Wilkinson	1916–1922
11	Sir Ransford Slater	1922–1927
12	Brigadier-General Sir Joseph Byrne	1927–1930
13	Sir Arnold Hodson	1931–1934
14	Sir Henry Moore	1934–1937
15	Sir Douglas Jardine	1937–1941
16	Sir Hubert Stevenson	1941–1948
17	Sir George Beresford-Stooke	1948–1953
18	Sir Robert Hall	1953–1956
19	Sir Maurice Dorman	1956–1961

The Governors of Southern Rhodesia 1923–1965 and 1979–1980

When in 1889 the British South Africa Company was granted the right to administer the territory lying to the north of the British possessions in South Africa, the new Colony's first name was Mashonaland. It was administered by a Resident Commissioner until 1894 when the colony was renamed, as Southern Rhodesia, and the post restyled, as Administrator. The British South Africa Company renounced its administration of Southern Rhodesia in 1923 and it became a self-governing Crown Colony. Between 1953 and 1963 Southern Rhodesia was, along with Nyasaland and Northern Rhodesia, part of the Central African Federation. In 1965 the government of Southern Rhodesia made a unilateral declaration of independence. In 1969, the last Governor appointed by the Crown resigned. However, as part of the British Government's plan to restore Rhodesia's constitutional position to legality and to introduce direct rule in preparation for the standard British pattern of planned and phased decolonisation in Africa, as agreed at the Lancaster House Conference held in the autumn of 1979, Lord Soames was appointed as the last Colonial Governor of what was now renamed Southern Rhodesia at the end of the year. His brief was to organise elections against the transfer of power within six months.

There were two Resident Commissioners and four Administrators between 1890 and 1923. The nine Governors since 1923 were:

1	Sir John Chancellor	1923–1928
2	Sir Cecil Rodwell	1928–1934
3	Sir Herbert Stanley	1935–1942
4	Sir Evelyn Baring	1942–1944
5	Admiral Sir William Tait	1945–1946
6	Major-General Sir John Kennedy	1946–1953
7	Admiral Sir Peveril William-Powlett	1954–1959
8	Sir Humphrey Gibbs	1959–1969
9	Lord Soames	1979–1980

The Governors-General of the Anglo-Egyptian Sudan 1899–1956

On the reconquest of the Sudan in 1898, from which the Egyptian Government and its British advisers had been driven out by the Mahdist rebellion in 1881, a joint Anglo-Egyptian administration was set up under a Governor-General. The Anglo-Egyptian Sudan became independent in 1956 and changed its name to the Sudan.

The nine Governors-General of the Anglo-Egyptian Sudan were:

1	Sir Herbert Kitchener	1899
2	Sir Reginald Wingate	1899–1916
3	Sir Lee Stack	1917–1924
4	Sir Geoffrey Archer	1924–1926
5	Sir John Maffey	1926–1933
6	Sir Stewart Symes	1934–1940

7	Sir Hubert Huddleston	1940–1947
8	Sir Robert Howe	1947–1955
9	Sir Knox Helm	1955–1956

The Resident Commissioners of Swaziland 1907–1968

On the termination of the Boer War in 1902, Swaziland was administered as part of the Transvaal colony. In 1906 it was made an independent command under a Resident Commissioner. During the colonial period Swaziland was recognized as one of the three High Commission Territories, from 1907 its chief administrator being responsible, along with those of Basutoland and Bechuanaland, to the British High Commissioner for South Africa, a post combined with the Governor-Generalship until 1931. The High Commissioner's post, which became co-terminous with that of British Ambassador to South Africa in 1961, was abolished in 1964. Swaziland became independent in 1968.

The ten Resident Commissioners were:

1	R. T. Coryndon	1907–1916
2	De S. M. G. Honey	1917–1928
3	T. Ainsworth Dickson	1928–1935
4	A. G. Marwick	1935–1937
5	C. L. Bruton	1937–1942
6	E. K. Featherstone	1942–1946
7	E. B. Beetham	1946–1950
8	D. L. Morgan	1951–1956
9	Sir Brian A. Marwick	1956–1964
10	Sir Francis Loyd	1964–1968

The Governors of Tanganyika 1920–1961

Tanganyika, from 1891 to 1918 the colony of German East Africa, was captured by the British in World War I. In 1916 the territory was brought under the jurisdiction of a British Administrator for German East Africa, the post being restyled that of Governor in 1920 consequent upon the grant of a mandate to Great Britain over the territory by the League of Nations, less the area of Ruanda-Urundi which was awarded to Belgium as a mandate. In 1947 the nomenclature was changed from a Mandate to Trust Territory. Tanganyika became independent in 1961, and in 1964, after union with Zanzibar, it changed its name to Tanzania.

The nine British Governors of the colonial period were:

1	Sir Horace Byatt	1920 (1916)–1924
2	Sir Donald Cameron	1924–1931
3	Sir Stewart Symes	1931–1933
4	Sir Harold MacMichael	1934–1938
5	Sir Mark Young	1938–1941
6	Sir Wilfrid Jackson	1941–1945
7	Sir William Battershill	1945–1949
8	Sir Edward Twining	1949–1958
9	Sir Richard Turnbull	1958–1961

The Governors of Transvaal 1902–1910

The Boer Republic of Transvaal was annexed in 1877 and governed by an Administrator until the British withdrew in 1881. It was reoccupied during the Anglo-Boer War, and from 1902 was administered by a Lieutenant-Governor responsible to the High Commissioner for South Africa who was simultaneously Governor of Cape Colony. Responsible government was granted in 1906. In 1910 the Transvaal became one of the four colonies which united to form the new Union of South Africa, thereafter administered by a Governor-General until South Africa withdrew from the Commonwealth in 1961.

The two Governors of the Transvaal were:

1	Viscount Milner	1902–1905
2	Lord Palmer	1905–1910

The Governors of Uganda 1893–1962

In 1890 the Imperial British East Africa Company began to establish a presence in the lacustrine area of East Africa. In 1894 Buganda was declared a Protectorate, administered by a Commissioner answerable to the Foreign Office. After the transfer of the eastern highlands to Kenya in 1903, the Colonial Office assumed control of Uganda and the post was redesignated Governor in 1905. Uganda became independent in 1962.

The five Commissioners and the twelve Colonial Governors were:

1	Sir Gerald Portal	1893–1894
2	Colonel H. E. Colville	1893–1895
3	E. J. L. Berkeley	1895–1899
4	Sir Harry Johnston	1899–1901
5	Colonel J. H. Sadler	1902–1905
6	Sir Hesketh Bell	1906–1909
6a	Major H. E. S. Cordeaux	1910 (did not assume office)
7	Sir Frederick Jackson	1911–1917
8	Sir Robert Coryndon	1918–1922
9	Sir Geoffrey Archer	1922–1924
10	Sir William Gowers	1925–1932
11	Sir Bernard Bourdillon	1932–1935
12	Sir Philip Mitchell	1935–1940
13	Sir Charles Dundas	1940–1944
14	Sir John Hall	1944–1951
15	Sir Andrew Cohen	1952–1957
16	Sir Frederick Crawford	1957–1961
17	Sir Walter Coutts	1961–1962

The British Residents of Zanzibar 1914–1963

From 1840 to 1913, Zanzibar was administered by a succession of Consuls and from 1873 Consuls-General, responsible to the

Foreign Office. Between 1895 and 1904 the Commissioner of the East Africa Protectorate (later known as Kenya) was simultaneously Consul-General in Zanzibar. In 1913 Zanzibar came under the control of the Colonial Office and the title of the administrator was changed to Resident. Zanzibar became independent in 1963, and in 1964 joined Tanganyika to form Tanzania.

The ten British Residents of the colonial period were:

1	Major F. B. Pearce	1914–1922
2	J. H. Sinclair	1922–1924
3	Sir Claud Hollis	1924–1930
4	Sir Richard Rankine	1930–1937
5	Sir John Hall	1937–1940
6	Sir Guy Pilling	1941–1946
7	Sir Vincent Glenday	1946–1951
8	Sir John Rankine	1952–1954
9	Sir Henry Potter	1954–1959
10	Sir George Mooring	1960–1963